PHILIP F. NAPOLI

BRINGING IT ALL BACK HOME

Philip F. Napoli is an assistant professor of history at
Brooklyn College, where he also directs the Veterans Oral
History Project. He was one of the chief researchers for
Tom Brokaw's *The Greatest Generation* and *An Album of
Memories*. He lives in New York City.

BRINGING IT ALL BACK HOME

BRINGING IT ALL BACK HOME

· AN ·

ORAL HISTORY

· OF ·

NEW YORK CITY'S

VIETNAM VETERANS

PHILIP F. NAPOLI

HILL AND WANG

A DIVISION OF FARRAR, STRAUS AND GIROUX

NEW YORK

Hill and Wang
A division of Farrar, Straus and Giroux
120 Broadway, New York 10271

Copyright © 2013 by Philip F. Napoli All
rights reserved

Published in 2013 by Hill and Wang
First paperback edition, 2014

The Library of Congress has cataloged the hardcover edition as follows:
Napoli, Philip F., 1960–
Bringing it all back home : an oral history of New York City's Vietnam veterans /
Philip F. Napoli. — 1st ed.
    p.   cm.
Includes bibliographical references.
ISBN 978-0-8090-7318-4 (hbk.)
    1. Vietnam War, 1961–1975—Veterans—New York (State)—New York—Interviews.
2. Vietnam War, 1961–1975—Personal narratives, American.   3. Vietnam War,
1961–1975—New York (State)—New York.   4. New York (N.Y.)—Biography   I. Title.
II. Title: An oral history of New York City's Vietnam veterans.

DS559.5 .N367 2012
959.704'30922—dc23

                                                          2012034731

Paperback ISBN: 978-0-8090-3153-5

Designed by Abby Kagan

www.fsgbooks.com
www.twitter.com/fsgbooks • www.facebook.com/fsgbooks

To Marilyn, love of my life

CONTENTS

BRINGING IT ALL BACK HOME

INTRODUCTION

> There is no history of mankind, there is only an indefinite
> number of histories of all kinds of aspects of human life.
> —KARL POPPER, *The Open Society and Its Enemies*, 1945

This book explores the American experience in Vietnam by linking our soldiers' early years with their behavior on the battlefield and their progress after the war. It uses oral history to understand how veterans make sense of the most intense period of their lives in light of the knowledge gained in later years.

There are many accounts of the Vietnam veteran's experience. In 1997, the World War II fighter pilot and Princeton University literature professor Samuel Hynes published *The Soldiers' Tale*, his personal reflections on the stories men write about war. In one chapter Hynes reviewed the narratives that American veterans have written about their war in Vietnam, highlighting the gap between public discourse and the war the veterans say they really experienced.[1] Of course, veterans themselves helped to create the public discourse: in Ron Kovic's *Born on the Fourth of July* and many other staples of the Vietnam literature as told by Vietnam veterans, Hynes found what he called the "myths of war . . . the simplified narrative that evolves from a war, through which it is given meaning."[2]

The memoirs and novels he studied suggested that the Vietnam conflict's particular "myths of war" included an emphasis on dead children, on killing, on the bewildering directionlessness of the fighting, and on destruction as a deliberate military policy.[3] According to these narratives, he concluded, "You might say, indeed, that the war in Vietnam was ironic from the beginning, that its essential meaning was the *absence* of a single coherent meaning in its events."[4] Such meaning as does emerge in these works reinforces one idea: "the loss of faith" in the American ability to fight Good Wars.

This Vietnam myth, Hynes emphasized, worked and was broadly accepted because it provided a narrative structure for the telling of the story of America in Vietnam. This was, according to the title of one oral history, the Bad War.[5] Soldiers could not feel good about fighting a bad war. The stories of veterans' lives after the war therefore included "irrational violence, sleeplessness, alcoholism, the inability to hold a job or preserve a marriage or feel love" with depressing regularity.[6] This story, the myth of the veteran that Hynes found embedded in the literature about Vietnam, echoes something the veteran Bernard Edelman once said to me: the assumption was that "the war was fucked-up, therefore the veterans must be fucked-up."

In fact, the Vietnam myth articulated in these personal narratives did not match the war fought by the majority of veterans. Hynes noted that as early as 1980 more than 70 percent of Vietnam veterans were reporting to the Veterans Administration that they were proud to have served and 66 percent said they would do it again. The story of their war was, Hynes asserted, "as valid, as truth-telling, as valuable, as the worst accounts of slaughtered innocents and damaged lives. The soldiers' tale of Vietnam is *all* of the stories. We must not choose among them."[7]

The only way to present a counternarrative is to listen to a wider range of voices. This work is focused on Vietnam veterans who either grew up or live in New York City, because the city's estimated eighty thousand veterans represent a diverse and inclusive sample of those who went to Vietnam. I have sought to find a balance between those who saw Vietnam as a guilt-inducing series of mistakes and atrocities and those who seem not to suffer from nightmares and disabling wounds. There are stories here of substance abuse and post-traumatic stress disorder (PTSD), but also stories of redemption; stories of grief, but also of service; stories of pain, but also of transcendence.

As these veterans also remind us, their experiences in Vietnam have implications for the lives of those who've fought in Iraq and Afghanistan. Rudy Thomas Sr., who earned three Purple Hearts while serving with the 173rd Airborne Brigade in Vietnam, emphasized the relevance of his war experiences to a new generation of returning soldiers. He said:

For the past twenty-eight, twenty-nine years I've been a disabled-veterans specialist for the State of New York Department of Labor. I see veterans from Vietnam and I see veterans from Iraq and I understand. I don't like what I see now. I see a lot of young people with problems that they're not even aware of, just like myself. I had no idea what I was going through.

The veterans I see from Iraq and Afghanistan, they have problems. They're not really familiar with what's going on, and I think it's my duty to open their eyes and let them see what's happening. I had a young lady two days ago. She was fine, and then I started questioning her. I said, "You've been up all night, right?" She said, "How do you know that?" And I just started laughing.

I am experienced. I've been there, done that. I'm up all night. Sometimes I look up, open up the door, and look out. What the hell am I looking out the door for? There's nobody at the door. But it's something that I do. I look out the window, you know, and I catch myself doing it. What are you doing? There's nobody out there. But it's something that happens. And I see it in a lot of young veterans coming back now.

What they don't understand is the problems that they're having affect not only them but the family also. The family doesn't understand what they're going through.

So I tell them a lot of times, "Sit down with your family. Talk to them. Tell them what's going on with you so they will understand. Hopefully, they will have a better idea of what's going on in your mind so they wouldn't get the wrong impression from what they see."

Just as Thomas stresses that remembering and sharing can promote understanding between individuals and among family members, Neil Kenny maintains that shared stories create connections across generations. As a Vietnam combat veteran, Kenny reaches out to the younger generation of men and women returning home from combat. He described his relationship with two of these young men. One Marine was *struggling down in Charleston, South Carolina. When I met him up here, he said, "I want real Italian food." I said, "It's a real Italian restaurant." He says, "What's good?" I said, "It's all good." He said, "I've never had real Italian food." And this kid was in Iraq, fighting for his country.*

The second young man, also a Marine from Staten Island, was having trouble with PTSD.

I go to Carmine's house, and I'm talking to his mother. I said, "Where the hell is Carmine?" "Oh," [she says], "he's up in his room."

I [went up to his room and said], "You know, Carmine, you can't be staying in your room like this, bro. You got to get out. You got to do something." I said, "When you were in that courtyard in Fallujah and you were down because you were hit, and you were defenseless," I said, "you didn't really think you were going to get out of that courtyard." He started crying.

He says, "Neil, you read me like a fucking book." I said, "I'm not reading you like a book, my friend. I'm only about three chapters ahead of you."

That common experience, the shared sense of what military service and combat can mean, enabled Kenny to reach out to this Marine. He has not finished living the chapters of his own book, but he is willing to share what he has learned.

All the people profiled in this book understood that their remarks to me were on the record and intended for publication. All were given the opportunity to edit their words, and some did so. Final responsibility for what appears here, of course, rests with me. No pseudonyms appear in this book. Throughout the text, all words spoken to me by my interviewees are presented in italics.

1

MAKING SOLDIERS: THE BOYS WHO BECAME THE MEN

On December 7, 1941, the attack on Pearl Harbor galvanized public opinion in favor of war. In June 1942, a "New York at War" parade up Fifth Avenue attracted about 500,000 participants and 2.5 million spectators. The parade was intended, according to *The New York Times*, to "visualize the magnitude and intensity of the city's contribution to all phases of the war program." The *Times* pointed out that the crowd was larger than in "any other single American city with the exception of Chicago, and there were twice as many people along Fifth Avenue as live in Detroit or Los Angeles."[1] By 1943, it was estimated that 600,000 New Yorkers were in the armed services.[2] By one account, some 800,000 New Yorkers served in the military overall during the war years.[3] For many children of these World War II veterans, their parents' military service was a conspicuous point of pride.

The New York veteran Ed German is a painter and the host of a public radio jazz program that airs on WPPB, on Long Island. He lives comfortably on Long Island, in a home filled with works of art and the music he loves so much. He is both a public and a private personality, carefully sharing stories that reveal bits and pieces about himself and the world he grew up in. Recently, he published his autobiography, *Deep Down in Brooklyn*. He says of himself, "I don't consider myself an African American. I am an American Negro. We've been Slaves and

Nigras and Niggers and Colored and Spades and Spooks and Coons and Splibs and Afro Americans and Blacks, but Negro conclusively describes for me who I am and the journey that my continental ancestors took."[4]

German's parents, originally working in agriculture, were from Georgia and came from a large family: *Between my mother and my father*, he says, *I had twenty-two aunts and uncles, eleven on each side of the family.*

German's family left the South in the early 1940s, as part of the great African American migration to the North. They moved first to southern New Jersey, where his father worked as a sharecropper. The African American population in New York City had more than doubled from 1900 to 1920 and then doubled again in the 1920s. By 1940, African Americans represented 6 percent of the city's total population.[5] They would make Harlem famous as a cultural enclave, but they also populated many other neighborhoods, like Williamsburg and Bedford-Stuyvesant in Brooklyn.

Eventually, the German family moved to Brooklyn. Ed's father got a job as a building superintendent there, and his mother did domestic work. German was born at 533 Halsey Street in Bed-Stuy. His father, born in 1916, had fought in both the European and the Pacific theaters as part of a quartermaster company, picking up some French and German language skills along the way. All his uncles served in the war as well. German has never forgotten learning about his father's service.

When I was a little boy living on Willoughby Avenue and my parents used to leave the house, we kids often would do what my mother and father [called] plundering. We'd just go up into their room and just looking at stuff, you know, opening doors and closets. And I remember one day I looked in my dad's closet, and I saw his old Army uniform. It was in a clothing bag. I unzipped it, and I looked, and I said wow. I was only about eight years old when I saw it. I saw the medals on the outside of it, and then I looked in the inside jacket, in the inside pocket of the jacket, and there was a little leather folder in there, and I pulled this leather folder out, and I looked in it, and his Honorable Discharge was in there.

After the discovery of his uniform, German senior began to share stories of his war experience. They left a lasting impression, especially the story of his war wound.

He got shot one day in the wrist. And he told us the story. He said while he was in Germany, I think, he said he had bought a new watch. I forgot the name of the watch, but it was a really stylish kind of watch to have at that time, and he said he bought a new watch. And he was driving the jeep and he had his left hand holding on to the top of the window of the driver's side window and he was showing off his new watch, you know, because he was—that's what he said, he said he was showing off his watch. And he was just driving along and a bullet hit him in his wrist. And he used to show us a small bullet mark on his leg, too. I don't know how he got that one. But he was over there from 1943 to 1946. He came home in 1946.

German would later write in his memoir: "I can see from all of this that he's been somewhere far away and done something important."[6] By the time German returned home from Vietnam in June 1969 with his own military discharge papers and the Purple Heart medal he'd earned for being wounded in action, the idea of the uniform as a symbol of pride had changed drastically for him.

The historian Joshua Freeman writes, "In the memories and memoirs of working-class New Yorkers, the neighborhood looms large."[7] This certainly seems to be true for the Vietnam veteran John Flanagan, who was born on November 6, 1946, in Brooklyn, New York. He recalls his home and the surrounding area with a degree of bitterness mixed with anger. In his memory, the block was mainly Irish, although there were a significant number of Puerto Rican families too, and the overcrowding was intense, with as many as four families sharing a two-bedroom apartment and adults sleeping in shifts.

I was the fifth child of first-generation Irish. All four grandparents came from Ireland. Most of the uncles worked "longshore" or became policemen . . . my father worked for the city in the Parks Department. We lived on Fortieth Street between Third and Fourth Avenues. It was my grandmother's house. My grandmother lived on the top floor. We had the second floor and the basement. We didn't have a lot of money at all. Money was tight, and I mean all the time. Having a grandmother living on the top floor who owns the house didn't make it any easier. She was a widow and always had one or the other of her sisters that were maidens that were living up there.

Since we lived in the house with her, we were always no good, and all of my cousins, since they didn't live there, they were always so good. So we were always being told how bad we were and how good they were.

Flanagan had two sisters and a brother, who was two years older than he was. Shortly after Flanagan's first birthday, his brother died.[8]

That sort of destroyed my father. He was just bitter, drank an awful lot, and we had some really terrible times with him. Although I recognize all of the things he went through—what I had to go through with him—I just absolutely hated him. I hated the house and to be there with him.

When they got the autopsy, they found that [my brother] had some kind of lead poisoning. It wasn't until my mother died [and] we were going through some stuff that I came across the letter from the doctor and the results of the autopsy.

I got a remembrance of the funeral; he was laid out in my grandmother's living room, my mother's parents. They lived above a delicatessen. I've got a memory of that—of seeing a baby lying in a crib and the baby not moving—from an angle of being real low, and later on I find out that when he died, they laid him out in their front room and it took two days to get a children's coffin in. So they in fact did lay him out in a cradle.

Immediately after his brother's death, his parents became very protective, but as he got older, the Flanagans began to loosen their grip a bit, and Flanagan participated in the kinds of urban street games that many children played in that era.

We were playing stickball all the time. You sort of watched them from the sidewalk forever, and then when you got old enough where they trusted you to count and keep score, you could be the scorekeeper, and then when they needed somebody on the outfield or something like that [you could go into the game]. So it was a lot of fun sort of growing up there. We played that and we played box-ball, you know, Chinese handball.

Eventually, a portion of Flanagan's street was removed to enable the building of the Gowanus Parkway. It cut right through a large swath of the Sunset Park, Brooklyn, neighborhood he grew up in. While the construction project is often blamed for devastating the neighborhood, in the eyes of a young Flanagan it opened all kinds of potential for fun. It became "Contractor Central," as he calls it, with all its materials and equipment. Flanagan and his friends cleared out a big area, moving rocks and rubble so they could create their own urban baseball diamond.

While his father did not serve in World War II, Flanagan was influenced by other veterans who fed his patriotic pride.

I remember on Flag Day and Memorial Day having to help my father string a gigantic American flag from my grandmother's two top windows on the top floor that would hang down almost to the basement. I mean, this was a humongous flag and very heavy, too.

Joey lived upstairs, and he didn't have a father. His father was killed during World War II. I thought that was just "Wow; he's got a hero father." Plus, I had an uncle who was a tail gunner on a Flying Fortress that got shot down and bailed out over Germany. He and his crew, on the anniversary of the shoot-down, would do a conference call with all of the guys. My uncle Frankie and my uncle Herbie, they were in the Navy.

My father, he stayed home; so he didn't sit very well with me at all, because everybody else was a hero and my father is a turd sitting back. Later I found out that because he was the oldest son in the family, he had to go to work and support my grandmother because she was a widow.

At the same time, Flanagan recalls the anxieties of the early Cold War years. For him, patriotic pride mixed with a desire to participate in correcting the problem.

I vividly remember sitting on the stoop at my girlfriend's house on Fourth Avenue and Forty-Fourth Street. We listened to Kennedy talking during the missile crisis and having the sense that it's going to blow up; we're going to have a nuclear exchange, and that's going to be the end. We're going to die within two days. I remember those things and wanting to do something about it.

I was very happy to be an American and I understood what it meant and I understood the freedoms that I got. I ain't got much, but I got a lot of freedoms that other people don't. I could do the right thing, I could protect people, and I could eventually get married and have some kids and a car and maybe get a house on the island like my brother did. So that's where the patriotism came. Of course, growing up Catholic, every morning we said the Pledge of Allegiance and prayer; I mean, that's just the way it is. You waved flags; you went to parades; you were proud to see your uncles marching in the Veterans Day Parade, and that . . . patriotism is there.

However, given the family's relative poverty and what he describes as a constricted sense of his personal horizons, he didn't believe that he had much of a future to look forward to.

My goals were so limited. What I thought I was going to be able to do was nothing. I remember the view of my life that I had in my head; I could see a block of, you know, eight years, which is elementary school, and then the four-year block that's half the size as, you know, high school, and then it was just black. There was nothing—you know, nothing at the end; there was no mountain to go up; there was no "here's what I want to be when I grow up." You take a look; your uncles are cops and that stuff and you say, "Okay; I'll probably end up being a cop."

By 1965, the military seemed a natural and appropriate way out.

While the U.S. military sent advisers to Vietnam in the mid-1950s and there were more than sixteen thousand American personnel there by 1963, the American war effort significantly expanded shortly afterward. Following alleged attacks on U.S. Navy patrols in the Gulf of Tonkin, Congress passed the Tonkin Gulf Resolution in August 1964, authorizing President Johnson to use force, at his discretion, to protect South Vietnam. As a result, the Selective Service began to conscript larger and larger numbers of New Yorkers. At the time, certain groups of young men, college students and parents of young children among them, were allowed to defer the draft. Those who had completed their high school education and had not enrolled in college (or perhaps had left college for one reason or another) were the first to be drafted.[9]

After Flanagan graduated from high school, his certainty that he would be drafted increased. As the war in Vietnam grew, some friends and co-workers of draft age were maneuvering to get into the National Guard and reserve units. He and his friends took a number of the appropriate civil service exams. Flanagan did well but was told he would have to work on his physical fitness, not something he was inclined to do. Instead, he and his buddies visited various recruiters, because they were told that the recruiters might be able to steer them into their preferred branch of service. After listening to all the pitches offered, and hearing repeatedly that he would need to sign up for four years for the more interesting service options, including officers' training, he decided to schedule a date for his induction into the military, effectively volunteering for the draft. As he writes in his autobiography, "This way I knew I was going to go soon, but that it would be only for 2 years."[10] Draftees served for two years; volunteers for three.

Postwar baby boomers were influenced by a generation that had confronted incredible challenges. In 1932, as a result of the Great Depression, one-third of the city's manufacturing facilities had shut down, and 1.6 million New Yorkers were receiving some form of relief.[11] In a piece written in 1955, the *New York Times* writer Meyer Berger would describe a resilient city that had just gone through "the tensest quarter-century in her 302 municipal years. In that period," Berger wrote, the city "struggled out of black depression's pit to her greatest opulence. She maintained her population lead and painfully let out her stays to prevent utter traffic strangulation. She tore down more slums in those twenty-five years than in any other quarter-century in her history; replaced them with airier housing set in green playgrounds and doubled her park space." In this era, the Lincoln, Queens-Midtown, and Brooklyn-Battery Tunnels were dug, along with additional routes out of Manhattan. That quarter century also saw the construction of the George Washington, Triboro, and Bronx-Whitestone Bridges and the completion of the Sixth Avenue and Eighth Avenue subways. As the war removed the last vestiges of the Great Depression, it brought new tensions and fears, including worries about blackouts, threats of a water shortage, and a rise in delinquency.[12] But there was work to be done and a hungry population willing to do it. Working-class New Yorkers labored in factories and served on the police force; they worked to keep the transportation systems running and the city sanitary. They would also become grandparents and parents, raising the generation that would eventually be asked to serve in Vietnam.

Edward Blanco, a retired government worker, was born in Manhattan but raised in Williamsburg, Brooklyn. *My mother and father are from Puerto Rico,* he says. *They met here in this country.* His father arrived in New York City after completing his U.S. military service in 1946, and his mother arrived in the same year. During that time, there was a surge of immigrants from Puerto Rico into the continental United States, New York City especially.

Blanco lived on West Twenty-Ninth Street until his parents' marriage failed, when he moved with his mother and sister to the Sumner Avenue public housing projects, in Brooklyn, where he lived until he went to Vietnam. His mother worked in the garment district as a seamstress. Many first- and second-generation Jewish and Italian workers who had dominated the garment industry until that time had retired or left the business. This meant new employment opportunities for minorities, including Puerto Ricans, and African Americans, and women like Ms. Blanco.

Blanco recalls the projects where he grew up as a tough neighborhood.

It's low-income families. At that time, there were no doctors or lawyers or, you know, any professionals living in the projects. There were people who worked in factories; my mother worked as a seamstress. People were on public assistance. When I first moved into the projects, there [were] a few nonblack or Hispanic families, but very, very few. The projects were brand-new; they had just built them. And so there were a few Jewish families and a few Italian families, but within four or five years they were gone. There was a Jewish family that was there much longer. They were, like, older people, and I guess they didn't have anyplace else to go. But it was mostly black and Hispanic families.

As he thinks back, he remembers how he and his friends were outside all the time, playing in the parks—softball especially. There were a lot of drugs in the neighborhood, and kids occasionally had run-ins with the police and with the youth gangs in the area.

My project had a gang. Just to give you an idea of what kind of neighborhood I lived in. All the projects had their own gangs, and the neighborhoods had their own gangs. And the gang that was in my project was called the Buccaneers—mostly a black gang with some Latinos and Puerto Ricans—and then there was the Chaplains, there was the Stompers, there was the Black Knights. The Buccaneers were a relatively small gang, but they were pretty fierce. And we would get invaded by Stompers and Chaplains in the nighttime in the summer and spring.

One time the Stompers came to my project. There had been a gang fight, and [the Buccaneers] killed a Stomper in front of my project building, a seventeen-year-old kid who had just graduated from high school that summer. He was supposedly the president of the Stompers. We had chains to separate the grass from the walkways, and people used to take those chains, cut them, and use them as weapons. And what I heard was they stomped and chained him and they killed him with the chain. Soon after that the Stompers lost another guy. He was knifed and killed by the Buccaneers. Now they had lost two guys.

I wasn't into any gangs, but I knew guys in the Buccaneers; it was good to know them. [Laughs.] And I saw this guy coming. I always remember because he's got white pants on, a dark shirt, and, like, a little hat—like a straw hat, and he's got a cane. [Gestures.] And I see him walking and he gets past the first light and then he enters the second light and he's walking, but then as he leaves, like, the second light, I see in the first light where he has been about five, six, or seven guys. So I said, "Holy shit; I think these are the Stompers coming back and this guy might be with them. I don't know who the fuck he is." And he comes up and he says, "Do any of you motherfuckers jitterbug?"

And I panicked . . . just took off because I . . . didn't know what these guys were going to do. So he yelled out, "Get that motherfucker," and I was running. I was like sixteen years old or something, and I was running like crazy. And they started chasing me, and I ran into a building and I ran up to my apartment and I didn't have the key and they caught me. But when they saw me, they saw I wasn't the Buccaneer. But they got pissed because I had made them run and chase me, and he said, "Let's kick his fucking ass." And the other guy said, "Nah." Anyway, they argued about it for like a second or two, and they just took off.

I knew people who died of ODs and stuff like that. But most of my closest friends and I stuck to playing softball. We didn't get into any heavy drug use or gangs. We had a softball team, and we just kind of stayed out of that kind of trouble.

Blanco attended the local junior high school and had the gift of a math teacher, Mr. Gibson, who had a tremendous impact on his life. Mr. Gibson wanted more minorities to get into one of New York's selective high schools, Brooklyn Tech, in Fort Greene. So he identified several young boys to groom for admission into the school. He took these children under his wing and tutored them, gave them additional homework, and tried to push them academically. They took the admissions test in the eighth grade and failed. So he pushed them twice as hard. In ninth grade, Blanco and three others passed the admissions test and started Tech in the tenth grade.

It was me, this guy Jeff, and Arthur; we went to Brooklyn Tech, which was a very good high school. I didn't realize it at the time. I mean, I didn't even think about those things. But it made a difference.

While World War II stories did influence Blanco and push him toward military service, he remembers that his father's story probably involved as much invention as truth.

I would visualize that he was in action, but later on I realized he didn't really see any close-up action. He may have been on an island that got bombed or something, but . . . he had a little vaccination scar here. And when I was a little kid, he told me it was a bullet wound.

He also links the images of war on the silver screen to his own interest in the service.

I would watch a lot of World War II movies, you know, John Wayne and everything. And then when the news started talking about Vietnam, it caught my interest and I was in high school. In '65, I was just graduating; it was my last year in high school, and that's when the Marines landed [in Da Nang] in March of '65. And I was just paying attention to it, and even before that I was paying attention to it. I was just,

"There's something going on here." And I kind of was getting interested in joining.

By the time Blanco graduated, a lot of his slightly older friends from the neighborhood were already gone. They had either joined the service or been drafted. While Blanco could have gone to college, he decided not to. Everyone in his class at Brooklyn Tech was planning on college, and they thought he was crazy. But Blanco wanted to serve. At age seventeen he asked his mother to sign the papers to allow him to go into the military. She refused. He had to wait until he was eighteen.

He got a job with ITT, bringing in $72 a week—good money at the time. He also took the test to qualify for work at the Metropolitan Transit Authority (MTA), and while he did well on the exam, he found he couldn't work there until he was eighteen. He returned to the MTA when he turned eighteen and got an offer for $112 a week (it was the starting salary), more than his mother was making. Thinking he ought to stay home and help his mother, he took the job but quickly began to reconsider his decision.

The war was blowing up, and my friends were all there, two of them were already in Vietnam. And I said, "Nah, I'm going to go." I really wanted to go there; I wanted the adventure of it, you know. Throughout the ages, young boys have been wanting to go to war for the adventure and the excitement; I'm no different.

At first he aspired to be a Marine, in part because he loved those old movies so much.

They ate up my mind. I wanted to be a Marine, and they were an elite unit. I was going to go into battle and be with an elite unit; I don't want to be with some scrubs that got drafted, you know. That's the way I'm thinking back then. I don't feel that way about draftees now, but back then . . . But I said, "I'm not going to join for four years. I just don't want to join." So I did a lot of research, and I realized that Airborne to me was an elite unit, too, you know. And if I got drafted, I could volunteer for Airborne; that means I would be in an Airborne unit, like the 101st Screaming Eagles. And to me that's as good as being in the Marines.

I figured I was going to get drafted eventually; everybody was getting drafted—everybody. I was 1-A [immediately available for military service]. But I couldn't wait; so I found out that I could volunteer to be drafted. I went down to the draft board and waited until they opened, got in, and volunteered to be drafted. I didn't tell my mother or anything. I just made believe that I had gotten drafted.

The Hamill family, from Brooklyn, are well-known in New York. Pete, the oldest of seven, is a widely acclaimed novelist and has had a long career in journalism. In 1965 he covered the war as a reporter. He went on to write for *The Village Voice, New York Newsday,* and the New York *Daily News.*

Pete's brother John, now in his sixties, works for the Federal Emergency Management Agency (FEMA) as a director of external affairs. He has a full head of gray hair and walks with a limp at times due to the shrapnel that remains embedded in his knee, a gift of the North Vietnamese. When we spoke about his Combat Medical Badge, John told me that it was *the only medal I ever received that meant something to me.* He wanted that badge for the hard-earned knowledge it represented, just as he wanted to serve.

I met John through his younger brother Denis, who is a New York *Daily News* columnist. In 2004, Denis wrote a column about John's service in Dak To in 1967—one of the bloodiest battles of the war. They agreed to sit down and talk to me about the Brooklyn they grew up in and the impact Vietnam had on their lives. We met in Denis's home in Queens.

John described himself as one of the lucky guys. *I got to experience Vietnam and the '60s both here and abroad, and I'm still on my feet. I mean, I've done some damage, you'd say, since, but I consider myself lucky.*

Denis explains further:

I did a column about this a couple of years ago. I was walking with my little guy, and I stopped to look at this wall where we [his childhood friends] all used to carve our names in the wall with can openers. I was fifty years old, and I looked at it and I said, "Holy shit. All these guys are dead." Glen blew his head off. Bat died on drugs, got hit by a car, you know. The Doyle brothers are all dead, about four of them. And there's just an endless march of guys from AIDS and from shooting dope. And it is just an endless parade of guys who were my friends in the '60s who are all gone.

Denis described the Brooklyn he grew up in as a collection of small towns: a big, notorious place, with clearly delineated neighborhoods, like the one he lived in. Now known as Park Slope, when the Hamills lived there it was simply called South Brooklyn. John says:

It was a really small world. [The] same kind of hermetically sealed feel that you had in some bad ghettos, you know. So you didn't feel poor, because nobody had much. I mean, you could play ball and make people move their car if it was on the corner.

They lived and played on the street:

John: *The fucking house was so hot.*

Denis: *There was no such thing as a playdate.*

John: *[Laughs.] That didn't exist. The playdate was "Get the fuck off of that." My mother wouldn't let us stay in the house, because we would wreck it. So we'd go out and come back in when it's dinnertime.*

John continues:

It was a neighborhood, as my brother Pete described—but it's very accurate—that the Depression never left. It was a place that never got to boom time, postwar, or any of that. So it was factory and dockworkers, essentially; some civil servants. I mean, we didn't know any white-collar people hardly.

As boys from the neighborhood became men, they sometimes did better than their parents, moving into civil service or back-office jobs on Wall Street or becoming police officers or sanitation workers or taking other uniformed service jobs.

Denis portrays his brother John as a young man who dreamed of moving beyond Brooklyn and beyond the Staten Island housing project where they lived for a time. He recalls John reading *I. F. Stone's Weekly*, the New Left magazine *Ramparts*, and Paul Krassner's *Realist* as well as newspapers like the *Daily News* and *The New York Times*. To Denis this seemed very unusual for a seventeen-year-old.

He had this sense of history about Vietnam when it happened that it was the biggest event of his generation.

He was really smart and I was a fuckup. I mean, school for me was a big pain in the ass, and I was more interested in chicks and sports and eventually drugs and everything else. But Johnnie became very politicized during the war. He was in his teens. We'd go to these meetings in church basements in Bay Ridge. I remember going to one where there was a guy from the Green Berets speaking to all the pink-faced men in Bay Ridge and Johnnie stood up in the middle of them all and told them what [he] thought about it, the war. He stood up in this room full of guys and he was booed down and the people were telling him he was a pacifist and a punk and all that kind of stuff. I remember that very clearly.

John recalled the same incident:

I said, you know, "I don't think this is such a great idea." I didn't think that we had the justification yet, you know. It was "Show me." Weeks later, John joined the military, thinking he might as well see for himself. And there were other influences as well.

You want to run away from home when you're seventeen, you know. That's part of it. And it is a rite of passage in America, isn't it? I mean, in Brooklyn to, you know, join the military.

I was a sophomore in high school the day Kennedy got killed, and four years later, to the day, I was in Vietnam. So, you know, after Kennedy and when that started, I said, "This is going to be the defining moment. There's no question about it." This country's never going to be the same, the world's never going to be the same, and it's like missing the last boat; you know, in a way I thought it was, you know, our generation's event. I didn't feel such an obligation so much as I felt a sense of wanting ownership of the facts of it, you know, to be able to say, "I know what this is about. I don't speculate about it. I don't have opinions. I have experiences."

For Denis, John's choice was enormously painful:

I couldn't believe it. Of course, I wept because it was the end of our childhood. I mean, it was, we were just getting into marijuana and the Beatles and, you know, and Donovan and Dylan and all of that and the '60s were here and we were having a great time and he was going to Kingsborough [Community College]. And boom, he dropped out of school and went into a recruitment station and joined the Army and then went Airborne.

The Hamill family actively tried to dissuade John from reporting for his swearing in. John recalls:

May 8, which is my brother Brian's birthday, of 1967 was the day I was officially inducted into the Army at Fort Hamilton in New York. Had been a big party the night before, where my older brother took out three grand in cash and says, "Here, take this and go somewhere, but don't go in the Army." Well [laughs] . . . [it was the] first of several decisions I still question, but at any rate . . .

I wanted to do it.

2

PROFESSIONALISM: RICHARD EGGERS

Richard Eggers was wounded in battle in early 1966. When I sent him a photograph I had taken of the First Cavalry Division, his former unit, holding the flag during a ceremony at the Vietnam Veterans Memorial in Washington, D.C., he replied: "Good memories." Indeed, the military suited him; he considered making it his career. Eggers's story is that of the professional American soldier who fought in Vietnam because he believed in his country and its mission and saw a place for himself in both. Although his future did not work out as he might have hoped and he left the Army after Vietnam, he maintains the values he associates with his life as a soldier.

Eggers was born while his father served in the Army during World War II, and he was raised in Westchester County, just north of New York City. He recalls: *In Larchmont, the men worked, and the women were at the clubs and they raised all of their children and they volunteered.*

Eggers's father was wounded on Guadalcanal. While Eggers recalls his father's imposing six-foot-five-inch stature, he doesn't remember the elder Eggers speaking much about his wartime experience. At one point, Eggers's dad told him that he received the Purple Heart because he "didn't duck quite fast enough." Perhaps, jokes Eggers, his dad was too big to fit into a foxhole.

Eggers's grandfather Otto Eggers was a longtime associate of the well-known architect John Russell Pope. In 1939, after Pope died, Otto and his partner completed the construction of Pope's design of the Jefferson Memorial in Washington, D.C. Eggers and his partner would go on to run one of the most respected architecture firms in the country, Eggers & Higgins.

Eggers recalls a childhood in which he and his siblings did not want for anything, as the family was relatively well-off. Nevertheless, by the time he reached high school, he recalls, he was a bit of a troublemaker.

In addition to architecture, the Eggers family had a tradition of serving in the military. His father was a graduate of the New York Military Academy in Cornwall-on-Hudson and felt that a military school would be good for his son. Even so, the young Eggers ended up attending a military college *more by chance than by choice.* He recalls that his grades were good but that in 1960 that wasn't so rare. When the Pennsylvania Military College accepted him, he decided to go. *As it turned out, it was wonderful. It was a marvelous experience; I loved every single moment of it.*

There was one area where Eggers would break with the family tradition. He had grown up in a family of staunch Republicans, but he registered as a Democrat in 1959 so that he could vote for John F. Kennedy in the 1960 primary, a decision that irritated his father. *It was an assumption not only in my house but in my family in general that you were a Republican.*

In the end, he received a solid education at the military college, graduating with a major in economics and a minor in English in 1964. He also belonged to ROTC, and by the time he left that organization, he was a commissioned second lieutenant in the U.S. Army Reserve. At that point in his life it appeared to him as though the military would be his career. About this, at least, his father was very proud. Eggers liked the Army, too. He says, *I liked the life; I liked the structure.*

After graduation, Eggers postponed entering the service until January 1965. Knowing that he could not commit to a regular job, he looked into working at the 1964 World's Fair in Queens. Through family connections, Eggers got a job bartending at the Schaefer Beer Garden. It was a fateful choice, as he met his wife-to-be on the way there. Barbara Williams, from Douglaston, Queens, worked at the New York State Pavilion and attended American University in Washington, D.C. They fell in love and married on November 28, 1964. As it turned out, his new father-in-law was also a veteran, which had a significant effect on Eggers.

He landed at D-day. In fact, there's one piece of film that I've seen. He was in a boat, in this landing craft, you know, with his tank, and the boat had been hit and was sinking. And there's a shot of it, and he's out there waving.

In January 1965, Eggers was assigned to Officer Candidate School at Fort Benning, Georgia, for training, just as the war in Vietnam began to escalate. By June 1965, the United States had placed 82,000 combat troops in South Vietnam, and General William Westmoreland, commander of Military Assistance Command, Vietnam (MACV), was asking for more. By 1968, 525,000 U.S. troops were stationed in South Vietnam. As part of this buildup of U.S. forces, on July 28 the president announced he would send the revamped First Cavalry Division (Airmobile) to Vietnam. The unit left for Vietnam in August 1965.

While the First Cav headed for Vietnam, Eggers remained in the United States, continuing his training. In retrospect, he does not believe that the men conducting the training had an adequate sense of the kind of combat Americans would confront in Southeast Asia.

I don't think that they had any clue as to the tactics that were necessary to fight in Vietnam, because Vietnam was completely different than any other war we had ever fought . . . there were no lines; there was no place that you could say this is your own. The only place that was your own is where you were at that particular moment. Outside of that, everything else was up for grabs.

As a result, the image of warfare that Eggers and others took to Vietnam was similar to what they saw in the movies. It would have little to do with what they would actually experience.

You gotta remember, war, in my mind, was almost a game, because when you were in training, there was no live ammunition except in this evasion course where they were firing over your head. You knew that you weren't going to be hurt or killed.

In November 1965, the First Cavalry Division met the troops of the North Vietnamese Army, the People's Army of Vietnam (PAVN), and beat them in battle. Depicted in the 2002 Mel Gibson film *We Were Soldiers*, the Ia Drang Valley battles took the lives of over three hundred Americans, including Eggers's good friend from college, the platoon leader John "Jack" Geoghegan. When Geoghegan was killed in the Ia Drang Valley, Eggers says, *I was just absolutely stunned.*

War, which had been a game, an imaginary experience invented for him through Hollywood movies, became intensely real. The reality of Geoghegan's death was brought back when he saw *We Were Soldiers*, in which the actor Chris Klein plays Geoghegan.

I saw it at my college with a lot of the guys who were with Jack, and Bravo and Charlie Company . . . in the Ia Drang Valley. I was actually ducking, because the surround sound in that movie was close to realistic combat; it brought back a flood of memories.

As the Ia Drang battles were taking place, Eggers's life changed.

I was in class, and we had a break, and I went down to the men's room and was standing in front of the urinal, and this captain walks in and says, "Lieutenant Eggers?" I said, "Yes, sir." "Saddle up, dude, you just got orders to go across the pond." That was the phrase, "going across the pond," over there. Promptly at which every bit of blood drained right out of my body, and I peed on my shoe as I was standing there. That's actually what happened.

I immediately called my wife on the phone and told her. She started to cry; I said, "Yeah, I know, but I'll be back." And I packed up my bags— they cut orders for me right there—went right straight back to Fort Knox. We had Thanksgiving, and it's funny. Our final meal at Fort Knox, Kentucky, the end of the month on a second lieutenant's salary, you're broke. And we had hot dogs and baked beans—that was our Thanksgiving dinner.

Eggers and his wife drove from Kentucky back home to Larchmont, New York, and stayed with his parents while his orders came through.

While in town, Eggers recalls eating at the famous '21' Club and seeing *The Sound of Music* on Broadway, enjoying his time at home as much as possible before saying goodbye. On December 30, 1965, the Eggers family drove him to JFK, and his wife's family was there as well; the two World War II veterans both came to see him off.

We got out there to the airport, and my father-in-law said goodbye and shook my hand and all this kind of stuff, and my father wasn't looking at me. He couldn't look at me, he said, later on, so he just put out his hand and said, "Take care of yourself"—turned around and walked away, because he was crying. But he didn't want me to see that he was crying. My wife was crying; I was crying; we gave a big hug and a kiss, then I got on the plane and swoosh! Off we went.

By the time he arrived in Vietnam, he knew that Jack Geoghegan had been killed. In an assignment area at Tan Son Nhut Air Force Base, he was asked what he wanted to do, where he wanted to go. He was offered a post in a rear area, but refused. Instead, Eggers asked to be assigned to Geoghegan's old battalion. That position was filled, so they offered him a spot as a platoon leader in B Company, First Battalion, Seventh Cavalry Regiment, and that's where he ended up. By that same afternoon he was boarding a C-130 aircraft on its way to Anh Khe in the Central Highlands. He landed at a sprawling base in the mountains surrounded by jungle.

Eggers met Sergeant Montgomery, a noncommissioned officer and grizzled veteran of the Korean War whose job it would be to assist him. Eggers immediately acknowledged Montgomery's greater experience and knowledge. He knew he would have to rely on Montgomery's help.

I came to respect the guys who knew. They just knew what to do. They didn't get frazzled; they didn't get excited no matter what was going on. They told me straight out front, and this guy had been in the Ia Drang Valley, so hell, this guy's a pro.

Life in the Central Highlands was not like anything Eggers had ever experienced. The soldiers took salt pills, gamma globulin shots, and quinine pills and used water-purification tablets. Eggers shares a story of his first night out in the field. During a search-and-destroy operation, his unit came upon a village, but the homes were eerily empty. He spent the night in one of them and describes finding a way to spice up his unappetizing C rations.

I hadn't eaten anything at all for breakfast. So it was quiet, and I crack open a can of C rations, some ungodly concoction, and sitting over on a shelf in this guy's hooch was this French champagne bottle filled with these lovely multicolored orange/yellow/green/red peppers. They were about this big and long, about an inch long. And so, you know, one of the guys says, "Hey, Lieutenant, why don't you use, why don't you add some spice to your life and put some of that?" What do I know? The thing is filled with vinegar, homemade vinegar, so I pour some of that in there, and I shake out some of the little peppers and I take out my knife and cut the peppers up, and I knew they were going to be hot. I mixed it up in the thing like this, and we stick it in the fire that we had going there, so it just got warm. It wasn't hot; it just got warm. And I remember taking one spoonful of that stuff, and I thought, "Mother of God," I thought I'd died. The only thing that put it out was peanut butter with crackers.

Even nearly forty-five years later, his time in the field remains vivid. He recalls eating vintage World War II C rations. While they didn't taste that good, they were filling and had the carbohydrates and proteins the body needs to keep going. Sleep was elusive, and when you could grab it, your auditory senses were primed to the specific sounds that indicate threat. His sense of hearing became so acute he could hear the sound of a single round being chambered or a safety being turned off on a rifle.

Whenever that happened, and you could be asleep and hear that, I swear to God, your eyes would open up.

Anxiety was always running high. One night while the unit was on perimeter guard duty, they heard rustling out beyond the barbed wire. They shouted commands for whoever it was to stop moving. It didn't, so they opened up. It got quiet again.

[We thought, we'll] get it in the morning, whatever it was. Whoever it was is out there, and they're not going anywhere. [It turns out] we'd killed a cow.

The next morning they took what is called an "army mule," a little flatbed cart, and loaded the cow in the back. That night the men barbecued the cow.

Not long after, Eggers and his unit were transferred out of the Central Highlands to the seacoast to participate in what was called Operation White Wing/Masher. His unit was placed on an outpost beyond the "golf course" at An Khe, where it served as an early warning unit for the base.

Following the detection of enemy soldiers nearby, his unit conducted a helicopter assault into an embattled landing zone in January 1966. He remembers being under fire, with his RTO [radiotelephone operator] Stanley Semler nearby:

I mean, they were shooting at us. It's the damnedest feeling—and anybody else that you talk to, I'm sure, will say the same thing. You're flying along in a helicopter, okay? And I'm sitting there in the door with my feet hanging out on the rails, and I'm holding a baseplate,[1] my hands are over here on the side; Semler is over here beside me or right behind me, and you're looking down and you can see rounds coming up at you. The only thing that you can see are the tracer rounds—all these things were loaded, four rounds of ball, one round the tracer. And you're seeing the tracer rounds going up and over. These are .50-calibers.

Now, I've seen what .50-calibers do to people. You don't want to know, it's terrible—absolutely terrible. And you're wondering to yourself, "Why aren't we being hit?" And they're going over the helicopter and under the helicopter. I'm wondering where the other three rounds are. I can see the tracers.

So we fly in and we fly in fast . . . You could hear over the pilot's radios that it was way too hot; this was bad news. I mean, we're getting hit—bing, chung, bing, like that. I have the baseplate in my hands, and I felt this foot in my back go boom, like this.

He was kicked out of the chopper, landing in a rice paddy. As soon as he hit the ground, Eggers was off and running as fast as he could, carrying the baseplate for the mortars.

You don't think; there is no thought to this process. It's you or him, I guess. He's shooting at you when you're shooting back at him, and you just do what you have got to do. It was your job, you know. You take as many of them down as you possibly can.

This was his first real firefight, and it lasted only about five minutes. It was the first time he could ever remember firing in someone's direction and watching him fall down. His unit did not lose any soldiers that morning.

At those times you don't think of yourself as a commander; you think of yourself as a soldier with command responsibility. And thank God for Sergeant Montgomery, God bless him.

It's likely they were being fired upon by the Vietcong—South Vietnamese Communist guerrilla units—although there may have been PAVN—North Vietnamese regular soldiers—operating in the area. The unit spent the night in a village, Eggers and Semler sleeping in a house with a bed made out of a slab of mahogany. He used his backpack for a pillow and slept heavily. *I slept just like a bear. I hibernated that night. It was my first real, honest-to-goodness shooting.*

The following morning they went out on patrol in an area with tall brush. As they moved down a path, they heard the sound of automatic weapons fire. Then they saw a line of ten uniformed North Vietnamese soldiers moving quickly along a tree line to the north, where the weapons fire had come from.

And all of a sudden, all hell breaks loose; that line of guys that I saw going in there, it turns out later, was an automatic weapons company of NVA regulars. These are professional soldiers, just like us. And they opened up. They had dug in; they had moved very quickly into this little dike area. They opened up on us and, Mother of God, there were bullets flying everywhere. I reach for my radio . . . [Claps.] I got hit.

Eggers and Semler, a native of Stockton, California, were both hit by a burst of fire from the same weapon.

Semler got shot in the neck somewhere, and he went down and I went down. The only thing I remember about it is this force picking me up—I was hit in the arm—picking me up off the ground and spinning me around. And when I came down, my M16 was halfway underneath me in the water and this arm was over my eyes, and I'm underneath the water. I thought I was dead.

I couldn't see, I couldn't hear, and I could feel nothing, because the pain hadn't hit me yet. And so I actually said, "Oh, shit, I'm dead," and then the arm flopped down in the water, and the pain hit me. I have never felt pain like that—never. When a bullet hits you, hits bone, it shatters everything. How I still have movement in this hand, as far as I'm concerned, is a miracle of God. God wanted me to have both hands still. Because it blew the entire back of my arm out, all of it out.

After what seemed like an eternity, a medic emerged, wrapped his arm, gave him a shot of morphine, and moved on. As the firing decreased and he began to move, he could hear North Vietnamese bullets striking the paddy dike against which he rested. He watched a South Vietnamese Air Force propeller-driven aircraft drop napalm on the tree line where the rounds had come from. From a hundred yards away he could feel the heat of the exploding napalm. All of a sudden he heard the sound of a helicopter that seemed to come to a dead stop almost on top of him.

And out hops the door gunner and the crew chief, pick me up, throw me in on top of ammo cases, arm banging around like hell, and I say, "Don't forget him," and the guys say, "Nope." That was my radio operator. And we picked off the ground and I can remember looking out, and I'm seeing [Semler]; he's just, he's lying there in the rice paddy like this— his eyes wide open and he's dead, just wide open like this, just like a crucifix, just lying there, like this. I can see his face here today. I actually heard him die. I could hear him dying; he was drowning in his own blood. He didn't move—there was no movement at all. I think the bullet went in and hit his spine and severed his spine, so there was no feeling . . . but he had to have known that he was drowning.

At the battalion aid station they wanted Eggers to walk out of the helicopter, but he couldn't. He was bleeding too badly. Someone quickly hit him with more morphine, and then he had to wait. As soon as someone did speak to him, Eggers remembers insisting that the doctors patch him up and send him back to his unit. Whoever was attending him told him, "Lieutenant, you ain't going anywhere but home." They took his helmet, weapon, and ammunition and placed him in a helicopter to fly him elsewhere for more medical aid. He remembers nearly falling out of the helicopter as it flew to the Eighty-Fifth Evacuation Hospital in Qui Nhon.

After debridement—a surgical procedure in which doctors and nurses attempt to remove foreign matter like dirt and other material from the wound—his arm was placed into a cast. The following day he was flown to Clark Air Base in the Philippines. The next thing he remembers is a bank of telephones they wheeled in so that he could call home.

My wife answered the phone, "Hello." And I said, "Hi"; there was this pause at the other end of the phone; she says, "Oh, hi, how you doing? How are you? Good to hear your voice." I said, "Well, let's put it this way. I was wounded." There's this long pause. "But you're talking to me, right?" I said, "Yeah, I'm talking to you and I'm on my way home." She says, "Okay." That's all she had to know. She never asked me where I was wounded. She never asked me how bad it was. She knew that I called her. I sounded like me, and I was on my way home. And that impressed me. Not then, but years later, thinking about it.

And I spoke with my father-in-law. Now, he was a vet from World War II; had landed at D-day, had his unit hit very badly; he was wounded, he had some nerve damage, he twitched, like that. And he was a tank commander. He was a major; he was the commander of a squadron of tanks or something like that. And he got on the phone and he asked me all kinds of questions, and I just . . . it was like a five-minute phone call, just that was it, that small, that short, and . . . done.

When it was time to go home, he was loaded onto a C-141 Starlifter aircraft and given new clothing. From there it was on to Hawaii, then Texas, then McGuire Air Force Base, and finally Valley Forge General Hospital in Phoenixville, Pennsylvania. By the time he arrived back in the United States, Eggers had dropped from his original weight of 183 to 155 pounds. His wound was extremely painful, and he had to have further surgery. He was hospitalized for much of the spring of 1966, often in traction. There is now a one-inch difference in the length of his two arms, the result of the destruction of the bone. And even now his arm aches when it gets cold outside.

There were other wounded soldiers at Valley Forge whom he will never forget, including a man with a spinal wound who had been hit by a .50-caliber round. He also remembers watching a young man get out of his hospital wheelchair and learn to walk all over again.

Talk about sheer guts and determination to live and go on. That impressed me so much. I can still see it in my mind's eye.

Witnessing the will of those soldiers moved Eggers deeply, and he left with a determination to get on with his life, despite his wound. To this day he considers himself fortunate to have gotten out of Vietnam alive with all his parts, *even if they were banged up a bit.*

He had only been in Vietnam for thirty-five days, but when he saw his wife for the first time, he had been through a lot. It was a relief to see her. By March 1966 he was being allowed day passes to visit his wife and family outside the hospital. Eventually, the hospital arranged an overnight trip to Atlantic City. In contrast to the experience of some other veterans, Eggers recalls being treated like royalty by a tourist association there.

Like Ron Kovic in *Born on the Fourth of July,* Eggers was invited by his hometown to be the grand marshal of the Memorial Day Parade. He agreed. The parade was the impetus for him to make his first visit back to Larchmont, and he has very warm memories of what took place. As he was dropped off at the arranged meeting place where the parade would begin, *you would've thought God walked in.*

He remembers being saluted and the pride that his father and father-in-law expressed.

I was proud, too. What the hell. I didn't know why I was there. I thought there were other people a lot more deserving of it than me. But there I was, the grand marshal of the blasted parade!

Eggers was not given a medical discharge. Apparently, his arm was not damaged enough, and he had time left on his military commitment. In early June 1966 he got orders to head to Fort Lewis, Washington, where he became a company commander. And he loved it. Still, as he puts it, he was *prime meat to go back* to Vietnam, and he didn't want to.

He could have stayed in. He and his wife discussed it, but he had

had enough of dead bodies. In addition, the Eggerses' second child had a serious case of bacterial pneumonia, and he just didn't want to be apart from his family at that time.

I liked the concept of the service; I was good at it; I was comfortable in it; my wife liked it too. We got to travel a little bit and do this and do that.

But Eggers was having doubts about America's involvement in the war. To him, it didn't seem that the country was committed to winning. He says:

The only way that this was going to be stopped was that we had to virtually take out Hanoi. If you want to kill the spider, you've got to get the spider in his nest. But there wasn't anybody out there who wanted to do it. That political risk internationally was way too big.

So, in early January 1968, he left the Army. Eggers went on to work for an insulation company and bought a home in Rockland County, New York. For the better part of two decades he didn't tell anyone he had served in Vietnam. *If somebody started to talk about it in a conversation, I just sat there. I never said I was or wasn't.*

Eggers didn't want to get into a political discussion with anyone. He was just happy that his war had ended and that he had survived. Then things changed a little. The war ended in 1975, and Eggers's brother-in-law returned from Vietnam. He had had a very bad time as a medic, though Eggers declines to say more, and died at age forty-five.

His brother-in-law's struggles led Eggers to begin talking more about his experiences. He took some goading and at times had to defend himself: *I said, "Look, I was just a soldier. I didn't kill any babies that I know of; I was just a soldier; that's all I was."*

Though he was no longer silent about his combat experience, Vietnam was still mostly out of his everyday thoughts until 1991, when several things happened. First, the Gulf War began. It seemed to Eggers that the country was entering the Gulf War with the determination to win quickly and definitively that he hadn't sensed in Vietnam. He remembers imagining what it would be like to return to the service.

That triggered something deep, deep inside of me, that I could no longer deny that part of my life.

Another factor was Eggers's younger son, who was learning about the Vietnam War in high school and asked his father to tell him more about his experiences.

For the first time, I said, "Okay, but you better have some time." And I don't know how many hours we talked. Over time I seemed to find a place inside of me that was more accessible. Gradually, it began to come out of me, and I began to talk about it to other people, if they asked. It became a source of pride eventually. But it was hard fought.

In the late 1990s he got a Purple Heart license plate for his car. Not long after, men from his unit began to contact him.

Today, he says that he is proud to have participated in the Vietnam War and that he did it because he thought it was the right thing to do. At the same time, he doesn't seek out veterans' reunions or other veterans' events. He doesn't want his veteran's status to define him, instead choosing to be oriented toward his family and his church. He is the father of five and has been married for more than forty-five years.

I don't want it to consume me. Some of these guys are consumed.

Looking back, Eggers associates military service with the virtues of leadership he believes he's displayed as an owner or manager of small businesses. He recalls being under fire and the instinctive effort to do his job without panic, knowing that mistakes could be costly. He and Semler were the only casualties during the time he led the platoon. And while the majority of the men in his unit were African American, he also had whites and Latinos and remembers that everyone got along. There was never a need to take disciplinary action.

At the end of our discussion, Eggers came to a realization:

I never thought about that, but here we are in the middle of a rice paddy, and I had a choice to go forward or back, and I went forward literally into a hail of machine gun bullets rather than go back. That was a conscious choice because I saw this dry spot and I figured I could get up onto it and be able to direct fire.

Leadership always presents difficult choices. And although Eggers's decision would lead to an injury and the death of PFC Semler, he felt it was the best decision to make for the platoon. His decision to be in the military was the right way to serve his country. For Eggers, every choice has its cost, but if it's the right one, the cost is well worth it.

Eggers argues that we never understood the enemy in Vietnam.

I think our presidents were in some way responding to generals who wanted notches on their rifle butts for further promotions. We were responding to the defense industry; they had to try new things like the concept of helicopter warfare.

Nevertheless, he asserts that politics aside, *I trained more young men to go over there, and I trained them the very best I could.*

Knowing what he does now, Eggers says he respects people who made the decision to resist service and flee to places like Canada, but that was not his nature. He couldn't have done it in 1965, and he would not do it today. For him, *war is obedience to orders; war is accomplishing your mission. The old phrase goes, "Ours is not to reason why. Ours is to do or die." And that's what we did. All of us did.*

3

FUTILITY: SUE O'NEILL

Soldiers—men and women alike—tell their Vietnam stories through the lens of their political and social viewpoints. Some came to see the American odyssey in Vietnam in terms that Richard Eggers might reject—as an effort that was pointless at best, barbaric at worst. While morale remained high throughout the armed forces during the first half of the war, after 1968, writes the historian James Westheider, "morale, cohesion, and discipline throughout the U.S. military establishment began to deteriorate."[1] Susan O'Neill's recollection of her time in Vietnam would bear out this assertion. What she remembers best is the futility of the war. But like Eggers, she found that the experience of serving a larger cause, in her case as a combat nurse working to save lives, shaped the remainder of her life profoundly.

For women as for African Americans, the 1960s was a time of widespread cultural change. Efforts were made to integrate women in the workplace more readily, to pay them more fairly, and to reform policies regarding sexual harassment and domestic violence. The decade also saw the development of the first reliable oral method of birth control, giving women command of their reproductive systems and therefore more influence over their futures. Like any other institution, the American military began responding to these changing realities. Recent writing on the history of American nurses during the Vietnam era argues that "the war both advanced the position of women and nurses in the army and preserved their subordinate status at the same time."[2] Female nurses gained new experiences and achieved dramatic gains in professional status while still occupying a second tier within the military bureaucracy.

Because women were not subject to the draft, all women who served in the U.S. Army volunteered. For O'Neill—née Kramer—military service was not a civic duty but rather a matter of expedience. She felt a strong financial obligation to her family, who had strained to put her through years of private Catholic schooling.

O'Neill became a New Yorker later in life than many of the other men and women I interviewed, having moved to the city to be close to her children in the past decade. She was born in 1947 in Fort Wayne, Indiana. Her mother was a stay-at-home mom, and her father worked in a factory; they were devout Catholics. While she had an older brother, O'Neill quickly became the "responsible" child, obligated to take care of her three younger siblings. Her parents were not well-off, but nevertheless wanted their children to acquire skills that would help them earn a good living. Unable to pay for college, they committed to making trade school educations available for all five children.

Her nursing career actually began early in life. The O'Neill children were divided between two bedrooms, with the girls sharing one room and the boys another. One of her younger sisters was often sick during the night, vomiting on the others in the bottom bunk. O'Neill would dutifully march into her parents' bedroom to announce that her youngest sister had been sick again. Often her mother would tell her to simply clean it up. A middling student, O'Neill did not work very hard at her academics during high school. However, given her parents' commitment to practical professions, along with a strong desire to leave Fort Wayne, she decided upon nursing school. She had no intention of becoming a secretary, and technology did not interest her. When she graduated from high school in 1965, she thought, *"Well, I can clean up after my sister, I can be a nurse."* So she chose nursing school.

O'Neill enrolled in a three-year program at Holy Cross School of

Nursing in South Bend, Indiana, which at the time was known as a service school. Students worked in hospitals in exchange for their education. While they still paid a tuition, it was much lower than it would have been otherwise, and it provided specialty training that sent students to institutions in other cities. Consequently, she spent time in both Louisville, Kentucky, at the Our Lady of Peace mental hospital, and Indianapolis, at the Riley Memorial Children's Hospital, where she trained in pediatrics.

One of Sue's good friends at school, Judy Kuchar, came from a conservative military family. Her father had been in active service, and her brother was enrolled in a military academy. Kuchar planned on following the family tradition and would eventually volunteer for the Army after completing nursing school. Despite this connection, serving in the military was, Sue says, the furthest thing from her mind. She was spending her time singing in South Bend, Indiana, coffeehouses, doing community theater, and working on the 1968 presidential campaign to elect Eugene McCarthy, an outspoken opponent of the Vietnam War.

When Kuchar decided to enlist, she made plans to travel to Chicago to sign up for the Army Nurse Corps. Tempted by the idea of a visit to a big city, O'Neill decided to go along for the ride but had no plans to enlist. She soon found herself in a room full of enthusiastic recruiters. According to O'Neill, the recruiters weren't exactly picky. She jokes that they were passing a mirror under her nose to make sure she was alive. That was the extent of the examination they gave her.

The recruiter turned to O'Neill and said, "Well, what about you?"

O'Neill's response was rather blunt. *"You've got the wrong person,"* she told him.

But the recruiter went on, appealing to her one vulnerability—her wish for financial independence. He explained that if she committed herself to joining the Army Nurse Corps, the military would give her a monthly stipend in her last year of nursing school. This tapped into her—as she terms it—*Catholic guilt*. She felt she owed her parents for her expensive education. She quickly figured out that she would be able to pay her parents back for at least one year of tuition. Further, as some recruiters did at the time, he tempted her with visions of international travel. "You could go to Japan; you could go to Germany. We have all these places you can go, including Hawaii," he told her.

She thought, *"Jesus. I've never been much out of Fort Wayne. That would be interesting."*

Still, O'Neill was smart enough to weigh the recruiter's claims against the practical realities of wartime, knowing she could end up in Vietnam. When she expressed her personal opposition to the war, his reply was classic. "You don't have to worry about that," he said. "There is a waiting list a mile long to go to Vietnam." He reassured her that she would never find herself there. In the end, the thought of being able to pay her parents back, and the idea of international travel, won out.

O'Neill now compares this decision to those she made during her time in community theater, where she had a penchant for taking roles that were often counter to the person she was. For anyone who knew her, the notion that Sue O'Neill would join the military would have seemed almost laughable.

With less than a day's thought, she signed on for the role of Army nurse. She called her father from Chicago. *"Dad, guess what? I just joined the military."* Her father had served in a noncombat role in the Navy during World War II. She assumed that he would be proud of her and her plan for straightening out her "wayward" life. Instead, there was dead silence on the other end of the phone for several seconds. In those days, long-distance phone lines could be faulty, and for a moment she thought their connection had gone dead. But then he spoke.

"I guess you know what you're doing."

O'Neill's next thought was *"Oh, shit. I don't know what I'm doing."*

O'Neill accepted her military payments for the first year. Occasionally, a form would arrive, and she would return it incomplete with a note claiming that she didn't understand it. This seemed to work for a while, as she did not hear from anyone in the Army. At the end of her training, O'Neill took her certification exam from the Indiana State Board of Nursing. Awaiting her grade, which delayed her military service yet again, she stayed busy working as a counselor in a Jewish girls' camp in New Hampshire. She recalls that being exposed to a class of very different young women was a learning experience. As they fantasized about their future weddings, set in their parents' picturesque backyards, all Sue could imagine was a wedding in her Indiana backyard, complete with dogs and *miscellaneous stuff*.

Finally, at the end of summer 1968 she received her grades and orders assigning her to Fort Sam Houston in San Antonio, Texas. Up to this time, she had only traveled long-distance by car. This was her first airplane ride, and she spent the flight vomiting. She suspects that it may have had a lot more to do with apprehension about her unknown future than motion sickness. When they arrived, O'Neill and the others in her unit were issued uniforms and addressed by a series of officers. One sergeant in particular was a dead ringer for the recruiter she had encountered in Chicago. He stepped up on the stage and made a remark that would stay with her forever. "For you nurses, you might have been told that there was a waiting list a mile long for Vietnam. Well, that's no longer the case. I say by the end of this year half of you will be in Vietnam." He continued, "The other half will be on orders for Vietnam." It was then that the reality hit. O'Neill remembers thinking, *"Oh my God. I asked to go to Hawaii, and Germany, and the Philippines, Fort Sam Houston, or anywhere else, but not Vietnam."*

The historian Kara Dixon Vuic has described the military training that nurses received. It is striking to note that men and women inducted into the U.S. Army during the Vietnam era received the exact same training with the exception of twenty-two hours. In those hours, the men had weapons training and other combat-specific instruction. Women, by contrast, learned how to fire a .45-caliber pistol. Much more time was spent on uniforms and insignia, as the Army insisted that women be appropriately dressed.[3]

O'Neill, like many nurses headed for Vietnam, felt grossly underprepared for combat medicine. She had dealt with emergency room trauma in her nursing training. She knew what it meant—and looked like—when people died from traumatic injuries. But for the most part her experience with death was limited to the elderly. Now she would encounter peers as patients.

When that hit home, O'Neill paid a visit to the people at the base education office to explain to them that sending her too close to combat would be a mistake. She asserted that she knew nothing about trauma medicine and feared that if she treated someone in Vietnam, she would hurt the person. The desk officer told her about an opening in the operating room. In her previous training, O'Neill had spent a couple of weeks in an operating room and had found the work interesting. It was then that the officer let the other shoe drop. Of course, he told her, if you go into the operating room, they're going to send you over there for sure. In the end, she figured that she would be sent no matter what.

"They're going to use me over there anyway," she thought. *"At least I will know something."*

As it turned out, the operating room course was the best and most informative one O'Neill had ever taken. She felt she learned a great deal about pre-op and postoperative care, although many of the skills would be unnecessary in Vietnam. Soldiers were more often than not patched up and shipped out to secondary-care stations as quickly as possible. Still, she realized that what she was learning would be extremely useful upon her return to civilian life. As part of the training she was sent to work in the amputee ward, where she not only treated the physical wounds but also gained exposure to the emotional and psychological dimensions of such wounds. Again, this was more real-life drama than she had bargained for, but O'Neill knew the experience would serve her well. During her operating room training, O'Neill received her orders to Vietnam. She arrived there in May 1969.

When she landed in Vietnam, a clerk-typist asked where she wished to be stationed. She knew nothing about the country and cared little for hard facts about the conflict. She replied that she would accept anything. The typist suggested a place in the northern portion of South Vietnam called Phu Bai, where the Twenty-Second Surgical Hospital was located. She accepted.

For the most part, doctors and nurses seek to remain unaffected by the cases that come before them. Giving excellent medical care requires distance, an ability to remain focused on the complicated tasks required to treat a patient, to save a life.

The first fatality that stuck in my mind was a kid. We didn't have many things going on at all at that point. They brought him in on a chop-

per, and he was put on a gurney outside the operating room while we made sure that everything was prepared. I was supposed to take his history. He looked okay, like he wasn't really hurting that badly, so we chatted a little bit. I asked him where he was from. He said, "Montana," and I kind of joked with him, I said, "Oh, I didn't know they had people over there." And he laughed and he said, "Well, they had me there," and all this . . . And then we brought him in.

We went to take him off the gurney, and he started to tank. He was turning gray, and at that point I had just readied all the scrub stuff. He had a chest wound and it was a little tiny hole in front, and we moved him and I was starting to shave his chest and the doc came through scrubbed and he said, "We don't have time, we don't even have time to gown," because he recognized [the nature of the wound]. They were starting to put him under, and they'd been alerted to the fact that his vital signs were going to nothing all of a sudden.

I was kind of a deer in the headlights. They said, "Just throw some Betadine on it and get me scrubbed," and so I threw on a pair of gloves and helped [the doctor] glove up. We didn't even have our gowns on at that point. We threw him into the surgical suite, and he started immediately cracking the kid's chest and just doing a straightforward front-type procedure. We got in there and it was a mess. Blood everywhere.

I was doing some circulating and working on getting the blood hung at all four extremities, and it was just massive amounts of blood we were putting in. We had this one kid. He was kind of the Black Power kid. He was a strange kid, not at all sociable with anybody, even the other black [operating room] techs, because he held himself above them. He supposedly had a checkered past as far as the clerks knew, and the clerks know everything. So we had this kid who was trained as an operating room tech, but he just didn't do anything. He kind of stood there. Because I had nothing better to do with him, I said, "Oh, great, he might not participate, but at least he can pump." So I showed him how to work the pumps that would squeeze the blood in, and I gave him one and I said, "You keep squeezing that until there isn't any more, and we'll hang up more and we'll put that one in your hand." And we were doing that; we were kind of punching one into his hand, taking it out, putting the next one in.

And [the tech's] eyes were just huge above his mask. It was like he was doing this as an automatic thing. I still remember being able to see the veins in his arms as they stood out against the clenching muscle. He was very lean, and as he pumped the things, he was putting a lot of effort into it. At one point I turned my back to get more, and all of a sudden there was this bang. The blood bag had exploded all over the surgeon, all over the walls, all over everything. So we sent him out.

In the meantime, they were working with the kid from Montana. They were trying to put sutures through his heart. But what had happened was the bullet, and it was a single bullet, had gone in, and it had done what bullets are supposed to do. It spun, it threw off shrapnel and turned his own bone into shrapnel, and it shredded his heart.

The surgeon was working the guy; the anesthesiologist was working like crazy. We were all just trying to get this kid to live. The surgeon would keep picking out the heart, kind of reaching under it and trying to suture it, and it was shredded. The suture would come up bloody.

And the surgeon just kind of gave up. I remember him kind of laying the suture right on the chest. It was like, what can you do? The guy's just had somewhere between twenty and forty bags of blood, and this isn't working.

I can still see that suture, on a suture holder, like a big pair of scissors almost.

Everybody just kind of left. It fell to me and one of the other techs to scrub the place down. It was just silence. You couldn't say anything.

Later . . . I thought about it. It's almost metaphorical. You just work your ass off, you work, you work, you work. And this guy who I'd had this small personal interaction with, who I'd talked with and I'd heard the last thing he ever said, and it was like, how could he die? We were working so hard. How could he possibly die when we worked that hard on him, especially from something as little as what he had. But he did.

Everything out there is serious after that.

O'Neill spent the remainder of the night scrubbing down the operating room, removing the traces of the exploded blood bag. She remembers finding dried blood behind her knee when she finally showered.

After that, it was turning to dusk. I went by, and they were bringing down the flag. They used to call it putting it to bed. They'd bring down the flag and they'd fold it and they'd take it off and put it away until the next morning, and I just remember thinking, "This is all for that flag? What does that mean? I mean, is this like some bizarre sports thing where you follow your team's emblem?" It made me . . . it just made me so angry. It made me so angry. It was so futile.

I think after that I really understood what people meant by "don't mean nothing," because it was like, it really didn't matter what you did. It came down to futility. It was just everything that I had felt about the war before. This was big-league. It wasn't the sort of thing where you go off and hold signs and stuff like that. This was the real deal, and it was even worse than I thought it was because it was far more futile. It didn't mean anything, and yet it meant entirely too much. It was just crazy.

Even in the brief time that I was there, I'd been exposed to a lot of people's different opinions about it, and it turns out I wasn't the only one who looked on this whole thing as being unseemly, unnecessary, and wasteful. But to see that graphic waste happening in that sort of form just devastated me.

To O'Neill, the reality of war and her role as a nurse went beyond issues of politics. It simply made no sense and at the same time cost the young people on the front lines everything.

After O'Neill had been several months at the Twenty-Second Surgical, the hospital was closed down, and she was transferred to the Twenty-Seventh Surgical Hospital in Chu Lai. She remembers treating a steady flow of casualties, many of them Vietnamese civilians. Later, she would transfer to a hospital at Cu Chi, the Twelfth Evacuation Hospital. She had been told it was the "worst hellhole in Vietnam," but she did not find it so. It was extremely busy with casualties from both the American and the Vietnamese sides, but she found the work interesting and in some ways therapeutic. She had managed to find her emotional distance.

She returned home in 1970 and married a man named Paul O'Neill, whom she had met in Vietnam. They became involved with Vietnam Veterans Against the War (VVAW) for a time, and then together they joined the Peace Corps, going to Venezuela in 1973–74. The decision to join, she writes, "had much to do with Viet Nam. We both disagreed with the war; we both wanted to travel and use our skills in a different cultural setting, in a country whose people didn't consider us the Bad Guys."[4]

Today, O'Neill lives in Brooklyn. Life has given her the chance to play many roles, including mother of three, nurse, waitress, lounge singer, storyteller, author, reporter, photographer, and teacher. She lives a full life, writing, traveling, and creating, while always "pushing her pacifist agenda."

In the introduction to her book of short stories, *Don't Mean Nothing*, named after a phrase that was common in Vietnam, O'Neill explains the differences between her war and that of the soldiers whose lives she was asked to save. She also writes again about futility, the daily arrivals of the injured and the dying, all for a cause she had never believed in from the start:

> There have been many novels, memoirs, and short stories published about Vietnam in the past thirty years. Most were written by men. *Don't Mean Nothing* has little in common with these, because hospital personnel—and female veterans in particular—served in a war that was substantially different from the one fought by male soldiers. To begin with, the goal of "our" war, though considered supportive to "theirs," actually contradicted it. Soldiers were trained—and expected—to kill the enemy. We were trained, and expected, to save anyone who came through the hospital doors, which often included the enemy. They lived with the guilt of killing; we, with the guilt of surviving. They lived surrounded by blood and death in which they had a direct stake; we faced a daily onslaught of maimed and dying men, women, and children dropped on us by helicopter from an alien world.[5]

4

WAR AND LIES: JOSEPH GIANNINI

The war transformed everyone who fought in it, to one degree or another. Joseph Giannini served as a Marine in Vietnam in 1967–68. Today he wants people to know what he saw and did and to understand it.

The first Gulf War rekindled his awareness of his military service. Giannini began to find ways to make people aware of the realities of war, as he understands them. He uses a wide variety of forms to do so today, including television, nonfiction story writing, participation in oral history projects, and public sharing of himself and his experiences.

In 2010, after the publication of Karl Marlantes's book *Matterhorn: A Novel of the Vietnam War*, Giannini wrote on Marlantes's blog, "We're on the same mission: Take them In Country. Make them see, hear, feel and suffer."[1] "In-country" is an expression used among veterans to mean "in Vietnam."

Giannini, JG to his friends, was born in Brooklyn, New York, in 1943. The family moved to Plainview, Long Island, when he was seven years old, his parents deciding that the newly minted suburbs would be a better place to raise Joe and his younger sister, Florence. He graduated from Massapequa High School in 1961 and went on to attend Hofstra University, where he was on the wrestling team. He graduated in 1966 with a bachelor's degree in political science. He got his draft notice at about the same time. He reported for induction at Fort

Hamilton, in Brooklyn, in March 1966. Giannini made a snap decision that would color the course of his life. As he puts it, *About thirty seconds before being inducted in the Army, I volunteered to go into the Marine Corps.*

Giannini did his U.S. Marine Corps Recruit Training, often called boot camp, at Parris Island, South Carolina. While he found that he was well suited to the demands of Marine Corps training, he did not like the drill instructors' methods for instilling Marine doctrine into the new recruits. As a college graduate, Giannini was given the job of "house mouse," working to assist the drill instructors with minor tasks. But he found himself rebelling against the environment at Parris Island, drawing comparisons in a letter home between himself and Howard Roark, the main character in the bestselling novel *The Fountainhead* by Ayn Rand. Like Roark, Giannini felt a need to repress his opinions.

Eventually, the effort to do so would fail, costing him his "house mouse" job and the small privileges that came with it. The importance of the letters Giannini both wrote and received during his time in the Marine Corps becomes apparent. He wrote home to his parents and sister several times at the end of March, highlighting for them the challenges he faced. He reported:

> *Discipline is kept very strict, anyone who steps out of line gets physically mauled by the Drill Instructors, they leave no visible marks . . . they sometimes seem sadistic and waste my time with trivial matters . . . This is "the epitome" of totalitarianism (collectivism). We do everything by the numbers. We aren't allowed to speak to one another. The mental boredom is quite frustrating. Howard Roark would never survive in this environment . . . We never get out of platoon formation out of the barracks . . . We don't go to the PX, either. Don't need any money. No place to spend it.*

Giannini graduated from boot camp on May 12, 1966. He requested his family not come to South Carolina for the ceremony, as he would have only a few hours of liberty and wanted to spend it with the other recruits. He was proud of his accomplishment. In a May 13 letter to his family, written as he rode on a Greyhound bus headed to Camp Lejeune for the next phase of training, he wrote: "Mom, Dad, Flo, I think I am finally turning into a mature young man. Never have I felt more confident in my own ability to do something, anything."

On June 8 he wrote that he had finally received his PFC designation, and he found that the new status suited him:

Oh, I made PFC (Private First Class). I was given my stripes! The Lieutenant handed out our certificates. I'm really proud to receive my first stripe. Only 24 privates made it out of the whole company. A stripe puts the finishing touch on our uniforms . . . Being a PFC is really different than being a mere private. I give the orders now. One private gave me some lip, we fought, he obeyed my orders after we fought. I'm in charge of seeing that the whole barracks is cleaned out every morning. This means I give orders to almost everyone, but I don't do any physical work.

Giannini completed Individual Combat Training in June 1966. By the end of July he was working at battalion headquarters at Camp Geiger, waiting to hear about Officer Candidate School (OCS). At Camp Geiger, he found what he called the MCW (menial clerical work) boring. He was accepted to Officer Candidate School, arriving there on October 5, 1966.

He graduated from OCS that December, and his mother put the lieutenant's bars on his uniform. There was a break in letter writing as Giannini went home on leave after graduation from OCS to wait for his orders. By the time Giannini arrived in Vietnam in June 1967, he was a married man.

Assigned to the First Battalion, Third Regiment, Third Marine Division, Giannini belonged to the Special Landing Force (SLF), a unit of two Marine battalions that could be called on to support other Marines who were in-country fighting on the ground. By July 4, 1967, he was on board the USS *Iwo Jima*, floating in the South China Sea, assigned to an 81-millimeter mortar platoon.

Before explaining what happened to him in Vietnam, Giannini wanted me to understand the sense of foreboding and fear that arriving in the place generated. He spoke of the heat and the smell, as many veterans do. But he also told me two stories indicating that communicating the atmosphere of Vietnam was key to my interview with him.

He was sent to a place near the demilitarized zone, or DMZ, to join his unit with two other freshly minted lieutenants he had met in OCS, Keith Gregory and Jim Grosshans.

We flew by C-130 from Da Nang to Dong Ha, and we spent the night at Dong. The next morning we went to the LZ [landing zone], the three of us, and we're waiting and we ask where is the First Battalion, Third Marines. This guy says, "You see all those clouds of dust out there?" It's like maybe three or four miles away, and we're like, "Yeah, what is that?" He says, "Well, that's . . ." I think he called it an "arc light." I said, "What the hell is that?" He said, "It's a B-52 mission, that's where your battalion is." So when I heard that, my vision was that we were going to land right in a firefight, and I mean there'd be a big battle going on. And we'd be right in the fight. The earth was actually rumbling from this arc light.

Giannini wanted me to know that combat made the earth move, both metaphorically and physically.

He continued his story:

We flew north. Dong Ha was a pretty big base then. It was mostly red earth, a lot of dust, and we flew north and we flew over jungle and then we came down in a small clearing. A little jungle, well, it was all jungle, but we came down in this clearing, and they said, "Get off." We got off, the three of us, and there was nobody there. It was like just all jungle. I said, "What the hell?" All of a sudden, I swear, just like ghosts coming out of the jungle, these Marines coming out of nowhere. "You the new guys?" "Yeah." "Okay, come with us." And we followed them, and they took us into a ravine. And down at the bottom of the ravine there were some more Marines.

What I didn't realize and I found out really fast was that we were in the DMZ.

I remember the first night; it was beautiful. Pitch-black; beautiful stars. They had been under some severe rocket attack. All of this I found out later, they had actually, there were a lot of Marines from my battalion, there were a lot of tanks. But the tanks were piled with body bags.

Transferred to Bravo Company within the battalion and stationed aboard the USS *Duluth*, he took over a rifle platoon that had just returned from an area just south of the DMZ. Being part of the SLF was a strange existence. On July 31, he wrote a long letter home to his wife:

There are a lot of things we are doing wrong over here. We just aren't meeting the V.C. on their terms. The concept of a force in readiness is a farce when fighting the V.C. They just won't meet us when we have such force. They'd rather sit back and harass us until we make a fatal mistake.

We are really driving ourselves but the returns for our endeavors are miserable. My men, and sometimes myself, are drained of physical endurance. They are so tired they can't stay awake when they know the V.C. are all around them. If we don't get some slack soon we might get into a real bad mess one night.

In a letter dated August 6 he responded to a request. His wife had asked him to supply her with arguments in defense of the war. It is tempting to speculate that she was being challenged by friends and acquaintances over Joe's military service. After all, by 1967, antiwar sentiment in the country was rising. Unfortunately, he had little to offer, except his sense of duty to his country:

I just received your letter asking for some good pro-war arguments. To tell you the truth there isn't much I can say to support this war. I believe we have made a mistake in getting involved in the first place. We should never have committed American troops to this dirty war. Now it's become a war of attrition, in which we are afraid to lose face . . . I live in a society that calls upon its young people to suffer a few hardships, like waging a war. You might say I'm paying for what I've taken for

*granted in the last 24 years. If I didn't come over here, I would be
cutting myself off from this society. This nation has committed
itself, I believe mistakenly, but to go against its policy would be
unwise for a person in my position. For me it has become a
personal struggle, I have to survive this perplexing mess. That's
my cause.*

However, in a letter to his father, dated August 5, he does cite one
more reason to do a good job: "Although I can't wait to get out of the
Far East, I've decided to do the best possible job I can. If I don't owe it
to myself, I owe it to my men."

In mid-August 1967, his unit moved into the Que Son Valley, south-
west of Da Nang, in Quang Nam province.

*What I didn't know about the Que Son Valley was that it was a very
hotly contested place. I think Marines might have called it "Happy Valley," but that's because it was just the opposite. We started on a battalion
sweep. I know now exactly the dates when this happened. It was August
12 when we went into the valley. Up until that time I had taken only four
casualties, three from booby traps and one from friendly fire. That night
I would lose my first Marine.*

He had sent Marines out beyond the company perimeter to listen
and watch for any enemy that might approach. A firefight ensued, and
in the confusion there was a friendly-fire incident.

*That was my baptism of fire. It was in the Que Son Valley. I only had
about twenty-six Marines. Twelve or thirteen were hit that night.*

This particular incident would have relevance later, after Giannini
returned to the United States.

As the days and weeks passed, he knew the war was changing him,
even as it happened, and he tried to make this clear in letters home. In
a letter to his sister dated September 12 he wondered:

*Whatever happened to the student that was so interested in
world organization and ways to keep the peace? I studied for 4½
years the efforts man has made and is making to bring world
peace. Now I find myself fighting a meaningless war, in*

contradiction to everything I believed in just a short while ago. I just can't go along with thinking that we have a good cause.

By the end of September, Giannini found himself locked in a personality conflict with a superior officer. As the conflict had escalated, he wrote home that the officer wanted to relieve him of command because he believed that Giannini "lacked maturity" and had grown too close to his men. The tension reached a peak during an incident Giannini will never forget.

[The officer] called me up for a meeting. We were on a hill looking down on a village across a small river, and he's telling me that he wants my platoon to go down the river about a mile because the battalion is going to cross the river in the morning. My platoon's going to be flank security. A mile down the river. This is ridiculous.

It's about dusk and this woman walks out of the village by herself. She's carrying empty water cans, and she's walking down to the river. I could see this clearly. I mean, she's not far away, maybe forty or fifty meters away. I'm looking downhill at her.

All of a sudden I'm standing there with [the officer] and someone opens up on her, a Marine. And they fire at her, but they miss. You could see the bullets, and [the officer] yells down to these Marines, "What's going on down there?" And they said, "We've got a VC across the river." And [the officer] said, "Well, if it's a VC, kill it." And I said to [the officer], "That's no VC. It's just a woman." And they just opened up, and she actually—they were missing her, it's weird, I mean, she actually bent down, got the water. She turned around and started to walk away, and I hear [smack], like that. A bullet right in the back. You could hear it. And she went down. I, at that point, didn't make any more protests. I just said, "She's not a VC." And he just gave them permission to open up, and the whole Marine squad opened up on her.

I turned around and I had this thought that I was losing my humanity, but I would just hold on. I felt like it was still there, but, I mean, I didn't cry. I just turned around and I walked away. But I felt like, you know, I was losing it. I was losing it. But, then again, I felt there was just a little bit left.

The next morning we went out early, my platoon. We get down to the river, and it's deep, and it's flowing fast. So we get across the river, and now we are making our way back to the battalion. And on the way back, we had to pass by the woman. She was still there. It must have been mid-day by now. She was just lying there in the sand. No one had come to get her or anything, and we passed by her. There were no repercussions. I didn't think about turning [the officer] in, but it was out-and-out murder and nobody said anything, nobody did anything.

He says it again, as if to drive the point home.

I felt like I was losing a bit of my humanity. But I would hold on.

The memory of this event echoes through his life. The sights and sounds are as vivid for him today as they were in 1967.

In the next letter to his sister he wrote:

I hate being away, I hate everything I'm doing and seeing. I'm getting by but I feel like I'm being skinned alive. I'm losing something out here, I just hope it returns when I leave this place. I wouldn't mind carrying such a heavy burden if I could believe in what we are doing.

On February 14, 1968, Delta One, a sister Marine company, was on point just ahead of Giannini and walked into a minefield. Six or seven Marines were badly injured. Giannini was ordered forward by his company commander, "Mad Dog," to assess the situation and report back. When he arrived at the scene, Giannini found Delta One's platoon commander crying from grief. The helicopters couldn't land; they were forced to hover off the ground for fear of detonating additional mines. As casualties were loaded on board, Giannini stayed with a Marine who ended up being the last one put onto the chopper.

When we got him to the chopper, he was right there. His head was right there in front of me. And what happened is, when the Marines went to pick him up to put him on the chopper, his head went forward. And I surmised that he must have seen his legs for the first time because all of a sudden his head fell back and his eyes were wide open. And you could see he was turning white. The blood was draining from his face. And that's it. That's the last I saw of him. He was gone in a swirl of dust. I don't know if he lived. I'm hoping that he did live. If he did live, I would say that he looked like he would be a double amputee. It was that bad. It was bad. But all these other Marines were the same way.

*Maybe the next day, I guess, we went back to Quang Tri. Back at the base, the battalion tells the company commander they want me to go out. They're going to send out a section of 81-millimeter mortars with me. They're heavy mortars, and they want us to establish a combat base out from the battalion. So, again, here we go the next morning, my platoon. We load up on slicks [*a Bell UH-1 helicopter used for troop and ammunition transport]*, with a section of 81-millimeter mortars. And my platoon, altogether seventy-eight Marines, we go out west. I don't know how many klicks [kilometers] out west, but pretty far.*

And they drop us on a hill, and here I am, by myself. I've got seventy-eight Marines. I've got a section of mortars which I'm not allowed to fire. Only battalion fires these things. You've got to go through the battalion fire center. I don't have authority to fire these things. I have to clear it through battalion. But as we're flying in, I notice we're not too far from the village and the minefield [where the Marines had detonated the mines].

We're on the hill. I'm by myself. We dig in. I send my listening posts out. I set my defensive fires. And while we're on the hill, one of my sergeants walks up to me. He's got a little pup in his hand. I mean, a little newborn pup. He said, "Lieutenant, I found this pup down the hill." He said, "What should I do with it?" I said, "It's got to be a pup from a VC tracking dog. Kill it, but do it silently. Slit its throat." And he just turned around, and he walked away with the pup.

So I'm out there by myself, and I decide I have to send out patrols. I just can't just be sitting there. They obviously know where we are. I mean, here we are on a hill among them. They know we're there. I call it Indian Country.

I had to be aggressive. So I sent out a patrol. I kept them away from the village and away from the minefield.

Anyhow, they went out and they started radioing the checkpoints, and they got on the ridgeline across from us, like a small valley. And all of a sudden there was a loud explosion. They'd hit a land mine. They radio back. They radio to me that the squad leader, Baker, stepped on a land mine. So I called in a medevac. They go out there to pick up Baker, and they're now taking him back to Quang Tri. And the rest of the squad comes in. Now it's getting toward dusk, and they radio out to me that Baker's dead.[2]

Every dusk and every dawn, we would do a thing called stand-to, where every Marine would get in his fighting hole and face outboard, and we would remain that way until it was stand-down. But when we stood down, you couldn't smoke. You couldn't have any fires. I mean, they could see you light a cigarette from half a mile away. And they would shoot at the flame. So, you know, we would run silent. Stand to for a while and then stand down, smoking lamp is out. Nothing.

Well, I ordered stand-to, and every Marine got in his fighting hole and faced outboard. This is what we did every dusk. And I went over to the 81-millimeter mortar position, which was in the center of our position on the hill. And I walk up to the sergeant, the section leader, and I said, "Fire mission." And he looked at me and he said, "No can do. You can't do this. You need battalion's permission." And I said, "Sergeant, I'm the commanding officer on this hill. You follow my orders. Fire mission." He figured it out pretty quick, I think. I gave him a fire mission and I gave him the coordinates and everything, and he fired the mission, heavy explosive, and he fired away. So I had four heavy mortars firing ten rounds apiece. That's forty rounds.

And while these rounds were starting to hit, battalion called. It was the executive officer. He wanted to know basically what the fuck is going on. And I said—they called him Five—"Five, I've got buku movement out here." And he said, "Lieutenant, you know, what do you mean by 'buku'?" I said, "Well, I've got a hundred enemy troopers advancing on us." He said, "Are you sure?" He said, "Because you're in a lot of shit. You know you can't do what you're doing. You have to go through the battalion fire control." I said, "I'm sure I've got enemy coming straight at us." He says, "You better be sure because you're in a world of shit [if not]."

Got off the radio. I went back over to the platoon section sergeant, and I said, "Fire again." So that's another forty rounds. And then all of a sudden the rounds were hitting. It was four tubes. Each one, ten rounds.

Eighty rounds had hit, high explosive. I ordered stand-down, and the Marines got out of the fighting holes, and they all were facing northeast. They were facing northeast looking at the village. It was burning. And the same sergeant who had had the puppy walked up. Sergeant King. He walks up to me and he says to me, "Lieutenant." I looked over at him, and the fire was making his face glow. And he said, "You know, Lieutenant, I didn't kill that pup." I said, "Okay, Sergeant."

Then he said, "Lieutenant." I said, "What, Sergeant?" He says, "Payback is a motherfucker, isn't it?"

The narrative conveys the ambiguity Giannini found in Vietnam. Who was paid back, and for what? Did the Vietnamese get what they deserved because Baker stepped on a land mine? Was Baker's death payback for Giannini's order to kill the pup? Morality in Vietnam, for Giannini, was not clear in that moment. All those meanings are possible, and Giannini is describing himself as someone every bit as compromised as the officer who ordered Marines to shoot a woman. He was angry and made angry decisions that intended destruction. This is what war did to him, and why now he is against unnecessary wars.

Giannini returned to the United States and eventually got a law degree. He remains a practicing criminal defense attorney to this day. Vietnam and his ability to draw on his experiences there continue to shape his life and work.

As he tells the story, *September 1989, we were out here [in the Hamptons] for the weekend, and my sister had come out with us.*

A police officer had been shot in Brooklyn. They were claiming that a Panamanian drug dealer had killed a police officer that was on [an] anticrime [task force] and they'd tried to murder his partner too. I'd been listening to it all day long, and I made a remark to Nikki, my second wife, and my sister, Flo, that it sounded like the police version was bullshit. Well, Flo got really angry at me: "How can you say that? What do you know? You weren't there."

About a half hour later I got a call, and it was a friend of mine who'd actually been a client; now he was a friend. He said, "Have you heard about the police officer getting killed?" He said, "They've arrested Renaldo, and you know Renaldo." I said, "Renaldo?" He said, "Yeah. Renaldo Rayside."

He said, "You know him." I said, "I don't know him." He said, "Yes, you do. He was in your office—he came to your office. One of his friends was accused of a murder. You represented his friend and got him off. He was in your office. His family is looking to retain you."

They do.

It turns out when he gets arrested for this Murder One—Attempted Murder One—he actually has my business card in his wallet. So I get on the case, and it's the biggest case of my life. It's really high profile. I mean, it's on the front page almost every day. Geraldo Rivera gets behind it.

It turns out that the officer who was killed is married. His wife is pregnant. She goes on all these TV shows. If it's a son, he's going to be a police officer. And everybody is rallying around this case to bring back the death penalty, which had been suspended for a while. So I get on this case, and to me it was a—it was a challenge. It was the most serious case I've ever taken on. This case actually went on, from the time of the shooting till the time of the trial was a whole year. And it was constantly, I call it on the front burner—on the front page. And they really ridiculed me. They were ridiculing me and my client.

I was putting this case together to go to trial, and my theory was that my client was innocent, that the police had been involved in this thing somehow. But I had no story. I'm sitting in the living room. And I had the case file sitting on the living room table, and it's huge. It covers the whole living room table—stacked. And I'm sitting there and it's like 3:00 a.m. in the morning and I'm trying to figure out, what am I going to say to this jury? How am I going to show them that he's innocent?

They have the two eyewitnesses: they have the surviving officer, and they have this young black kid, both claiming they saw my client do it. I'm sitting there, and then all of a sudden it just clicks. I had cross-examined the surviving officer, and I had really gone after him. He was crying on the stand. They had to stop my cross-examination to let him compose himself. He was crying on the stand. He wasn't angry. He kept crying. So I kept going after him; he kept crying. I kept going after him. I wouldn't let him go. And as I'm sitting there, trying to think, what am I going to say?

Something just hit me. I had run into this surviving officer, I'd say, maybe four or five times during the year leading up to the trial. For some reason when they were preparing the trial, they had these special offices in this high-rise office building. And I would go over there to talk to the prosecutors to get additional discovery—to look at evidence—back and forth all the time. And every time I went there, he was there. And my reaction was, what is he doing here? And the other thing, every time I walked in, they had him in the reception area, and I had to walk by him to go to where they were. And every time I went in there, he'd look at me and put his head down real fast. And I would say to myself, "That's a really strange reaction." If I was him, I'd be saying, "You're a fucking scumbag. You're defending a guy who killed my partner." He just put his head down and turned away from me, every time I walked in.

And then all of a sudden I'm sitting at my table, and I said to myself, "I know where I've seen that reaction before." It was the night that machine gunner was killed by friendly fire.

What happened is, a listening post had panicked, and they ran back, and as they were running back panicked, they were firing at us. And a machine gunner was shot in the head. When the listening post came in, they were standing there—why? This Marine was dying. And we had surmised now that he'd been hit by a small-caliber round because there was a small hole in his helmet. The round came straight in, then it deflected a little bit and went right in his eye. He's dying. These Marines are standing there, and I walk over to them and I just said one thing to them: "Did you receive any incoming?" I was trying to give them a way out. On occasion, the enemy would pick up our weapons and use them. That's what we were told—I never saw it happen. They would pick up our M16s and fire them at us. I was trying to give them a way out. And they just, all four of them just put their head down, and they wouldn't look at me. A few moments later I learned that this Marine had completed his tour and was due to rotate home on the next chopper.

I knew right then and there that one of them had killed this Marine. The same reaction that this guy had to me every time I saw him. Guilt. So I decided that night while I was sitting alone with this huge file that that was my story. I would summarize the evidence, but this is what it would come down to. I would tell the story—I wouldn't use the term "friendly fire." And this is how I would end my summation about an incident that happened in Nam. I was the one who started the cover-up. I wouldn't tell the truth.

I went to court that morning, and I started to sum up and it's a very long summation because they had called about fifty witnesses—between crime scene, ballistics, the officers who responded, the interrogation, hair evidence, fiber evidence, this and that. Fifty witnesses who testified, and the defense had called about six witnesses. And I was going through my summation, a very long summation. I was taking breaks. Every once in a while, maybe every forty-five minutes to an hour, I would take a break. And now I was into my last hour [or so] and I got up to my last hour, I told the jury, "I'm going to take you back to August 1967, Vietnam." The prosecutor jumped up and objected. He wanted to approach and talk to the judge.

So we went up to the judge, and [the prosecutor] said, "Mr. Giannini is about to tell a story about Vietnam. It's not appropriate for him to do that." And the judge, who was a really tough judge, had been the head of the homicide bureau in Brooklyn before he became a judge, he said, "You know something, it's been a really long trial, and if Mr. Giannini wants to tell some stories, he can tell some stories." So I went up and told that jury—I tried to tell it in the third person—in detail what happened on August 12, 1967.

I gave them the whole account of what happened and that I made a decision right then and there not to tell the truth. How could I? These parents are waiting for him to come home—to walk through the door— and he's dead. I actually told [them] the enemy killed him. He got killed by small-arms fire. And that was the official story. So I told that story— the whole story—to the jury.

I said that it was a cover-up, "and that's what happened here, and there's guilt." I pointed to the surviving officer. And you could see the guilt on his face. You could see him squirming. You could see it. There was the guilt.

The jury deliberated, I think for two days, and they found him, Re-naldo, not guilty on everything—the murder, all the serious charges.

I won the case. I won it because, I think, of that story. And I only could tell that story because from what I experienced in Vietnam.

One New York newspaper wrote: "One juror, who asked not to be identified, said the verdict was 'agonizing but the evidence did not support a conviction . . . It was a very upsetting case.'"[3]

A few weeks after this verdict was rendered, Giannini testified as a witness for the defense in the murder trial of the ex-Marine and Vietnam veteran Reuben Pratts. Pratts, a Brooklyn resident, had been charged with killing a man he found breaking into his sister's car and with wounding an accomplice. Giannini's testimony made direct reference to both the booby trap and the friendly-fire incidents he described to me, and the traumatic nature of those episodes. In what was believed to be the first successful use of a PTSD defense in New York state, Pratts was found not criminally liable for the shootings on July 11, 1990.[4]

Vietnam continued to be relevant, and Giannini believes the meaning of the war endures. During the recently ended war in Iraq, he participated in a number of antiwar demonstrations, and he hosts a local public access television program called *East End Veterans*, which airs on Long Island TV four times a week. The program aims to connect the lessons of Vietnam to the present global war on terror. I've been a guest on the show.

Reflecting on the experience of Vietnam, Giannini said:

It had an effect on me, of course, but it didn't make me bitter and it didn't make me angry. It made me more caring. Being so close to death and watching people die, in the end I came out caring more. I care more. I don't know if I would be this caring if I hadn't gone through that experience. I have a feeling there's a lot of people like me who came out on the other end and they were more human for what they've been through. I mean, we almost lost our humanity. I'm telling you it was a struggle. But in the end, it seems like we're more human.

5

FOLLOW ME: ANTHONY WALLACE

Like Richard Eggers, Anthony Wallace fought with the First Cavalry Division (though four years later, in 1970). Eggers was a white college-educated officer. Wallace, by contrast, was a noncommissioned officer, a black man, and a draftee. As such, he saw the war from a very different angle than Eggers did. Yet, like Eggers, he stresses that his experience in the Vietnam War was shaped by the leadership training he had received in his youth.

Wallace is a tall, strong, broad-shouldered man in his early sixties, with silver sideburns, a mustache, and a powerful handshake. In our interviews he has a tendency to lean in as he speaks, which lets you know he is fully engaged, intent, and focused. He is a natural teacher and an articulate speaker, with a gravitas that has something to do with his long connection to one of the most prominent Baptist congregations in New York: Brooklyn's Cornerstone Baptist Church. The church and its worship music have shaped and guided him his entire life, he says. He works to live by Christian principles, to preserve the teaching with which he was raised.

He believes, he says, that there is peace to be found in sharing and communicating his experiences with others.

Some Vietnam veterans can't talk about it. They don't want to talk about it, whereas I made the choice. It needs to be spoken about so people will know what a veteran goes through, what a soldier goes through, so when folks make a decision to send someone in harm's way, you understand exactly what you're asking that person to do.

Wallace's parents reached New York from the South, having joined the big northern migration that took place as southern agriculture mechanized in the 1930s and 1940s. His mother was from Alabama, his father from North Carolina.

When folks migrated from the South, you hoped first you could get a job and get a place to live, and then you found a church. You hooked up with people you already knew. Relatives of mine found Cornerstone. That's where we ended up.

Wallace's parents, Benjamin and Virginia, met on Greene Avenue in Brooklyn and married in 1947. Anthony was their first child, born on a day with twenty-five inches of snow on the ground that made getting to the hospital difficult. Two more children would follow, Cynthia and Vincent. His parents eventually found an apartment in the Marcy Houses, a then-new public housing project in Brooklyn, bordering Williamsburg and Bedford-Stuyvesant. Family legend has it that the Wallace family was one of the first to move in. The Marcy Houses were part of a large-scale effort by the city to build affordable postwar apartments. Completed in 1949, the buildings gave priority to World War II veterans, as long as their income did not exceed Housing Authority guidelines. Wallace's father was a Marine Corps veteran of the Korean War, which may have helped the family get into the complex.

Wallace recalls an ethnically diverse neighborhood with a unique flavor. He remembers Italian, Polish, Jewish, and German families.

At Christmastime everybody's home or apartment was your apartment. You ran from one kid's house to another to see what they got for Christmas. It was a joyous time. I have to stress, it was diverse.

As a young boy in New York City, Wallace had the freedom to visit other kids' houses, taste food from other cultures, and share other cultural traditions, which led to a certain innocence when it came to racism. On one occasion, his family traveled by train to visit relatives in South Carolina. As his mother unpacked the food brought along for the train ride, Wallace kept asking why they couldn't eat in the dining car, with its linen-covered tables. She chose not to answer. It wasn't until much later that Wallace realized why they wouldn't have been welcome there. Even though segregation in railway dining cars had been outlawed by the U.S. Supreme Court in 1950, Mrs. Wallace did not want her children to experience the racial tensions that might have arisen had they tried to eat in one. Segregation, a fact of life for southern African Americans in the 1950s, was not something he had so directly encountered before.

In some ways, he recalls an upbringing that echoes small-town life. In and around the Marcy Houses, child rearing was a neighborhood business. Living next door to the Wallace family was a single mom raising three daughters. Even though she was not a family member, she had a very real authority: *If Mrs. Madeline spoke to you and told you to do something, it was like your mother speaking or your father. You listened to [other adults in the neighborhood] as if they were your parents.*

Despite the communal nature of life in the Marcy Houses, Wallace remembers being something of a loner. His time was spent in school and going to music rehearsals and church. He loved riding the New York City subway system, watching the airplanes land at LaGuardia Airport, and visiting the Brooklyn Navy Yard. Wallace's mother worked part-time at the Industrial Home for the Blind on Gates Avenue, now P.S. 297. Wallace's father worked in a foundry in Red Hook. Wallace grew up with a sense of his family's place in the city's social hierarchy. He remembers playing in the band in junior high at I.S. 33, the only student playing a school-issued trumpet. His family was not what he would call poor, but there were real-world financial constraints that affected everyday living.

It was a combination of church life and church music that would ground Wallace through the tumultuous times ahead. Christmas and Easter music gave him an appreciation of classical music that served him well in school and became a source of pride. Music opened doors: his trumpet playing later enabled him to play taps and reveille during infantry training. He also played for church services at the Noncommissioned Officer School chapel. As he puts it, *The instrument gave you the opportunity to do something different.*

A church usher by the time he was eight, at age eighteen he was teaching Christian education and leading youth groups. The roles of student and teacher would prepare him for the rigors of military training and for military leadership. He developed a desire to inspire, instruct, and motivate others.

I wanted other people to understand and believe it [the Gospel] just as much as I believe it. So much so, that after I came back from the service, I was ordained a deacon, and I was one of the youngest deacons to be ordained in our church history.

After high school, Wallace attended Kingsborough Community College in Brooklyn for two years and at the same time worked at the Sherman Creek facility of Con Edison, the New York City power company. In 1969, he resigned from Con Ed so he could return to school full-time and finish his degree. He handed his letter in on a Friday and went home to find his draft notice in the mail. He returned to work on Monday and asked for his resignation letter back. His boss was happy to oblige, thinking this hardworking young man had changed his mind.

I tore it up in front of him, reached in my jacket pocket, and showed him my draft notice. He said, "No wonder."

Because Wallace had been drafted, the company was legally obligated to offer him a job on his return from service. In this way he had preserved his place at Con Ed, where he still works today, albeit now in a management position.

One of the ministers in his church offered to try to help him get out of the draft. Many others were urging him to find a way out of going to war, including his parents. In the end he felt resigned to going, and on a cold January morning, at the age of twenty-one, Anthony Wallace reported to Fort Hamilton, not far from the Verrazano-Narrows Bridge.

I went and I did what I had to do, and I don't regret that. If I had to do it again in another life, I would do the same thing. I said, "Maybe this was a chance for me to venture out. Maybe I won't end up in Vietnam. I'll end up in the Army band."

He recalls that he wanted to take the first steps into the Army on his own, saying: *The day I left it was cold, but sunny and bright. I walked to the subway. I didn't want anyone to go with me.*

It didn't work out that way. Going to induction, he ran into an old neighborhood friend, Willard Kelly, and they walked in together. Once inside, they found hundreds of men, some of them having ridden for hours on the subway to make the 7:00 a.m. start time. The experience made quite an impression on Wallace.

It was like New York, a diverse group. There were Latinos, blacks, whites. Some folks were apprehensive, of course. What I always think about was the people telling you what to do. There were clerks, specialists, ordering you around like they were generals. I laugh about it now, but that was their job. We stayed there all day, paperwork and more paperwork. Buses, charter buses, came to the base and loaded us up. Took us to LaGuardia Airport and flew us to Fort Jackson . . . We were still filling out paperwork, I would say, until one in the morning. You were tired, hungry; I don't think we really slept until the next day. Haircuts, uniforms, fatigues. Some folks were still shocked by the haircuts. In the meantime, while we're doing all this, we had a meal or two, but then they put you out there to police the base. It was an awakening, the first day or two in the military.

At Fort Jackson, South Carolina, Wallace was quickly recognized as someone with leadership potential and was made acting squad leader. He took responsibility for making sure everyone in his squad carried out his job; if one guy messed up, everybody suffered. In the best shape of his life, Wallace found the physical training easy. He remembers that he quickly determined that basic training was like a game, that he could learn from it, and that if he did his job as he was told, it could save his life.

In March 1969, his basic training complete, Wallace was shipped by bus to Fort McClellan, Alabama, for Advanced Individual Training (AIT). Here he was taught navigational skills and how to use weapons. Once again, he was made acting squad leader and was asked to play reveille on a bugle every morning at the personal request of a lieutenant. One bonus of being squad leader was not having to do KP duty. However, as Wallace would prove his whole life, he has never been above doing the work he has asked others to do. Once, he took the KP duty of a soldier whose family had come for the weekend, and found it suited his sense of order. Leaders do not always have to lead from the front.

Although Wallace does not like to speak about his experiences through the lens of race, one incident stands out for him from his AIT training. Having found the worship services at Fort McClellan unsatisfying due to their ecumenical nature, Wallace wanted to attend services at a Baptist church.

I had a little portable radio and I picked up local stations and they were broadcasting a service from Anniston, Alabama. I recall it said, "Come to Anniston Street Baptist Church," and they were singing and they were broadcasting a service. And it sounded good.

So one Sunday morning he put on his uniform khakis and headed down to the church in Anniston.

There was nobody outside, so I walked up the steps, and I remember it being a Gothic-type structure with one or two entrances. I walk up the steps, and to my surprise it was not a black Baptist church. It was a white congregation. So, of course, they were more than likely part of the Southern Baptists. Once I walked in, I almost had the sensation of saying, "Well, you don't need to be here. You need to turn around and walk back out." But that did not happen.

An usher came up and escorted me all the way down, it seemed as if to the first or second pew. As I'm walking down the aisle, uniform on, it felt like my ears were burning because I didn't want to look too much to the left or too much to the right. I felt like everybody was looking at me. I sat down and they gave me a program and I listened to the sermon. Then, after the sermon and the benediction, people came over to me and said, "Thank you for coming to our church." And then they asked me if I would come downstairs and join them for dinner. Now, that was kind of them, but I said to myself, "If I go downstairs, there is a possibility that the base and my family may never hear from me again."

Despite the racial fear dominating the country, especially in the South, and despite his personal trepidation, Wallace believes he had found acceptance. While it may seem like a small incident, understood within the context of 1969, with its urban rioting, assassinations, and Black Power protests, this became a defining moment for Wallace, one that would shape his views on race for the rest of his life. Fellowship, not race, mattered that day. When he politely declined the dinner invitation, they asked him to fill out a visitor's card with his name and address. Later, he would return from Vietnam to find a letter from the church, thanking him for attending and inviting him to come back if he was ever in Anniston, Alabama. To this day Wallace continues his search to locate the church—which no longer seems to exist—or at least a few of the congregants who were there that long-ago day in 1969. He says:

I haven't gone there yet, but I need to do that one day before I leave this earth. Perhaps there's nobody there that would remember that Sunday, but at least I could say thank you for allowing me to come and worship.

Wallace took his military aptitude tests and found that he qualified for Officer Candidate School (OCS). As a draftee, he was already obligated to serve two years in the Army, and agreeing to become an officer would add a year to his time and would almost guarantee a tour in Vietnam. This did not sound appealing. On the basis of his test scores, another option was to go to flight school. But with warrant officer training again came the requirement to enlist for a third year. He declined both opportunities. He was holding out hope for a place in the Army band or an assignment that might keep him out of Vietnam. Once he began "cultural sensitivity" training, however, his eventual deployment to Vietnam became clear. As he listened to instructions on how to treat Vietnamese women and children and learned basic Vietnamese words, it began to sink in.

They wanted you to have an idea of where you were going. So as this kind of training continued to take place, I said, "My goodness, guess what? I think you may be going to Vietnam."

Soon thereafter a third offer came Wallace's way, this time to become a noncommissioned officer (NCO). This opportunity did not come with an added year of duty, and he would emerge with the rank of sergeant. He jumped at the chance. The war was taking a severe toll on noncommissioned personnel, and the demand was growing. This provided opportunities that Wallace feels he may not have had otherwise.

They were looking for people who could take on leadership. It didn't matter if you were black, white, yellow, green. They needed bodies. You are OD [olive-drab] green. You bleed OD blood. In other words, everybody's the same. They tried to get folks to understand that it's not about being African American. It's not about being white. It's not about being from a farm. It's not about where you were from. They tried to get you to understand that you are now government property.

The U.S. government's color-blind, merit-based ideals squared nicely with Wallace's belief in equality. He would find himself at home in the NCO school, whose motto, "Follow Me," had a different meaning for Wallace. Wallace was reminded often of how those words are used in the Bible. Jesus would ultimately ask his disciples to follow him in a life of sacrifice, and Wallace would be asking his men to do the same.

The New Testament, Matthew, Mark, Luke, and John, when they speak about Jesus, one of the things Jesus would always say to his disciples was "Follow me." In essence he was saying, "Become fishers of men." So that motto at infantry school stuck with me.

There was one trainee candidate from New York, and one morning in the formation during inspection I saw he didn't shave. He had to give me twenty-five push-ups. He was grumbling and mumbling. He was a little upset with me. I sent him back to barracks to shave. He had to do it fast enough that he could catch up with the company to deal with the training that was going to be going on that day. You whip them into line. They had to understand, just as we have to understand, that following orders and attention to detail later on could be the difference between someone living or dying.

Though he considered himself a peaceable man, Wallace would find NCO school and weapons training fun. Exposed to rifles in basic and hand grenades in AIT, he now received more detailed instruction. He learned you couldn't pull the pin on a hand grenade with your teeth, John Wayne–style, unless you wanted a broken tooth. He learned that a .50-caliber machine gun could penetrate an armored personnel carrier at a thousand meters, and how to open C rations with a P-38 can opener. He learned well enough, in fact, to finish in the top five of his class and was invited to stay on and teach the next group. With just two years of college and nine months of military training, he had achieved the rank of buck sergeant, a remarkable feat. Wallace was proud of the accomplishment.

Now you are an NCO, and you have to help the officers do what they do. There is an unwritten belief that NCOs run the military, especially the Army. The officers are there, but the NCOs keep the military on track. If you don't have the NCOs, you're not going to get the mission accomplished. I felt like I was on top of the world as far as being a soldier. I had the attitude that I was going to be a soldier's soldier. Now, with that comes the question, "What am I going to do when it comes to combat? Would I be able to function, as they have taught me?" That's what we have to do. To find out.

In January 1970, traveling alone, Wallace took the subway to Forty-Second Street to catch a Port Authority bus to Fort Dix, New Jersey. A day and a half later he was on a DC-8 with two hundred other soldiers and military personnel, a few of them headed to Vietnam for a second tour. As it began to snow, the passengers started cheering, thinking the flight might be canceled. In the manner of how he came into the world, Wallace would leave for Vietnam with deep snow on the ground. After a long flight with stops in Alaska and Japan, his plane began its descent to Bien Hoa Air Base. His arrival in Vietnam left an indelible impression, as it did for so many.

That plane spiraled down when we got to Vietnam. Of course we were told they did that because we didn't want to be on a glide path that Charlie, the Vietcong, could line up and shoot at our plane. We landed, and when they opened the door, the heat was unbearable. Your body was in Vietnam, but your mind was still in Fort Dix, in the snow. The heat was the one thing; the other thing was the smell . . . It was like, "What have I gotten myself into?"

Wallace and the rest of the soldiers were loaded onto buses with wire mesh covering the windows and driven to the Ninetieth Replacement Battalion near Tan Son Nhut. They saw surprising luxuries, such as a PX and a swimming pool. A few lucky soldiers would probably stay, but for most of the soldiers their time here would be short-lived.

You're seeing all this, and you say to yourself, this is not that bad. If this is what I have to deal with, nobody's firing at you yet. We can deal with this.

It was a nice fantasy, anyway.

Every few hours an officer would stand up and call out a list of names and unit assignments, and another group of soldiers would be shipped off. Unit designations such as First Cavalry or 101st Airborne meant very little to these newly arrived soldiers. The majority of the men arriving in Vietnam in 1970 came as replacements, individuals inserted into whatever unit happened to need additional manpower at the time. Wallace was assigned to the First Cavalry Division, a combat unit. He would be departing for the field in Tay Ninh province, near the Cambodian border and west-northwest of Saigon (today known as Ho Chi Minh City). The only problem was Wallace would never really be told exactly where he was. For him, this was just one small indicator of how the military was handling this particular war. While it was the best-documented war in American history, very often U.S. soldiers were given little information about its purpose and their place in it, both practically and metaphorically.

At battalion headquarters, another way station, conditions were far more spartan. He was given a rucksack and a weapon and was reminded of the laws of warfare and the Geneva Conventions as he eyed guard towers and combat latrines. Finally, helicopters arrived to take Wallace and the others in his unit, B Company, 2/7, First Cavalry Division, to Fire Base Jamie, near Nui Ba Den, where he would meet his squad for the first time.

He was apprehensive about being what many derisively referred to as a "shake-and-bake" NCO, a noncommissioned officer who had achieved his rank quickly. Those fears, however, dissolved when a seasoned soldier, Thurman Wolfe, approached him with words of encouragement: *"It's not as bad as you think."*

In early March, while in the field in Vietnam, Wallace would learn that his friend from home Willard Kelly had been killed on February 12 in a Claymore mine accident.

He's gone and I've got to finish nine months in Vietnam. So tears start coming down my face. How am I going to make this? My goodness. My goodness. I got to push. I'm going to make it home. I kept saying, "I'm going to make it home." I have to tell myself that because I couldn't let down the squad. That night, after I learned that, it was on my mind. But I also could not allow it to prevent me from doing the job I needed to do in dealing with these men. So I tried to put it aside, but it was always there.

Wallace steeled himself to take command: *I knew what to do.*

As a squad leader, Wallace was open to what the members of his squad had to say. Like many other veterans, he recalls the enormous physical labor of simply carrying all his gear in the field. The men of his squad offered advice. He was told to carry his M16 ammunition on his belt rather than in his rucksack and not to wear underwear in the field because the chafing would break down his skin. They informed him that two canteens of water should be on his pistol belt and not in the rucksack. When soldiers made contact with the enemy, their rucksacks might have to be dropped, and they might have to go a long time without water. While Wallace remained in command, his squad helped him learn how to conduct himself in the field.

By 1970, there was speculation in the press about U.S. activity on the Cambodian border. The official U.S. policy, announced by President Nixon in 1969, was that the United States was beginning to disengage from Vietnam. In reality, units like Wallace's were being moved closer and closer to the Cambodian border, where they were poised to expand the conflict into another country.

When we go on these assaults or you're moving through the bush, you never really had a sense of what your operations were going to be. You didn't see the big picture. The higher military ranks and the president, they knew they were sending us toward Cambodia. Every place we went to, and you piece together where they are, you see this farther west, farther west. We just knew we were getting closer, because the closer you got, the more contact you made with the enemy.

On April 14, 1970, as his unit bunkered down for the night at Fire Support Base (FSB) Atkinson, in Tay Ninh province, three figures walked up to a night defensive position and tripped some flares.

They were startled by the instant light that lit up the jungle, and they were in front of our position. Like a robot I stood up, because my men were in front of me in their bunker and they were sitting there. They started firing, but I fired over their heads. Basically, you were trying to protect yourself and your unit, so those rounds went out there. You could not say which rounds hit. I can't tell you how many people that I personally killed in each of the contacts I made.

After that, my hands started shaking. Of course it was fear, but the other thing that upset me was the fact that I fired at another human being with no hesitation. Much of that came from the training, but at the same time you want to survive. It seemed to happen in slow motion. When the men went down, it didn't seem like they went down instantaneously. It seemed like some movie where they just melted away. In the morning we went to see them and to examine them and see what intelligence could be found.

Later that night he was wounded.

Wallace possesses a copy of the battalion after-action report he obtained from the National Archives. In it, the battle at Fire Support Base Atkinson is recorded in the dry language of Army bureaucracy.

On the evening of April 15, at 2200 hours F.S.B. Atkinson received incoming rocket and 60 mm and 82 mm mortar round [*sic*]. Early warning of the impending ground attack came from use of the ground radar on the firebase. Cobra gunships, flare ship [*sic*] and air strikes with napalm were called in for support. By 2400 the incoming had stopped. The base defense was so alert that not one of the enemy got as far as the perimeter wire. The following morning's sweep of the area located 55 N.V.A. [North Vietnamese Army] killed along with three wounded taken as prisoners. A total of 8 Americans were killed in action.

Three of them were in Wallace's squad. It was a bloody week for American forces in Vietnam. One hundred forty-one Americans died that week, the highest total since September 1969.[1]

Wallace's perspective was somewhat different.

As he recalls it, he and his men—Thurman Wolfe, William Di Santis, and Joseph Di Gregorio, known as Pepe—were sitting in front of the bunker and preparing for some to remain awake and on guard while the others slept. When the fight started, there was no time to give commands; everyone heard the commotion out front at virtually the same time and opened up as soon as they possibly could. They also knew that they had to move inside quickly.

We had to get into the bunker. We were not going to stay out there. We got in the bunker, and when we opened up, they opened up. When we opened up, the bunkers on the right and left opened up. That's how it started. That was real.

Wallace's bunker was not in action for more than five minutes, probably less.

Their training had taught them to keep their rounds low and close to the ground, because rifle rounds have a tendency to elevate. Wallace was also taught to detonate Claymore mines outside bunkers. Enemy soldiers would be trying to break through the wire perimeter at the front of their position. As the situation intensified, Wallace's overriding recollection is of a choking sensation and an inability to see what was going on, because of the smoke.

It just amazes me how quickly the air filled up with smoke. You couldn't see anything. That was a little unnerving. It's not like television, where you think you can see everything that's happening. It wasn't like that. You could not see anything before your face. You couldn't see the enemy and are just firing blindly. All these things are going on in your mind when smoke is there and you see nothing. The other thing that you smell is one of the ingredients in the explosives called cordite. And of course [there were] the sounds of the rounds being fired from the weapons.

The bunker was loaded with firepower: an M79 bloop gun, an M60 machine gun, and two M16 rifles. To this day Wallace can remember the distinct sounds of each of these weapons. Wolfe was firing the M60 almost continuously, and Wallace could see that the ammo belt was nearly empty. He turned to get more ammunition, since there was no one to act as assistant machine gunner. That's when they were hit. Wallace believes that a rocket-propelled grenade or mortar hit the bunker.

The concussion blew all the sandbags and the shrapnel into the aperture of the bunker. That's why, with my back facing the aperture, I got hit in the back. My comrades were hit in the chest. Once that happened, it was like you were helpless. At that point I could do nothing more—you had to wait and see what the outcome would be.

Wallace never lost consciousness.

I thought I was going to die, and I remember it as if it was yesterday. I said, "God, if this is dying, I'm ready," because I felt no pain. It was like, I'm cruising, and I was ready to step over from earth to heaven, and my life passed before me. From a youngster to an adult to that spot to my own funeral to the extent that I saw myself in a flag-draped casket in the church in Bedford-Stuyvesant. I could see right across family members seated there, and it was as if I'm looking down on all of this.

As Wallace waited, he expected the bunker to explode again, from either enemy fire or secondary explosions from the ammo stored there. It didn't happen. Dizzy and light-headed, he began to feel as if he were floating. As lights from the rounds flashed, he could only make out some lacerations on one of his hands. What he couldn't see was that his entire back, from his shoulder blades to his ankles, had been torn to hamburger. Later he would learn that blood was filling his lungs. He was asphyxiating. He had no idea whether his fellow soldiers had survived.

All of a sudden I heard movement above me, and there were two, perhaps three soldiers pulling sandbags off. They pulled enough off and spotted my arm. Then they uncovered me, and I remember these guys dragging me across the firebase.

He recalls feeling angry that his rescuers broke up his sense of peace.

It was because they broke up that feeling of just going my way. If I was dying, I was going peacefully. Once they touched me, it was broken up. They dragged me, and they threw me in a helicopter. Someone else was in there. This other soldier, he and I are hugging each other and just saying, "Hey, man, what's going on?" Suddenly the helicopter began to rise, to lift, and when it lifted, it banked to the right, and I looked out to the two pilots I see . . . on-screen in front of it there are tracer rounds being shot up at the helicopter. I'm saying to myself, "I survived whatever happened, but now we're going to get blown out of the sky." I said, "I don't want to end this way, in a ball of fire."

By the time the helicopter landed at the Twenty-Fourth Evacuation Hospital, he was in shock. He does remember the Quonset hut being cold and bright. Medical personnel cut off his fatigues and the chain around his neck. They asked for his name, rank, and serial number.

The last thing I remember was someone saying, "We're going to take care of you, soldier."

When Wallace woke up after surgery, he found himself looking like a mummy, his entire body wrapped in gauze.

The next thought I had was that, "Well, Wolfe, Pepe, and Di Santis must be okay, because I'm okay."

A nurse came up, and Wallace told her he wanted to walk. *She looked at me and said, "Soldier, you can't walk."*

I said it again. "I have to walk. I want to walk." She didn't listen. She went off and got the doctor.

When the doctor arrived, he gave the okay. They helped Wallace up, arranging the IV and blood tubes.

I didn't know what a hangover was, but when I sat up, my head was spinning. It was like I had been knocked out and just couldn't gain my balance. For a few seconds after I sat up, it cleared. Then they helped me to stand, and I gained my balance and I shuffled from my bed. I didn't walk anymore for at least another fifteen to twenty days.

Wallace would spend the next week in a Stryker frame—a human sandwich board that would allow the nursing staff to flip him over, because he couldn't do that for himself. He remembers the relief in getting turned onto his back.

It was a blessing to be able to get turned over. Then you could relax your chest and abdomen.

The next day the company commander visited. Immediately, Wallace asked about his bunker mates, but the answer was too slow in coming, in his opinion.

Nobody said anything. They didn't say anything. Then they went on to tell me that they didn't make it. They took a hit basically in the chest.

The commander informed him that they had found seventy-two North Vietnamese dead out in front of his position. This did little to alleviate the pain he felt over the loss of his men.

Wallace's wounds needed to be cleaned and dressed three times a day, an extremely painful procedure. Whenever he was asked if he needed painkillers, he said no. He wanted to feel what was going on. As they used Betadine to loosen the gauze, he remembers feeling cool, but as the crusted, blood-covered dressings were removed, he needed someone to hold his hand because it was so painful. One day he finally asked about his wounds. The nurse tried to make light of the situation, but her humor was lost on him. He spent the next few hours concerned that his wounds were treatable enough that he would soon be sent back out. He asked: *"How does it look?" They said, "Oh, you have a few scratches." Why did they want to tell me that? All they are going to do is patch me up, and I'm going back out there.*

The day the presenting officer came to award him his Purple Heart, it began to dawn on him that the military was not the organization he thought it was. The honor was bestowed with little ceremony.

On behalf of the president of the United States, boom, you know. They read off this speech, in a grateful nation, you are awarded the Purple Heart. They pin it on your pillow. Once they did that, they move on to the next guy. It was like an assembly line.

Wallace assumed that the military had informed his family of his wounds, but he was mistaken. The Red Cross helped him write the letter that would inform them of his status and condition. Later, during a stay at Camp Drake in Japan, as he was preparing for his trip home, the Red Cross arranged for him to speak with his family for the first time since he had been wounded. In Japan, Wallace decided it was time to see the damage for himself. As a corpsman was changing his dressing one day, he asked for a mirror.

When I looked at it, that's when I realized, "No wonder they're sending me home," because I could not believe the damage. Some of the wounds were still open.

In addition to the physical wounds, Wallace recalls the psychological impact of his injuries. He frequently reached for his imagined M16 when he heard a loud sound. He knew that the man returning to the United States would be very different from the one who had left New York such a short time ago. His experience was a profound watershed, and he wondered about the Army's ability to help him cope with his return. The Army, he says, didn't train him for this. It had taught him how to be a soldier, not a veteran.

There were several stops along the way as he contemplated his return. He was flown from Japan to Seattle, Washington, where he remembers sipping hot chocolate given to him by a Donut Dolly—a Red Cross volunteer providing services to U.S. military personnel—that upset his stomach. After a few days at an airport base hospital, he was flown to Maryland and then to St. Albans Naval Hospital in Queens. The excitement he felt at landing at Floyd Bennett Field in his hometown of Brooklyn can be heard in his voice even today. The first familiar face he saw was a church friend, Mary Foster, who worked at the hospital. He learned that rumors had been circulating about his condition.

They had [heard] all kinds of rumors of what had happened. Worse than it really was. They came running through the doors. Here I'm lying there with an OD blanket covering me up, and I'm lying there, and my brother gets down on his hands and knees and begins, I think with my right foot, going all the way up, goes all the way up to my head and goes down the left side, feeling my body. He gets down once and determines that everything is there, comes back up, and he lifts me up and he hugs me. And I have to tell him, "Ease up, ease up!"

He had not lost any limbs. He was reunited with his family. He was home. It was a good day.

Since he was a semi-ambulatory patient, the Army gave him duties—he worked for an orthopedic surgeon. When he received the okay for overnight passes, he attended Brooklyn College, studying to get his bachelor's degree. He was required to wear his dress uniform to get off base. Attending class at the openly antiwar campus was the first challenge he would face in his new, somewhat uncomfortable identity as a veteran. No one would know that underneath his uniform, some of his wounds were still open. Brooklyn College, like many college campuses around the country in the spring of 1970, was the scene of much antiwar activity, and sometimes Vietnam veterans received a hostile reception from college students and faculty.

One of the younger students made a comment about me being a Vietnam vet. You have your ribbons, and they tell a story [about you and] your unit. But the professor said to that student, "I never want to hear you say something to this man or any other young man like him. He has done more for you than you will ever realize." And that shut this guy up. Here I am sitting in class in an Army uniform just coming back from Vietnam and dressings literally still on my back. I'll never forget that professor straightening that young man out.

What Wallace gave up in Vietnam he counts as the cost of the gift he received—an opportunity to live another forty years and counting. He compares his fate with that of Wolfe, Pepe, and Di Santis and considers himself blessed. Nevertheless, the wounds went deep. While his physical wounds would slowly be covered by scar tissue, the emotional wounds would take much longer.

Today, while he insists that the surgeons and medical staff did excellent work, each night Wallace has to lubricate the skin on his back where the skin grafts did not completely take. Without daily applications of ointment, the grafts would tear. On a trip with Wallace to the Vietnam Veterans Memorial in Washington in 2009, I witnessed a small sliver of shrapnel work its way to the surface of his skin, drawing blood. It's as if his body were still working to purge his experiences.

You can't just forget it just like that. I know, for me every day, there's a reminder, if not in mind and heart, there is a reminder in body because I have the souvenirs. My souvenirs are some scars. My souvenir is that shrapnel in my body.

Last week I went to the doctor. I had to get X-rays, and the technician said to me, "What's the stuff in your body?" She said, "It looks like snow." The shrapnel shows up in the X-ray as white pieces against the darker muscle and tissue. I look at it in amazement and then say to myself, "None of this cut my spine." [It is] in my lungs and farther down, but none of it cut my spine. None of it pierced my heart, and it's all around. So I can't take that lightly, but then I feel that some of the worst wounds and scars are that ache . . . it's not a pain, but it's an ache. You live with that. I'm not complaining, because I'm here.

So I say, "God, I thank you for this extra time." Then, when I say thank you, of course I have to think about Willard and I think about Wolfe and I have to think about Pepe and I have to think about Di Santis. I have to think about them because if I didn't think about them, I would be selfish and I don't want to be selfish. I don't want to be selfish when I think about these young men, because they had just as much right to live as I do. That's why folks don't forget it so quickly.

6

THE BELIEVER: JOAN FUREY

The majority of American women who served in Vietnam did so either as members of the Army Nurse Corps or as civilians attached to the American Red Cross or Army Special Services. Joan Furey and Sue O'Neill were two of about eight thousand American women who served in Vietnam as members of the Army Nurse Corps.[1]

Joan Furey, now retired after a thirty-year career with the U.S. Department of Veterans Affairs, was raised in Flatbush, Brooklyn. She had a stay-at-home mom, while her father worked at a locally owned A&P grocery store on Church Avenue. In those days, it was possible to raise a family on a workingman's wages. Furey has a number of relatives with military service backgrounds, including her father. With combat zone experience of her own under her belt, she now believes her father, a World War II veteran, probably suffered from some form of post-traumatic stress disorder. Her mother told her once that when he returned home from World War II, he experienced sleeplessness, a racing heartbeat, and other symptoms often associated with PTSD. At the time, he was diagnosed by the family doctor with "soldier's heart." She doesn't know if he ever received any kind of treatment for his condition.

Back then, Furey lived in a primarily Irish Catholic section of Flatbush. She attended Holy Cross Catholic School on Church Avenue between Bedford and Rogers Avenues, right around the corner from her home. Members of her extended family lived nearby, including two aunts, who lived across the street. Within twenty blocks, there were members from both sides of the family. Consequently, Furey grew up in a tightly knit group, with church playing a big part in her life. In 1957, the Furey family moved out of Brooklyn to Port Jefferson Station, Long Island. With several family members already living on Long Island and a desire to send their children to good schools, the Furey family felt it was a good move. Her father continued to work at the Church Avenue store, commuting from Port Jefferson Station to Brooklyn. Eventually, he transferred to an A&P out on Long Island.

Furey attended public school in Port Jefferson Station. It was the first time she had ever had friends who were not Catholic. This caused her concern, because as far as she knew, her new friends were condemned to hell.

There were five children in the Furey family. Furey recalls that she was a relatively average student, getting B grades. She liked sports and played on both the hockey and the softball teams at her school. When she was fourteen, Furey became a member of the Future Nurses of America and worked as a candy striper at a local hospital. She ran the information booth, giving visitors room numbers and helping serve patients meals. Occasionally, she helped the nurses by running errands or transporting patients. For Furey this stands out as an important time in her life. She enjoyed the work and the environment; she felt comfortable there.

Furey also read a lot as a young woman, including a series of books about Sue Barton, a student nurse. The character, created by Helen Dore Boylston, moved around from job to job quite a bit, serving as an operating room nurse, an emergency room nurse, and in other nursing jobs. The books gave Furey her first impression of the nursing profession, as well as a sense of the opportunities it might provide to a young woman. She read every book in the series.

At sixteen, Furey got a paying job at the hospital, working in the kitchen as a tray girl, helping put food trays together and delivering them to patients. She held this job until she finished high school. It probably surprised no one when, upon graduating, she applied to the nursing programs at Kings County Hospital in Brooklyn and Pilgrim State Hospital on Long Island and was accepted at both. She elected to attend Pilgrim State, partly because it was close to home.

Back then, most everybody went to three-year-diploma hospital schools of nursing. I'm not sure there are any more. They were very inexpensive, so if you came from a lower-middle-class family like I did, where there was not a lot of money, it was a very economical way to get a good education.

In retrospect her choice was strangely appropriate. During World War II, the War Department had taken over Pilgrim State and expanded the facilities. At one point it was so large that its land area actually touched on four municipalities: Huntington, Babylon, Smithtown, and Islip. Part of the facility was renamed Mason General Hospital and was used to treat combat-traumatized soldiers returning from World War II. John Huston took a film crew to the hospital and documented its activities in a movie titled *Let There Be Light*, which is about how the War Department treated, with as much compassion as psychiatry had to offer at the time, the psychiatric casualties of World War II.

At that time "combat fatigue" was a recognized psychological problem associated with exposure to military combat. During the Korean War, the American Psychiatric Association published the first edition of its *Diagnostic and Statistical Manual* (*DSM-I*), which contained an entry for "gross stress reaction." This was something that could occur to soldiers in combat—a "temporary condition produced by extreme environmental stress," according to the sociologist Wilbur Scott.[2] But in 1968, when *DSM-II* was published, "gross stress reaction" was omitted. It took an alliance of psychiatrists and Vietnam veterans until 1980 to get a replacement diagnosis inserted into the manual. In the end, that diagnosis would become known as post-traumatic stress disorder, a condition that Furey would, to some degree, suffer from.

For Furey, a mystique surrounded the role of nurse and it made her feel important.

I remember after your freshman year you got to put on this white apron. We wore striped dresses, and then these really starched aprons. You had to learn how to sit down with them. I can just remember feeling really special when all that happened. It instilled in you a level of pride.

Furey did well in nursing school, taking a leadership role there. At the time, the military began actively recruiting Army nurses. Furey finished her nursing education while resisting recruiters' offers to pay tuition and a stipend. Instead, to earn money, she worked at several part-time jobs, including one in the hospital kitchen. After graduation in 1967, as the "big" war in Vietnam was under way, Furey continued to work at Pilgrim State but began to itch for a change. She considered a possible move to Manhattan, among other ideas.

There are so many factors that are going on in your head when you make the decision [to join]. One of the things I wanted to do was to get away from Long Island and see the world and have some adventures. I had never been away from home in my life.

There were other motivations. The Army had begun placing advertisements in *The American Journal of Nursing*, and they were a powerful draw. They suggested that Army nursing could fulfill her desire for a satisfying professional career, permit her to get out of Long Island and see other parts of the world, and at the same time act on her patriotic impulses. She still remembers one advertising slogan: "How to bandage a war: one soldier at a time."[3] She began to think about it. Perhaps it was something she should do; she could give back to her country in the same fashion that her father had during World War II. She thought that because there were no sons eligible to go fight—her brother was still too young—she had a responsibility to take the family spot, so to speak, playing a role that no one else could fill.

There was the matter of American domestic politics.

It was really the peak of the war, and all these college students were demonstrating. I was very angry about all that. I guess all those kinds of events came together at one point for me, and then I just thought, "I should . . . I need to do this. I have a responsibility. I'm a nurse. I can help these people who are being injured."

She also felt the impact of the political climate of the time. She recalls the anti-Communist sentiment that seemed to be in the air. Communism appeared "on the march," threatening to take over the world, with Vietnam as one component of that larger struggle. And a part of her motivation was deeply personal.

There were questions about myself that I needed to have answered. I felt an obligation as a nurse and as a citizen, but also there was this other part of me that really needed to strike out on my own, to find out something about myself, to put myself to some sort of test. That was certainly a big part of it—that was for sure.

This combination of factors led her to a decision. On the way home from work one day she stopped by the Army recruiter's office in Patchogue. She remembers saying something like, *"I'm a nurse, and I want to go to Vietnam."* They said, *"Sign here."* Obviously, it was not quite that simple, but she remembers it happening very quickly. Naturally, the next step was to go home and tell her parents. She walked in and announced: *"I joined the Army, and I'm going to Vietnam."*

There had been no discussion. Her parents were stunned.

Meanwhile, her friend Lorraine, who had joined the Army right after graduating from nursing school, was back from Vietnam. Joan recalls people talking about her strange behavior. In fact, when Furey tried talking with her, Lorraine would not speak about Vietnam. Furey didn't understand her attitude. In time, she would understand all too well.

Furey entered the military at Fort Hamilton in Brooklyn in June 1968 and reported for basic training in July. After her basic training, the Army sent Furey to San Francisco for advanced nursing training. Furey remembers being fascinated with the 1960s counterculture. She remembers fondly the nightclubs, the music scene, and the dancing. It opened her up to a world that she had never known before, but she didn't falter in her commitment to the U.S. military and its servicemen.

I was one of these people who believed in the war. I believed that if our government was sending us to war, it was good. We needed to be there, and we were fighting for freedom and democracy. I bought it hook and line. I was brought up to buy it hook, line, and sinker. No question about it.

The hospital where she was assigned, Letterman General Hospital, at the Presidio, was a tertiary-care hospital. They received casualties who had been evacuated from Vietnam to Japan and then on to the United States. This was Furey's first exposure to war casualties. She worked first in the emergency room. The wounded came in from Japan in the middle of the night and would be triaged into the various units for the kind of care that they needed. She was then transferred to a post in the intensive care unit (ICU), which was where she really wanted to be. It was here that Furey began to see the reality of what combat could do to a human body. The hospital did a lot of reconstructive surgery. Furey cannot escape the memory of the youth of the patients, all of them amputees. She recalls the pain, both hers and theirs, and it is still apparent when she speaks about it.

Of course, these were young men, still kids in many ways, and they sometimes played that way. Furey recalls how the soldiers would race down the long halls in their wheelchairs, up and down ramps, knocking people over, riotous, upbeat, and full of laughter.

One memory stands out as she recalls seeing a handsome young soldier.

I was twenty-one. He was standing sideways, just kind of staring out. The hospital was right near the ocean, right underneath the bridge. I was staring at him when he turned around and looked in my direction, and I saw that the whole right side of his face was just scarred. And gone away. Literally, the right side of his face had been blown away.

Ultimately, Furey would take care of this man in the intensive care unit as doctors tried to graft skin and attempted to rebuild his face. Furey estimates that he may have had as many as seventeen or eighteen operations.

In seeing the guys with amputations and the other kinds of injuries, it only made me want to go more. I wanted to take care of them, I wanted to help them. I got to Letterman in August of '68, and by November '68 I went and volunteered to go to Vietnam. I just wanted to go. That's why I joined the Army. I didn't join the Army for any other reason. I joined the Army to go to Vietnam . . . I really wanted to go to the war zone, very honestly. I wanted to help take care of these soldiers. I wanted to do my part. By virtue of my own family history, with my father having been in World War II, I felt I had some kind of obligation to serve in a war. I wasn't in the Army to make it a career. Then I was afraid, when they started sending people to Korea from our hospital, that if I waited, I could end up in Korea, and that's not what I was there for.

She came home for Christmas in 1968 and told her parents that she had orders for Vietnam with a January departure. Her mother cried. She dreaded worrying about a loved one away at war again. Furey's father became a little teary-eyed but was very proud. Of course, they both feared for her safety. But Furey had set her course. She returned to Letterman, packed her belongings, and took the long flight to Vietnam. She remembers the trip clearly. Traveling on Flying Tiger Line, a contractor taking American passengers to Vietnam, she recalls being the only woman on the aircraft filled with 140 men on a trip into the unknown.

I was sitting in a row with a pilot. Of course, you understand, the only other time in my life I had flown was when I flew back to New York from San Francisco on R&R. Back then, people didn't fly like they fly today. I had been on a plane once in my life. Now I was on a plane. I was going to be on this plane for twenty-four hours. And the last people you want to be on a plane with is a bunch of pilots because they tell you all these stories about flying. Oh my God. I was very scared, anxious, and a nervous wreck.

Furey recalls writing a letter home to her mother on that plane ride, in an attempt to explain her decision. She told her mother that the antiwar demonstrations upset her and that she felt, as an American citizen and as a nurse, that she had to take some sort of stand. To her, she could best demonstrate her patriotism by going to Vietnam, though she says: *I'm sure I didn't use that word.*

She also recalls telling her mother that the journey to Vietnam represented an experience that would *help me learn things about myself that I needed to learn. I thought it would be a personal challenge. I felt it was important that I put myself in a situation where I don't have all the so-called luxuries that surround us in this country.*

At the remove of forty years she views this as a *typical twenty-one-year-old statement.*

She went with a noble intention but found herself unprepared for the reality of Vietnam. One of her first realizations that Vietnam would be far different from what she had imagined was the bus ride from the airport.

I remember getting on this bus. And all the windows were wired. They had screens and wires on them. This is Vietnam. It's hot, you know. I'm thinking, "Why is everything so weird?" So I'm writing, and again I'm the only woman on the bus, so I said to one of the guys, whispering, "Why do the windows have wires on them?" and he said, also whispering, "That's so when they throw grenades, they bounce off." I went, "Oh, shit! I would have never thought of that!" It's like you start to realize what this really is. Until you've actually been there, I'm not sure anybody really gets what war is. It's a whole other experience.

And then began a series of events that would slowly chip away at her naive patriotism. She remembers spending several days at the replacement center at Long Binh where all new arrivals took a class intended to teach the American mission in Vietnam. She recalls some of what they were told.

They spent a lot of time on the fact that one of our jobs was to "win the hearts and minds of the people." This is, believe it or not, the first time that I heard this. I remember thinking that was kind of odd. I'm still stuck in the World War II mentality. These were our allies. We were there to help them. They want us here, so why are we trying to win hearts and minds? I remember being just so totally confused.

Furey confesses readily that at the time she was not a deeply politically aware person. *All I saw was what was on TV: people were getting injured and hurt, and we were fighting Communism, and that was enough for me.*

Entering the war zone was undoubtedly exciting, although it produced anxiety as well. Furey remembers her first night in a trailer at Long Binh, before she received her assignment. As she listened to the rockets go off, she couldn't sleep. She asked a friend what was going on, and her friend reassured her that the rockets were probably outgoing rather than incoming.

On the advice of a friend who was an Army captain, Furey requested to be stationed at the Seventy-First Evacuation Hospital in Pleiku, in the Central Highlands of Vietnam. The captain explained how hot Vietnam was and told her that being stationed at Pleiku, located at the base of the mountains in the Central Highlands, would be cooler. Furey didn't know that Pleiku was an evacuation hospital in the middle of one of the most active combat zones in Vietnam.

For Furey, as with so many veterans, the trip to her new unit in the field remains an indelible experience. She recalls that rather than taking a scheduled flight, you went to the airfield and announced your destination. You would be placed on a list and then begin the wait for an aircraft going in your direction. At least that's the way it worked most of the time. But Furey was traveling with her friend the Army captain, whose first name was Barbie. Barbie's brother was a helicopter pilot, a distinction that enabled her to move among the helicopter pilots at the airbase and ask if anyone was headed to Pleiku. Apparently, someone was, and Barbie asked for a ride.

Because one of the things is if you were a nurse in Vietnam, you were golden. What they wouldn't do for you . . . People were just incredible. They treated you with the utmost respect. You [could] have anything you wanted.

One of her lighter moments in Vietnam, Furey recalls, was her arrival at the hospital. As the helicopter landed, the hospital staff charged out toward it with stretchers, prepared for what they thought were wounded soldiers. Instead, two nurses climbed out—with an enormous footlocker.

It took us a while to live that one down.

Nursing staff lived in hooches, temporary huts usually built out of plywood. Divided into cubbyholes or rooms, each hooch housed at least six individuals. The United States did not expect to need more permanent facilities, based on the premise that the American presence in Vietnam would be short-lived.

Furey requested an assignment to the postoperative intensive care unit. Ordinarily, this position went to nurses with more experience in-country. Generally, new staff worked in regular units for six months before transferring to the ICU. However, the hospital was short of nurses at the time and Furey had previous experience, so she rotated into the ICU rather quickly. Despite her training, she found herself unprepared. For one thing, she saw many young children and infants injured by the war.

I was stunned that we had a number of Vietnamese children and babies. Some of them had diseases, but some of them had been injured in the war. We took care of them. You know, you didn't expect this. You're expecting American GIs. You weren't really prepared for the fact that you're going to have to care for children.

Little could have prepared her for her first such experience, which was caring for a Montagnard baby who had been badly burned. The Montagnard, or Degar, are a tribal people indigenous to the Central Highlands of Vietnam. Some Montagnards worked closely with the American military.

Montagnard people carry their babies on their backs in what are really like shawls. They cook outside in big pots. This woman had been bending over a pot, and a baby fell into it and was burned on one side of its body.

Periodically, a medical team from the Seventy-First Evacuation Hospital would go out to the Montagnard villages in the Pleiku area on MEDCAP (Medical Civic Action Program) missions to provide basic health care. Occasionally, the medical personnel brought people from the villages to the hospital for treatment. Personnel from one MEDCAP mission had found the baby and brought it back to the hospital for treatment. The baby was admitted to Furey's unit, and Furey cared for her. The mother stayed with the child, at times sleeping just outside the hospital area.

In fact, we put up mattresses out there for them to sleep on, because when they had a family member in the hospital, they wanted to be there.

The American medical staff found that they could not save the child's arm. An interpreter explained to the family that the baby's arm needed amputation.

They were there the day of the surgery. The baby went in and had the surgery, came back without the arm. It had been removed at the shoulder. The mother and father came in to see the baby postoperatively, then they left [without the baby], and we never saw them again. They never came back.

I was stunned because they had been there. Someone had always been near, around the clock. What they told me was, in their villages, if you lose an arm, you are useless to the village, because everyone has to do their share of the work. For them it's easier to walk away and just leave the baby with us than to have to take the baby back and have to figure out how to deal with it in the village. Literally, we had the baby, and we ended up having to send the baby to an orphanage. This was like, one of those things that is like, "Whoa." It's a culture shock, because you don't even . . . because they seemed like caring . . . I think they were caring parents, but it was just not something that they were capable of dealing with.

It was my first week there.

Furey remembers hearing about the Communist treatment of the Montagnards and how it helped form her perception of America's objectives in Vietnam.

They were often attacked by the Vietcong and the North Vietnamese, because they were considered sympathetic to the Americans. They were often targeted. The villages were ransacked, shelled. They were shot. The villages were overrun. We had a lot of Montagnard casualties. We took care of them. I just love[d] them to death. They were a very simple people. But they had terrible diseases. Their hygiene was awful. I went out with the MEDCAP teams occasionally to their villages. You always have somebody with some kind of disease or illness. We found people with plague and tetanus.

The most difficult cases often involved children.

I had one kid. It was just devastating to me. He picked up a white phosphorus bomb, which is something that they shoot off at night that lights up the sky. I guess this thing hadn't gone off. This kid picked it up off the ground, and it exploded. The thing about white phosphorus is it just burns and burns and burns until it gets neutralized by a specific chemical compound. It wasn't a compound that was readily available out in the field. One of the infantry units found him and rushed him into the hospital. This kid, this eleven-year-old kid . . . just, third-degree burns . . . it was awful . . . on his entire body. He died. He died . . . to see that, an eleven-year-old kid burned to a crisp. It was really awful. You are expecting to take care of soldiers. I never really thought about civilian casualties, or what happened to them, or who took care of them. I never really thought about kids. All of that was totally unexpected.

She went to Vietnam, however, to care for American servicemen.

The first patient I was assigned to care for was a young guy who had multiple injuries, like most of them did, and he had a spinal cord injury, a cervical spine fracture. So he was placed on a Stryker frame . . . But this patient, he had a crushing injury to his body—broke his spine, his lungs collapsed, he had all kinds of internal injuries, so he had all kinds of tubes attached to him. Chest tubes on either side, gastric tube. He had a Foley catheter, I don't know how many IVs, and then he had Crutchfield tongs attached to his skull. These are tongs that are screwed into the skull on which you can hang weights to provide traction to the spine. He had a cervical neck fracture, so the tongs were keeping his spine in the proper position. So I was charged to take care of him. So the nurse orienting me to the unit is going over everything, and she tells me, "You're going to have to turn him every two hours." And I remember thinking, "Turn him? I don't even want to touch him." I had never seen anything like this in my life.

So there you are. You've got Crutchfield tongs [screwed to his head]; you've got chest tubes coming out. You've got IVs. You've got a Foley catheter. And you've gotta flip this guy 180 degrees, in one movement, and I'm thinking, "You cannot do this, because how does all this stuff move and not get pulled out?"

I just remember thinking, "I can't do this." I was overwhelmed. At that point in time, I wanted to run out of the room. But obviously that wasn't an option. But I was assigned to another nurse, and she walked me through this whole thing. She taught me how to do it all. What to look for. How to position the tubes, all of it. You put this here, you put this here, you place [that] back here, and then you flip. Ta-da!

Till this day, I'm always amazed that I actually learned how to do that and by the end of the week was able to do it by myself. I didn't need any help.

Furey says somehow she learned how to cope. Within two months she found herself teaching new nurses to do what she could not have done just months earlier. By the end of three or four months, Furey says, *I was untouchable. I was like a crackerjack. There was nothing hidden or thrown at me I couldn't handle.*

Eight nurses were killed in Vietnam; their names too are inscribed on the Vietnam Veterans Memorial in Washington, D.C. The possibility of enemy attack was real. When rocket attacks occurred, the medical staff would place mattresses on top of the patients who were too ill to be removed from their beds, and the staff members stayed with them. Putting on flak jackets and helmets, they would crawl across the floor from bed to bed, in the dark, to monitor the patients until the attack was over. Furey recalls:

Was that frightening? Yeah. But after a while, it was just part of what you did. You didn't even think about it.

These experiences changed her forever. Looking back, Furey says:

You really didn't appreciate it until you got home: that your entire emotional makeup was changing by virtue of the fact that you are really removing yourself from your old reality. The way you evaluate pain and suffering was changing, the way you acted, the responsibility you took on. All of that and more, which would later affect you so dramatically.

The historian Elizabeth Norman's book *Women at War: The Story of Fifty Military Nurses Who Served in Vietnam* includes statistical data compiled by the Naval Support Activity Da Nang Hospital during the 1968 Tet Offensive. The statistics supply context for Furey's remarks:

- From January to June 1968, the death rate in the hospital was 2.92 percent.
- The greatest number of deaths were due to rifle/pistol injuries, followed by artillery/rocket/mortar injuries.
- The average time a soldier spent in Vietnam before injury was 5.3 months.

- The average time from injury to admission was 2.8 hours for men who could be saved.
- The average time from admission to surgery was 1.9 hours for men received alive.
- The average length of hospital stay for soldiers in Vietnam was four days.
- During the Tet Offensive the hospital had 2,021 admissions and 8,430 wounds.
- Extremity wounds accounted for 68.2 percent of all recorded injuries. Penetrating wounds of the head, thorax, abdomen, or a combination were found in 61 percent of all deaths.[4]

The unremitting nature of the work is clear.

At times, the tension would cause someone to snap. When that happened, hospital personnel would step in and care for their own. For Furey, this happened on one occasion when the Seventy-First received an unusual influx of casualties. Furey found herself unable to think rationally, overwhelmed by the desire to help and to heal; finally, she gave in to a feeling of intense frustration and failure.

I'd been in-country [for a while], and there was a mass-casualty situation. There was a big firefight. You were just getting casualties. They were lined up in the hall. They sent me this expected patient through triage. Expected patients were patients who came in through triage, and it was decided that their injuries were such that they could not be saved. Nothing could be done for them. So basically they would put a tag on them that said, "Expected," and they would bring them into our unit, and we would basically provide comfort until they died. That was what our job was.

We kind of put him down at the back of the unit. ICU is like a big Quonset hut. There were fifteen or sixteen beds on one side, fifteen or sixteen beds on the other side, and there was like this half wall separating the two sides. Otherwise, it was a big open ward. I'm in charge of one side.

I went up to this patient, and the truth of the matter is he did have a small entry wound right here. [Furey pointed to the center of her fore-

head.] *So I decided, I just decided that they were wrong in triage. That the patient was not going to die. I proceeded to just focus in on [the fact that] I was going to take care of this patient.*

I always said it probably was like a fugue state. The first thing I did, because he had this bloody saturated dressing on the back of his head, I went and got a dressing kit and I got the gloves. I took off the field dressing. As I did that—this is kind of graphic, but I'm trying to make a point, okay?—half of his head, literally, came off in my hand, blood poured out all over me. What did I do? What I did was just place the mass of tissue and bone that was on the dressing back on his head. I put it back, and I didn't even respond. I just put a new dressing on over it.

So here I am, covered with blood, and I decide I have to get him blood, give him blood. Well, you don't give blood to an expected patient. Blood is a valuable resource in a war zone, and you don't use it on someone who is not going to survive. In the meantime, the corpsman is trying to get my attention because we have these other patients coming in. I'm not responding. I tell the corpsman to go get me blood. He says to me, "Lieutenant, this is an expected patient. You shouldn't give him blood."

I said, "I want you to go get him some blood. He needs blood." Well, he wasn't going to get me the blood. I decided I'd go get the blood. So I went to the refrigerator. I got the blood. By that time, he'd gotten a nurse from the other side, who happened to be a very, very close friend of mine.[5] In fact, he had gone to school at CI [Central Islip State Hospital on Long Island], and I had gone to school at Pilgrim. We knew each other. We went through basic training together. Jude came over. He looked at me and he said, "Joan, you can't give this patient the blood."

I said, "Yeah. He just . . ."

He said, "Joan . . . he's an expected patient."

I was saying something like, "No. They're wrong."

"Joan, give me the blood, and walk away from this patient."

Now, he told me later, "The look you gave me . . . if looks could have killed . . ." I gave him the bag of blood. I just walked away. I went over to wash my hands. He came over to me as I was washing my hands.

I turned around, and I said to him—I just looked at him and I said,

"You know, Jude, I feel like I'm Lady Macbeth. I'm never going to wash the blood of Vietnam off my hands."

Over time, her frustration with the war rose. She had arrived committed to the vision that the U.S. mission in Vietnam was to save the people of South Vietnam from Communism.

But it was clear to me that many of them were sympathizing with the North. As much as I didn't understand then politically what was going on, you did get the feeling that we were not there because anybody really wanted us there. Yet we were having all our guys blown up. Just people getting all these devastating casualties and injuries, for what?

By Thanksgiving 1969, her feeling solidified as staff at the hospital began to talk of participating in an antiwar protest that would attract public attention. Some thought of going to the mess hall and sitting silently, refusing to eat the traditional turkey dinner, but the base commander made it clear that soldiers doing so would be subject to disciplinary action. Anyway, Furey had no intention of participating in a public protest. Eventually, 141 soldiers stationed in Pleiku, including members of the medical staff, signed a letter to President Nixon denouncing American involvement in the war and proclaiming their opposition to it. It became big news as reporters arrived to cover the fast. Furey describes what happened next:

That day a particular patient whom I had been caring for went very bad on me and had to go back into the OR [operating room] for emergency surgery. I followed him in there. We weren't all that busy; I never would go in there, but I had gotten very attached to this particular patient. His name was Timothy. I don't remember his last name. He had a pretty serious chest wound. When they opened up his chest, it was just awful what came out of it. It was just devastating to me that he had developed such an overwhelming infection. I think I just kind of snapped.

Furey's patient, quite possibly, was Timothy Ernest Badostain of Avalon, California, the only Timothy to die in Vietnam that Thanksgiving.

So I said, "To hell with this. I'm gonna tell these people." So I came marching out of the OR, and I said to the guy who was organizing it, "Are those television people still here? I have something to say." That's what provoked me. Just seeing one more needless death.

Furey was the only officer who spoke to television reporters, and the story was carried by the nightly ABC network news. Articles about the Thanksgiving Day fast also appeared in *The New York Times*.[6] While worried about the possibility of court-martial for participating, Furey can recall no disciplinary repercussions for soldiers involved. But, she says, the protest *was not well received. At all. We even had patients who came in and asked, "Is this the antiwar hospital?"*

Thinking back on it, she is still proud.

It made me feel good that I publicly took a stand, consequences be damned. I'm glad I did it. I still feel the same way.

On December 7, 1969, after the storm had blown over, Furey sat down and wrote her mother a letter in an effort to explain her fast. Her mother was so touched by what Furey wrote that she had it published in a local newspaper—on the day Furey arrived back home from her year in Vietnam. The letter read:

> *I took part because I am a concerned American, because I love my country and I love my people and I do not wish to spend the rest of my life watching us destroy each other—in Vietnam, in Africa, Egypt, Israel, Nigeria, Europe and the United States. I took part in it because it was a sacrifice—a very small one, granted—but it was represented as suffering for something better. I fasted for an end to war, for the end of destruction, needless death and bitter hate. Yes, I fasted for peace on earth and goodwill to all men. There is nothing left to do!*[7]

Gender had a large part in shaping the experiences of nurses who served in Vietnam. The nurse-patient relationship was clear, in one way: it was a nurse's obligation to care for the patient and get him well enough to be moved to the nearest hospital facility. And yet the boundaries were not always clear. As Furey puts it: *The fact is that there were very few American women in Vietnam, so we were magnets for attention.*

In telling her story, Furey reminded me that the nursing personnel in Vietnam were very young. The nurses Elizabeth Norman interviewed for her book were most often in their early twenties when they served in Vietnam.[8]

Many soldiers wanted sexual interaction with the nurses. At first, Furey found the attention flattering. Then it quickly became overwhelming.

Everybody wants your attention, and everybody wants to sleep with you. It's not really what you're necessarily about.

It was not uncommon for romantic relationships to develop between nurses and soldiers, though not often with patients. The sexual revolution, discovered by the media in the early 1960s, meant that for many young women sex before or outside marriage was newly permissible. At times, these relationships were not as honest as they might have been under different circumstances.

Furey recalls: *I did fall in love with a pilot, which wasn't uncommon, and since we were right next to the airbase, we had a romance, and then he was off to fly medical evacuations.*

In addition to being in love, Furey found the relationship convenient. A way to protect herself from all the male attention, a solid relationship marked her as off-limits. As she says, she hoped to create a situation in which *I belong to him and everybody knows it. Maybe people will leave me alone.*

When he was off on piloting missions, they would write, maintaining their emotional connection.

When I first met him, he told me that his wife had been killed in an automobile accident. When you are twenty-two, you don't think people make that kind of stuff up. So I was head over heels in love with this guy.

One morning, after the base had been under attack all night, she got a phone call. It was a colleague, who told her, *"Joan, you need to know something before you get here." I said, "What's that?" She said, "Bill was brought in this morning, and he's really seriously injured."*

This was the guy. But this is an example of how crazy it was. So I was talking to her, and then there's this silence on the phone. She says, "There's something else you need to know." "Okay, what?" She said, "He has his next of kin listed as his wife."

Furey was stunned.

Her job required that she report for duty in the ICU, where she cared for a man she loved who had betrayed her. She remembers looking at his chart.

I'm in love with him. I'm having this relationship with him. And I find out not only that he lied to me, but he's lying on my side [of the ward] critically injured and I have to take care of him. I mean, you just get a little blown away with that kind of stuff. I can't tell you how many women can share some more stories.

Now, there were some people who ended up in very good marriages and relationships. But I think there were more people than anybody really knows who ended up having pretty devastating experiences in that regard.

The experience was so devastating for Furey that she felt unable to deal with the social life of Seventy-First Evac anymore. She changed her schedule so that she could avoid interaction; going on the night shift permanently, she worked from 7:00 p.m. to 7:00 a.m.

She later discovered that the experience was not uncommon.

Many more women than I think people would like to know left Vietnam thinking they were engaged to marry somebody, and then they never heard from the person again.

The long-term consequences of betrayal—feeling deceived by the war, by lovers, and by the nation itself—run very deep for Furey.

When I came back, people did not know I had been in Nam. They didn't want to know. Unlike a man of that generation, no one questioned if a woman went to Vietnam. So you could really isolate yourself in a way; nobody would ever come near you with any question about that. I didn't talk about it for thirteen years.

Furey returned from Vietnam in 1970. She suffered from depression and experienced a great deal of emotional pain. She was extremely angry and confused. Nevertheless, like many Vietnam veterans, she worked to become professionally successful, acquiring bachelor's and master's degrees in nursing.

Most of her anger centered on the American involvement in Vietnam. As she points out, 1970 was one of the peak years for antiwar demonstrations in the United States. By the time she left Vietnam, she had come to fully oppose our involvement there. She had seen so much, and it all seemed senseless. She considered joining Vietnam Veterans Against the War.

At the same time, she felt that protesting somehow betrayed the very men she had cared for. This set off an intense emotional conflict.

On one occasion, she attempted to—but could not—speak to an antiwar rally at a high school in Nassau County on Long Island. As she approached the podium, she wanted to tell the students about the reality of war. She wanted to make it clear that the devastation she experienced and saw firsthand could never be repaired. She understood the war in ways that even soldiers fighting on the ground could not. It turned out to be far more difficult for her to speak her mind than she had imagined.

As I looked out, I started talking [and] I felt like if I said that, I would be betraying all these guys I took care of. I was just overwhelmed with guilt. I walk[ed] offstage.

So despite her anger, she could not bring herself to join the antiwar movement in an active way. At the same time, she felt unable to connect with the civilians surrounding her in her new college environment. The pain and suffering she had seen and experienced isolated her from her peers and gave her a sense of alienation that made her feel surprised and hurt. Despite her feelings about the war, in a strange way she wanted to go back to Vietnam, to rejoin and serve again. She just didn't fit in stateside.

I'm twenty-three years old. My friends are all out partying, drinking, and having a good time. I didn't see anything worth laughing about.

Furey now sees that she suffered from some degree of post-traumatic stress disorder. She remembers beginning to have intrusive thoughts of Vietnam and drinking in order to make them go away and to help her sleep.

Sometimes I would just be so angry and upset it would be the only thing that would calm me down. I can remember walking around my apartment with a glass of scotch, drinking.

Furey recalls the difficulties of dating while studying at the State

University of New York, Stony Brook. Draft deferrals, allowing students to avoid service in Vietnam, were common.

So all of a sudden this is a guy who had a draft deferment, and you're a woman who was in Vietnam. Talk about a disconnect!

In the meantime, Furey continued to work as a nurse, but her attitude had changed, and not in a good way.

Things did not go well for her, primarily because she felt little compassion for her patients and their intolerance for pain. On one occasion, she needed to walk a forty-year-old woman down the hall who had just had her gallbladder removed. The woman felt pain and did not want to walk. Furey could sense her own temperature rising and remembers thinking, *I used to get people up and walking after their bodies were blown in half almost. And you're telling me you have too much pain? I had no use for that.*

At the same time she knew that her attitude was inappropriate and that she had no right to judge the patient based on her experiences in Vietnam. She realized that she had a problem; something inside her had changed.

The crisis came soon after. One night she got called down to the ER to help after a group of drunken teenagers driving in a car struck a tree. For Furey, this was eerily familiar, reminding her of a mass-casualty situation in Vietnam. She found herself doing everything as she might have done it in Pleiku.

We got everybody settled off to the operating room, off to the wards and whatever. After everybody had gone, I just pulled the curtain on me, and I collapsed into this wheelchair.

She remembers thinking, *I can't do it. I cannot do this anymore.*

She realized that this was the very thing she had been fighting against, giving up nursing. And if she did give it up, what would she do? Her entire life had revolved around nursing. Mrs. Florczek, an old acquaintance who had served as a nurse in World War II, came in and opened up the curtain and found her sitting in the wheelchair contemplating quitting. Furey will never forget what she said:

"Joan, I just want to tell you one thing. When I came home from

World War II, I thought I was going to lose my mind. But I didn't. And neither will you. You'll be okay." That's all she said, and she walked out.

Furey quit that job and never saw Mrs. Florczek again. She returned to school, to get her master's so she could teach. She didn't realize until years later how much Mrs. Florczek's words helped her find her way.

She was not alone. Elizabeth Norman's study of fifty nurses who served in Vietnam found that forty-three of them changed their area of specialty after returning home. A number of veteran nurses elected to leave nursing, for a range of reasons, including the fact that some found "they could no longer deal with patients and their problems."[9]

By 1975, Furey was teaching nursing as South Vietnam fell to the Communists. She remembers getting drunk as she watched Pleiku surrender. At that moment in time, it appeared to Furey—and to many, many other Vietnam veterans—that everything that had happened, everything she had struggled for, every effort she had made to save someone, had been for nothing. Furey abandoned the premise that her work and sacrifice had been of value, that the war itself had meant anything.

She didn't know about post-traumatic stress disorder. She felt terrible, out of control, and in crisis. Furey stopped drinking, and she has been sober for more than thirty years. She dealt with her alcoholism but did not begin to deal with the realities of Vietnam until 1982.

When the Vietnam Veterans Memorial was dedicated in Washington, D.C., in November 1982, as badly as she wanted to be there, she felt attending would lead to a relapse and that she might begin drinking again. She did not go.

But a number of developments would prompt her to acknowledge her status as a Vietnam veteran. The first was the development of the Veterans Administration Vet Centers in the early 1980s. These were storefront counseling centers for Vietnam veterans who were looking for help but unwilling to deal with the Veterans Administration bureaucracy. Veterans' advocates believed, probably rightly, that Vietnam veterans were put off by institutions of the size and scope of the VA. These supporters felt the veterans might seek care more readily in casual environments that invited open conversation and facilitated access to treatment. This storefront method mattered, and it helped many people. But Furey remained angry: *I got livid because I thought it was too little too late.*

The second stimulus for change was the publication in 1983 of Lynda Van Devanter's memoir, *Home Before Morning: The True Story of an Army Nurse in Vietnam.* In it Van Devanter described her drug and alcohol use and provided accounts of her romantic relationships with doctors. The book provoked outrage among a number of other Vietnam nurses, who felt compelled to protest against the image of Army nurses it painted. Furey too was angered.

She just totally told secrets and presented all this stuff. It violated confidentiality—this thing that what happens in Vietnam stays in Vietnam—and presented women in a bad light. Initially, my response was "How dare she?"

Furey was especially unhappy with Van Devanter's open acknowledgment of her struggles with PTSD when she came home.

I thought that, you know, you're not supposed to talk about that because then people are going to ask me, us, the other people who served. And I didn't want to talk about it. None of us wanted to talk about it. It was almost like somebody was exposing you to the world, even though they were talking about their own experience.

The consequence, though, was that Furey was increasingly driven to speak up about the Vietnam War she had experienced and to acknowledge her own struggles with PTSD.

On Memorial Day 1983, with six years of sobriety behind her, Furey made the trip to the Vietnam Veterans Memorial in Washington. While there, she began to recognize that she had some of the symptoms of post-traumatic stress disorder. She had kept busy, working at a VA hospital in St. Petersburg, Florida, but at the same time she knew that she was hiding something from herself. She didn't trust her own feelings.

Furey admits that her first five years back from Vietnam were the most difficult years of her life. She struggled to create an emotional balance and find a community that supported her. There were far fewer female veterans, which made it even more difficult for them to locate each other. Furey had not stayed in touch with anyone from her Army days. To her it seemed as though she had experienced Vietnam all by herself.

Asked to become almost superhuman, caring for badly wounded soldiers and civilians day after day, seeing the war from the perspective of the triage and surgical units, Furey developed whatever coping mechanisms she could. She is still proud of what she did in Vietnam, even if she was disillusioned by the war.

Today, she understands the act of relating her life story as part of a larger effort to find comfort with her own life. Vietnam is central to that effort.

I [am] struck by the fact that the stories of Vietnam don't really end. You know, everything you approached in life, everything that you responded to in life, was always interpreted through this lens of Vietnam. The effect of the experiences literally carried on for years. I think the reason I spent so much of my professional life working in this field of PTSD and veterans' health care was to . . . figure out a way to get people to understand what this experience is about so the next generation of people don't have to go through that.

It's been like this probably lifelong journey to really understand what it was about that experience that was so powerful. That one year in your life—I mean, that's really all it was—this one year in your life could have that kind of impact on you or on any other person.

It's kind of mind-boggling.

7

WAR AND LOSS: MIANO, NOWICKI, AND GONZALEZ

The cost of war cannot be calculated in dollars and cents alone. Losses have to be reckoned in personal terms, too. The sons, husbands, brothers, uncles, and friends who died in Vietnam are one natural part of this calculus, but we must think too about the families they left behind. They are also casualties of the Vietnam War, even if they are not commonly recognized as such.

Take the number of Vietnam dead from New York City, 1,741, and multiply it by 20—the figure World War I historians have used to estimate the "entourage" or "circle of mourning" created by the death of a single soldier. By this calculation 34,820 New Yorkers were directly affected by combat losses in Vietnam between 1964 and 1975.[1] Since the population of New York City in 1975 was 7,895,563, these figures suggest that one person out of every 226 individuals had an experience like that of Vicki Miano and her family.

Death does not discriminate. Of the servicemen from New York who died in Vietnam, 496—just over 28 percent—were African American, 1,235 were "Caucasian," and 10 were of Malaysian, Mongolian, or "other/not reported" background. The Department of Defense did not count people of Hispanic descent as a separate category at that time, meaning those figures were likely folded into the numbers for Caucasians. By religion, the largest single group represented from New York

City was Roman Catholic, like Stephen Pickett, Vicki Miano's brother. Five were Muslim, and three were "other." Just over 68 percent had been in the military for less than two years. No women from New York City are listed as having been killed.

Like a lot of New Yorkers, Vicki Miano's family, the Picketts, had roots elsewhere. Her father was born in Ohio and grew up in Tennessee. Her mother was a Corona, Queens, native. When her parents married, they settled in Kew Gardens, Queens, later moving into their own house in Jackson Heights, Queens, in 1959. It was there that Vicki and her brother Stephen would grow up.

Born in 1947, Stephen entered the Army in 1966. As Vicki remembers the events, Stephen had an automatic student deferment because he attended Queens College full-time but made the choice to serve his country. Nevertheless, military records indicate that Stephen was actually drafted. People who knew the family said later that Stephen's mother had pressured him to go into the service. These contradictions are indicative of the tricks memory can play, and the ways we—all of us—can construct narratives that are in conflict with the documentary record. In any case, Vicki says: *I know from his letters and stuff that this was something that he did want to do.*

An Internet posting on a Vietnam Veterans Memorial website, left by someone who knew Stephen in high school, says, "I knew Steve at Regis High School in NYC where he was three years ahead of me. He was a non-conformist, wore sunglasses at odd times, and was generally 'cool.' He was a role model to me."[2]

Vicki and Stephen were very close. She recalls him as being more of a caretaker than either of her parents. Their mother suffered from asthma and was frequently immobilized by it; their father was often working and not at home, and the relationship between them was distant. Vicki holds on to memories of her brother taking her for ice cream at the corner store, bringing her along when he and his friends went out together—never treating her as a burden, despite the eight-year age difference between them. She says Stephen was kind, smart, and funny, the type of young person who left an indelible imprint on everyone he met. He had a facility with languages and had spent some time at a seminary in Indiana and contemplated joining the priesthood before entering the service. Stephen was in Vietnam for only nine weeks when he was killed in 1967. How he died remained a mystery to the family for over thirty years. They did not hear the details of what happened from the Army; families generally didn't get detailed information about such matters from the military itself.

Instead, Vicki learned the details of Stephen's death from a member of his unit. In 2001, she began to use the Internet to search for someone who might have known her brother on various websites that veterans use. One night she received an e-mail from someone who said he thought he might have known Stephen and been with him when he died. From him she learned that Stephen had volunteered to investigate an enemy bunker and been killed by a Vietcong booby trap. Pickett was one of the thirty-two American soldiers killed in Vietnam that week.

The family did not find out that Stephen had been killed until several days after his death. Vicki recalls:

It was probably midmorning. There was a soldier who came to the door, and my mother was sleeping and my [other] brother, Chris, and I were home. And he asked if our parents were home, and we both said no, because when my mother was sleeping and with her asthma, you just didn't wake her up quickly. And so he said, "When are they going to be back?" And I said, "Sometime in the afternoon," and he said, "Okay, I'll return." And there was a package at the door; someone had sent a Christmas present, and Chris and I were arguing about who was going to open it. And you know we were getting into this battle, and my mother said, "Who was at the door?" And we said, "Oh, it was some soldier." And I remember looking at her face; she knew right away.

I knew. When I told my mother that the soldier was at the door, I just saw her expression. She called my grandmother; my grandparents lived in Flushing. My father used to work in the neighborhood, and she said, "Go see if your father is in the luncheonette." And sure enough, we found him in the luncheonette, reading his paperbacks.

By the time the soldier came back, my grandparents were there, my father was home, my mother was there, and he came to the door. They let him in. [He] said, "I'm sorry; I regret to inform you but your son was killed on December 14." My grandmother starts screaming; that was her birthday. My father stepped down into the basement, and the next thing I knew he put his fist through the wall. My mother was hysterical—just hysterical. And my grandfather was just sitting there, you know—he was also crying. I mean it was just—whew, like I said—thirty-seven years ago, but you can remember it as if it was yesterday.

The following days and weeks were a blur of activity as Army personnel came and went and the family prepared for the funeral. It was a few days before Christmas. Vicki recalls the funeral ceremony at the church, Our Lady of Fatima, as a nightmare. The wake was packed with people from all over, including people who had never met Stephen. The family held the interment ceremony at the Long Island National Cemetery in Farmingdale, New York. She vividly remembers the twenty-one-gun salute and the soldiers folding up the flag and handing it to her parents on that very cold winter day.

After Christmas break, Vicki returned to school feeling alone and devastated. Life got hard after Stephen died. Her parents separated six months later.

I think that after Stephen died, everything just disintegrated and the whole world kind of, like, fell apart. I was thirteen, in junior high school at the time.

The impact of Stephen's death has been passed on to a second generation of the Pickett family. Vicki's oldest daughter, Stephanie, keeps a photograph of Stephen in her datebook. Vicki's nephew and a second cousin are also named Stephen and have learned much about the man after whom they were named.

Vicki still feels Stephen's absence. On Memorial Day 2011, at a gathering of Vietnam veterans at the New York City Vietnam Veterans Memorial on Water Street in Manhattan, she read the names of some of the 1,741 soldiers from New York who were killed in Vietnam. As she prepared to leave the podium, she looked up and said: *"This is for you, Stephen. I think about you every day. I love you."*

Vicki's story is disturbingly common. Pickett was killed on Thursday, December 14, 1967. The next day, Sergeant Edward Michael Looney of Marine Park, Brooklyn, was killed in Binh Dinh province, South

Vietnam. As the Pickett family was dealing with their loss, neighbors across the city were coping with theirs. Bridget Nowicki remembers how her family, the Looneys of Marine Park, learned about the death of her nineteen-year-old brother, Edward.

My brother had just gotten married before he went overseas, and they notified his wife. And the phone call came from his wife on a Sunday morning to let us know what happened. We were notified on the seventeenth.

I can remember before the phone call came, my mother—it was a Sunday morning—had asked me to go down [to] the store to get . . . The family joke was always bread, milk, and cigarettes, you know; so I'm sure it was one of those three things. And I can remember walking back home and hearing my mother screaming. And then when I went in, they were sitting in the living room, and I can't remember if somebody told me directly to myself, like said the words to me, or if I heard them. I can remember telling my father, "That's not true; don't say that; don't lie to me." I kept saying, "It's not true; it's not true; I don't believe it."

And I can remember my father getting upset; it was like, "It's true." Not getting mad at me, but being upset like, "It's true; stop saying that," you know. And I just remember saying, "I'm sorry." And I told him, you know what . . . I don't know if it was my Catholic background, but I said, "God must have loved him more than we did; that's why he took him." And it finally sank in.

There were signs that they had up, like they do now, like WE SUPPORT OUR TROOPS. They had signs that everybody would have in their windows: WE SUPPORT OUR BOYS IN VIETNAM. And I can remember one neighbor coming in and ripping it down and my father got very annoyed. He said, "Now is the time we really have to support them more than ever. You know, now we're there; now we've got to do what we have to do. I'm not going to have my son's life [be] in vain."

We found out, and then it's waiting for the body to be shipped home. He was buried the day after Christmas, which was tough. I can remember the neighborhood because my father and his family grew up there. There were always Christmas lights up, but I can remember that year that nobody put their lights on, because like the whole neighborhood felt it.

In 2001, out of the blue, the company medic and another member of Looney's unit contacted the family. The men had been trying to find the people they served with, and they flew in to meet and talk to Edward's family. They explained to Bridget and her father that Edward had not been alone when he died. The medic had been the one to place Edward on the helicopter that took him out of the field. The family had received a few letters, but for the most part it had seemed as though Edward had boarded a plane bound for Vietnam only to disappear off the face of the earth. With this one small act, two veterans helped to fill that void. Visiting more than thirty years after Edward's death, they gave the family a sense of closure.

When soldiers lost comrades in the field in Vietnam, they did not have time to grieve. Indeed, some commanders actively discouraged it, preferring that they focus on the tasks at hand rather than on the deaths of their peers—which inevitably brought to mind the risks of their service. Anyway, most did not have time. They literally had to soldier on. Many only felt the trauma of loss when they got home.

Jose Gonzalez served with the 173rd Airborne Brigade in 1967 through the terrible battles of that year. But for Gonzalez, coming home was even worse, because his unit continued to suffer casualties and he wasn't there. He says: *I got more devastated at home than I did over there, I think. Because everything over there was always, you had no time. You had no time, you know.*

While in Vietnam, he became close with another Puerto Rican soldier from Brooklyn named Geovel Lopez-Garcia. Lopez-Garcia had been sent home in November 1967 on emergency bereavement leave, missing the Battle of Dak To—one of the bloodiest battles of the war. When Lopez-Garcia returned in-country in December, Gonzalez was rotating home permanently.

And we saw each other again, two young kids. And then he gives me his address: "Go see my mother." I did.

The Tet Offensive opened in the last days of January 1968, and Lopez-Garcia was killed two weeks later. Gonzalez continues:

His mother, somebody called me, that he was missing in action, and the next day they confirmed it. [He was dead.] Then they brought him home at the funeral parlor, over there on Park Avenue and Tompkins. I went to junior high school right there when I was a kid. I walked in, I was in uniform, and his mother saw me. She lost it. I lost it. I walked out. I walked right out. I never saw them again. I never saw them again, and I didn't go to his funeral. I went on a drunk. I don't know how long it was. I was AWOL from my next duty station. I didn't care.

Statistics consistently reported elevated mortality rates for Vietnam veterans in the years between the end of the war in 1975 and 1983. While Vietnam veterans' death rates have stabilized in the years that followed, the stories of loss live on.[3] The widow of one Vietnam veteran told me a story about her husband, Ray, about his struggle with PTSD and cancer after the war, and what it all eventually cost her and her family.

I don't think things went too well for him over there. I heard stories, a lot of stories, that were very gory. These guys who went over were very young; Ray was about seventeen when he went over, and it was very hard for them.

Ray drank. At first she didn't think much of it, because, she said, at the time everybody was drinking. Ray didn't sleep much either, averaging three or four hours a night. He liked to work night shifts and had a very bad temper. On one occasion when he had their children with him, someone said something to Ray that provoked him and a fight began. It took seven New York City Transit Police officers to subdue him. Another time, at the VA hospital in Brooklyn, he lost control, and it took another half a dozen police officers to subdue him.

It was hard on me because you didn't know when he was going to explode. But I loved him, you know, so I was trying to help him. [I] tried to get him into therapy quite a few times. He went a few times. It was just very hard for him.

Sometimes, Ray would disappear for days on end. She heard that he would dress in his fatigues, put paint on his face, and walk—on the Belt Parkway from Brooklyn all the way out to Long Island. He could get violent, but never with their children. Eventually, she had to leave. Ray died in 1997. She believes that he too was a casualty of the war.

He developed asthma about five years before he died. They said it was cancer. We don't know if it was directly caused by Agent Orange. That we never found out. But because of the cancer, I think maybe Agent Orange did have something to do with it.

In speculating about the cause of Ray's cancer and its connection to his Vietnam service, she is on solid ground. The Veterans Administration presumes that certain "diseases can be related to a Veteran's qualifying military service." There are fourteen categories of disease on the current list. Lung cancer is among them.[4]

Almost a half century after the war in Vietnam, the bodies are still coming home; the costs are still being calculated. In 2009, the New York *Daily News* reported the story of Jose Sanchez. Born at Kings County Hospital in Brooklyn, Sanchez was killed fighting in Vietnam, and his body had only just been recovered—he was coming home. Sanchez had been killed in Quang Tri province, South Vietnam, in 1968, along with three other Marines. The news reported that Sanchez's mother, Virginia, died five weeks after learning that her son's remains had been identified. The *Daily News* reported: "Her mind at ease, Virginia Sanchez died five weeks later.

" 'Finally,' says son Peter, 'she could rest.' "[5]

8

WELCOME HOME, JIMMY: THE BACOLO TWINS

Jimmy and Mauro Bacolo are twins who were born in Red Hook, Brooklyn, in 1947. Their father, Mike, was a decorated World War II veteran, and they grew up wanting to be like him. Jimmy says: *We knew about my father. I mean, everybody knew about it. He didn't talk about it. Him and his whole generation didn't talk much about what they did.*

But Jimmy has studied his father's past. Mike Bacolo served in the Forty-Seventh Infantry Regiment, part of the Seventh U.S. Army that invaded North Africa. From there he went into Sicily with General George Patton and then landed in Normandy on June 6, 1944. He was wounded three weeks into the battle. Jimmy's uncle fought through the Battle of the Bulge and into the Rhineland with General Patton's Third Army. He says with pride, *Between the two of them they got five Purple Hearts.*

In part to carry on the strong family military tradition, Jimmy wanted to enlist in the Navy at age eighteen, but a petty juvenile crime record prevented it. Instead, he found himself swept up in the draft and sent to Vietnam as an Army artilleryman in 1966. His brother Mauro enlisted in the Navy, where he took part in the recovery of an H-bomb that had been lost at sea off Palomares, Spain, in 1966. He went to Vietnam later that year.

Today, both twins are retired—Jimmy from his job as a Staten Island Ferry repairman and Mauro from his work as a landscaper for the New York City Parks Department. Both men also suffer from cancer. Jimmy believes he may have been exposed to Agent Orange.

Recalling his service in an Army artillery unit, Jimmy emphasizes that his job was relatively easy. He was not a *"ground-pounder," "trigger-puller," or "grunt." We got lifted with the guns and placed down, but it was usually secure . . . what they would call an LZ [landing zone] or a fire-base. They were already secured by the airborne troops that went in there, you know? They would go in and secure it, and then the artillery would be brought in.*

Nevertheless, his time there wasn't without danger.

I was scared enough just being over there, knowing that you had 5 million people and 4.5 million hated your guts and you couldn't tell them apart, because nobody had uniforms. You know, they all wore pajamas, whether it was different colors or not. There was no battle lines; there was no secured areas. You could walk into a village one day, and the next day they're dropping rockets and mortars on you. Or at night, you know, there's a guy . . . he's cutting your hair in a village in the daytime, at nighttime he's lobbing mortars into your position.

By 1968, the Pentagon estimated that eighty thousand Vietnam-era veterans were being returned to civilian life each month.[1] These men and women were, as the journalist William Barry Furlong put it at the time, "peculiar." They were unlike returning World War II veterans. Furlong wrote, "The feeling of total anonymity strikes the Vietnam veteran right down to the neighborhood level."[2] Even after forty years, my interviewees reported feeling both isolated and anonymous when they came home.

Anonymity led to the effacing of a veteran's military identity. Sandy Goodman, writing in *The Nation* in 1968 about service members returning from Vietnam, described them as "invisible veterans." Goodman asserted that, "as a group, the Vietnam veterans resemble neither the noisy, assertive veterans of World War II, who clomped around as if they owned the country, nor the quiet, apathetic young men who shuffled aimlessly about after Korea, 'staring nowhere,' as one observer described them. Like the men of Korea, the Vietvets are relatively few in number . . . but unlike the Korean veteran, the Vietvet has no glassy, faraway look in his eyes. He knows exactly what he wants: to throw off his identity as an ex-GI and become a civilian again as fast as possible." Some hoped that shedding the identity of soldier might lead to an easy transition to civilian life. Goodman even quoted a Veterans Administration official who said—with what sounds now like painfully ironic optimism—that the Vietnam veteran's readjustment to civilian life is "the smoothest in recent history."[3]

In some ways, the return was smooth. In 1971, a Louis Harris & Associates poll conducted for the Veterans Administration indicated that both the general public and employers overwhelmingly respected returning veterans. Ninety-four percent of respondents indicated that Vietnam veterans deserved "the same warm reception" as veterans of earlier wars. Veterans—95 percent of them—believed that their family and friends greeted them warmly upon return, and 79 percent believed that "most people respect you."[4] And despite the impression that veterans were not welcomed home from Vietnam, there were parades and brass bands for the returning soldiers, Marines, and airmen. On March 31, 1973, New York City played host to one of the largest parades in its history, the Home with Honor parade.[5] Charles Wiley, at that time a writer for *The American Legion Magazine* and one of the parade organizers, many years later said about the parade:

On this day, unknown to the overwhelming majority of our people, one thousand servicemen, all of whom had volunteered and fought in Vietnam, all of whom had volunteered to give up a weekend to represent their service, marched a two-mile parade route through cheering, flag-waving Americans. The Army, Navy, Marines, Air Force and Coast Guard were there to be saluted on a day that was officially called Home With Honor Day. However, what happened after they completed the route-of-march made it one of the greatest homecoming parades in the history of the world. At the end of the route, the thousand servicemen sat in the grandstand while 150,000 people welcomed our men back from Vietnam by marching the two-mile parade route behind them. They tell you that there were no brass bands to welcome our men home. How about 120 brass bands to welcome them home? Probably the biggest massing of bands in history![6]

It took only about seventy-two hours for Jimmy Bacolo to move from the depths of the jungle in Southeast Asia to the cement jungle of Red Hook, Brooklyn. He felt as if he had to prepare himself for the emotional intensity of the moment.

Bacolo had gone over to Vietnam aboard a ship, a journey that took about twenty days. Coming home, he traveled on a commercial airliner. From his artillery unit he was sent first to Cam Ranh Bay for outprocessing. He turned in his combat equipment and jungle fatigues and was given a new set of clothing, including a garrison cap, which is generally worn only in the United States. After his papers were in order, he flew to Japan for a short stopover, then to Alaska for a refueling stop, and finally to Fort Lewis, Washington, in the Seattle-Tacoma area. At Fort Lewis, Bacolo was processed out of the service. After a short stay in San Francisco, he headed for New York.

It was 1968. As he flew over New York City, he looked down at the skyscrapers, the Brooklyn Bridge, and the Manhattan skyline. *You know, you were looking at America right then after being in Asia. It felt great.*

Several Brooklyn-reared soldiers from his unit were on the same flight. Together they flew to John F. Kennedy International Airport and then shared a taxicab home. Jimmy was the last to get dropped off because he lived on the waterfront, at Red Hook.

Coming home was rather emotional, being away for twelve months, going through Vietnam, just to get out of a cab and walk in the door without a few minutes of sort of downtime. I didn't want to just step out and step into the house, so I asked the cabbie to drop me off at Smith and Ninth Street, and he said, "Why? This is not where you live." And I explained to him that I used to always walk that Z shape to school and to work, so I needed that block and a half of zigzag just so I could sort of compose myself, you know? After being away for twelve months and most

After his return from Vietnam, John Hamill (at left) joined Vietnam Veterans Against the War and was arrested on the steps of the United States Supreme Court. As he was hauled away, John remembers a woman shouting out, "I don't think what you're doing is good for the troops." John replied, "Lady, we *are* the troops." (Photograph by Bernie Edelman, courtesy of John Hamill and Bernie Edelman)

John Hamill enlisted at the age of seventeen. Later on, he wrote his own caption for this picture: "IT WAS ALL OVER BUT THE FIGHTING—for John Hamill as he smiled for the camera, relieved to be done with the rigors of Airborne training in 1967. A month later he would join the hard-fighting paratroopers of the 173rd Airborne Brigade as a combat medic in the Central Highlands of Vietnam."

(Photograph courtesy of John Hamill)

Nurse Susan Kramer met her future husband, Paul O'Neill, in Vietnam. Paul took this picture at the time. After the war, they became involved with Vietnam Veterans Against the War, and later joined the Peace Corps. (Photograph courtesy of Susan and Paul O'Neill)

Joseph Giannini commanded a Marine rifle platoon. He has practiced criminal law on Long Island for more than thirty years and hosts a local television show, *East End Veterans*. (Photograph courtesy of Joseph Giannini)

Anthony Wallace in Tay Ninh Province, March 1970. After the war, Wallace earned a B.A. from Brooklyn College and returned to work at Con Edison, where he is still employed. (Photograph courtesy of Anthony Wallace)

Joan Furey worked as a nurse at an evacuation hospital in Pleiku, in the Central Highlands of South Vietnam, from January 1969 through January 1970, earning a Bronze Star. Much of the area was inhabited by indigenous tribal peoples known as Montagnards. Furey recalls: "This was a Montagnard's baby whose father brought her to the hospital in critical condition due to severe dysentery. We treated her, actually saved her life, and he was so overjoyed, he showed up with some rice wine and Montagnard bracelets for us . . . If you look closely at the baby, you'll note she has a bunch of them on her left arm. At the time, everyone said that meant she was a Montagnard princess, but I don't know if that's true or not." (Photograph courtesy of Joan Furey)

Jimmy Bacolo (at left) served in an Army artillery unit and later worked on the Staten Island Ferry. His twin brother, Mauro (at right), joined the Navy; after the war, he became a landscaper.
(Photograph by Philip F. Napoli)

Bernard Edelman poses at a temple in Vietnam. An Army journalist during the war, he is now Deputy Director for Policy and Government Affairs for Vietnam Veterans of America.
(Photograph courtesy of Bernard Edelman)

After joining the Marines, Ed German was wounded in a May 1969 ambush and returned home that June. Today German works as a radio personality on Long Island.

(Photograph courtesy of Ed German)

After leaving college, Robert Ptachik was drafted into the U.S. Army in 1966. He was wounded by a booby trap in 1967.

(Photograph courtesy of Robert Ptachik)

Upon returning, Ptachik became a founding member of the Brooklyn chapter of Vietnam Veterans of America. He is currently Senior University Dean for the Executive Office and Enrollment at the City University of New York.

(Photograph courtesy of Robert Ptachik)

Herbert Sweat served as an infantryman with the 173rd Airborne Brigade. Today he serves on the board of Black Veterans for Social Justice, Inc., a not-for-profit social service agency founded in 1979. (Photograph by Philip F. Napoli)

A retired New York City public school teacher, Neil Kenny served in Vietnam in 1968 and later struggled with PTSD. In 2005 he attended a Memorial Day event at the New York City Vietnam Veterans Memorial Plaza. (Photograph by Philip F. Napoli)

Neil Kenny in Vietnam. (Photograph courtesy of Neil Kenny)

Vince McGowan says, "I got my education in the Marine Corps with two tours in Vietnam." Today, he is Chief Operating Officer at Battery Park City Parks Conservancy in lower Manhattan and president of the group that puts on Manhattan's annual Veterans Day Parade. Here he observes Vietnam Veterans Recognition Day at the New York City Vietnam Veterans Memorial Plaza, March 2011.
(Photograph by Philip F. Napoli)

of the time walking on grass and weeds and bush and mud, I needed to find me back on asphalt and concrete.

Jimmy described what it was like to finally walk in the door:

And [long pause, taps with fingers] it was a school day, so my brothers and sisters, the younger ones, were in school. But my mom was home, as usual, sitting at the kitchen table drinking coffee because she always had a pot of coffee on, and I think she was eating toast or zwieback biscuits, which she loved with butter. It was emotional. We used to call her Tiny Tears because she would cry at the drop of a hat for anything; I mean, if a baby was born, she would cry. If somebody died, she would cry. If something was this, she would cry. She, my mother, was very emotional that way. She would always cry.

So I walked in the second door—we had a vestibule—and I still had a key because I always had a key to the house, and no matter when we moved away or where we went, we always had a key to get back to the house. And I just opened the door and walked in the first door, then I walked into the second door, and she heard the doors opening and she started to get up and I could just catch her from the corner of my eye at the table with the coffee and the zwiebacks and she turned and she got a little—I would say hysterical, more than emotional. I mean, she couldn't believe that I was home.

Jimmy's mother called his father's best friend. About ten minutes later three carloads of longshoremen showed up, including his father, his uncles, and his best friends.

My father was beside himself. He wasn't one for showing too much emotion at certain things, but he was taken aback, and it was good to see him. We had a couple of beers, and then he said, "Come on. We'll take you down to the neighborhood." We went back down to my uncle's bar, where all the rest of the longshoremen were because the longshoremen were strictly 100 percent behind the war or behind the troops, and we went down there and I met my cousins and other friends and all my father's longshoremen friends, and none of them went back to the ship that day. We stayed in my uncle's bar, and we all got smashed. We had a good time.

They had a sign out, which I still have. They took a piece of wood, painted it red, white, and blue, and they put Christmas lights on it, and they hung it up for Christmas out in the window. And it was still there when I got home in May: WELCOME HOME JIMMY FROM VIETNAM. *When my mother passed away in 1989, I went down in the basement. I found the wood sign dry-rotted but still painted with the words, and I brought it to my house, and I have it down in the basement covered up. That was the only welcome home I got—was the family and that sign.*

He came home in 1968. The New York City Fifth Avenue parade was five years in the future. By the time it rolled around, it was irrelevant to him. He compared his own experience with his father's return home from World War II, *when everybody had time to sort of relax a little bit. By the time they got everything secured, they got to the ships and all, they spent twenty-something days coming home. Here in Vietnam you were always flown home, individual or in groups, and within forty-eight hours from the time that I left Hill 29, I went to Chu Lai overnight, and from Chu Lai I went to Cam Ranh Bay overnight. That's two days. On the third morning I was flying home. Within seventy-two hours I was back in the States after being out in the field and in LZs and firebases. So in that seventy-two hours' time you went from one extreme to the next. Meanwhile, the battle, the war, was still going on and guys were still dying, and you were leaving guys behind that you knew well.*

Jimmy's sense that he had abandoned his fellow soldiers is a common refrain in Vietnam veterans' stories. Jose Gonzalez said the same thing, as did Joan Furey and many others I interviewed. World War II and Korean War veterans had long journeys home together, mostly aboard ship. Jimmy and his generation were separated and atomized by the service's procedures, which generated bitterness. Most often, people came home individually, not as part of a unit, as their tour of duty in Vietnam ended—at twelve months for people in the Army and thirteen months for Marines. The men and women returning from Vietnam never had the opportunity to effectively decompress before returning home. This lack of downtime led to resentment. Many returned home feeling like so much surplus baggage.

Jimmy's brother Mauro recalls a relatively safe time in the Navy.

We put things in the war; we took things out of the war. We researched the rivers, tributaries, and canals to measure the depth and breadth of them. We did water samples; we made charts. We turned them over to the Office of Naval Intelligence, the Army Corps [of] Engineers, and a sundry of other organizations that needed the charts. We worked for the Oceanographic Institute in Washington, D.C. The minute we went under way, we were measuring the water clouds. That's what the ship was, the Geodetic Survey ship AGS-15. That's what we did. It wasn't a horrid experience. I didn't earn any great ribbons; I didn't draw blood on my own.

He also describes homecoming as "uneventful." He was in the Philippines with his ship when his time was up.

I remember coming in, landing, it was morning; got in a cab and came home; it was bitter cold and I was home. The neighborhood had changed tremendously. A lot of the guys were on drugs, in jail, some had died, some were in Vietnam, others were in the military, several had died and I hadn't been aware of it. None of us went together as a group or unit; we all went our own individual ways, on our own.

At the age of sixteen, Mauro had left school to work at Ohrbach's department store on Thirty-Fourth Street in Manhattan. He joined the military the next year, in 1964, and got his GED while in the Navy, along with some college credits. He was married June 3, 1966, and reported to his ship in Bayonne, New Jersey, a week later. He arrived in Vietnam in September 1966, and his wife gave birth to their daughter in January 1967. Mauro saw her for the first time that May, on a two-week leave, and then headed back to Vietnam, finally returning to the United States for good in December.

My daughter was one month short of one year old.

When he returned from Vietnam, he had a drug problem.

He worked a variety of jobs, went to Woodstock in 1969, and hung out in Greenwich Village. He remembers the 1969 New York Mets victory parade in lower Manhattan.

I was on Broadway and Wall Street the day that the Mets won the World Series. I remember the windows opening and the roar and din, but I was on LSD. I wasn't a sports fan, so I could care less about the Mets. [But] I was sort of caught up in it . . . and when the paper came down, I was standing in the middle of Broad and Wall up to my waist in paper and trying to figure out why they were throwing this paper out.

Mauro went briefly to City College and then to the New York Botanical Garden's School of Professional Horticulture, from which he graduated in 1974. From 1979 to 1982 he worked for a young-adult landscape-training program, then bought a nursery in Park Slope, Brooklyn, which he ran until 1986. While he did okay, Mauro regrets the years he lost to drug and alcohol use.

I say to myself, "Look what I missed." I could have been a nerd like that. I could have gone to college and graduated because I would have been with a crowd that gravitated toward that.

In late 1986 he started rehabilitation, as an outpatient, finally getting clean for good in February 1989. He celebrated his twenty-third anniversary of being sober in February 2012.

While he doesn't blame the war for his drug use, he does attribute the lack of purpose and direction he felt after the war to the combined effect of his experience in Vietnam and social unrest in America.

I wanted us to be the winners; to vanquish the enemies, so to speak. But then all the politics involved, you know. So it changed me. Not so much my eleven-plus months there, but that whole period from '63 or '64 to '73 or '75, because . . . that whole ten-to-twelve-year period was all around Vietnam and the social unrest. You can't separate one from the other, because there was so much going on and I had four years in the military. I left with short hair; [then] I went long-haired hippie, drugs . . .

In 1975, when he heard the news about the official end of the war, it was a devastating moment for Mauro.

I remember the day. I was sitting in the apartment at 247 Garfield and they made the announcement and I broke down; I was in tears. I remember calling my brother Jimmy and [I] said, "Did you just hear the news?" He said, "Yeah." He was in tears too. I said, "But why, Jimmy? What happened?" It's very vivid. I can feel the sun coming through the window just sitting there in the little anteroom that we had off to the side overlooking Garfield Place, and I just sat there and cried. What happened, what happened? The war was over.

I wanted us to be the winners.

9

AGAINST WAR: FRIEDMAN AND LOUIS

The public memory of the war in Vietnam is dominated by several stereotypical images. The first is that of a dirty soldier in the midst of combat in a dense jungle. The second image is that of the civilian protester, voicing displeasure about American policy in Vietnam. The third is that of the returned veteran as victim. It has remained difficult for the American public to see beyond these clichés.

Plenty of veterans protested against the war—and continue to protest against present wars—and they speak with an authority that few others can match. They know what war means because they have seen it and experienced it. Some continue to live the consequences of the war in Vietnam every day. The experiences of Danny Friedman and Fred Louis reveal something of what it has meant to be an antiwar veteran.

The organization Vietnam Veterans Against the War has its roots in New York City. In April 1967, a Vietnam vet named Jan Barry, then known as Jan Crumb, marched in demonstrations under a banner held aloft by members of an organization called Veterans for Peace (VFP), a pacifist group made up mostly of men who had fought in World War II and the Korean War. VFP put up a sign reading VIETNAM VETERANS AGAINST THE WAR! mostly to see what would happen. In fact, as the historian Gerald Nicosia has noted, there was no Vietnam Veterans Against the War organization at the time, but Barry and five others would soon create one.[1] This veterans' organization would go on to deeply influence the lives of many and would have a significant impact on the national discourse about the war. Hundreds—some say thousands—of men and women moved through the organization, which continues to exist to this day.

Friedman grew up in the Homecrest section of Sheepshead Bay, Brooklyn, in a relatively liberal Jewish family. He had a stable upbringing: he lived in the same house from the age of six until he went into the Army. His parents, who both worked, volunteered at the local Jewish community center. His mother kept a kosher house, and the family kept the Sabbath, but over time religious observance became a less significant part of family life. While the family continued to go to synagogue on the High Holy Days, they did not attend on a regular basis. Still, they made certain that Friedman went to Hebrew school and had his Bar Mitzvah. Social consciousness was a component of their culture at home, albeit of a rather passive variety. He recalls:

We watched all the stuff on TV about the racial problems in the South with horror. We were offended by what was going on; we were outraged. We weren't activists; we didn't go join marches or anything. But mostly my friends in the neighborhood, we didn't really discuss stuff like that. It was just stuff that happened somewhere else. What we were involved in was the Giants and the Yankees and the Dodgers and the Mets and you know—the Knicks and the Rangers. That was important.

After he graduated from high school at the age of sixteen, he attended Kingsborough Community College for three semesters, until late fall 1966.

When he arrived at Kingsborough, the school was new, but many of its buildings were World War II–era barracks left over from a defunct military base. Friedman recalls taking part in the demolition of some of the older structures dotting the area. The school had the advantage of being close to home, and Friedman did not have a car.

In the mid-1960s, the antiwar movement was just beginning to take shape nationally. In March 1965 students and faculty at the University of Michigan held one of the first antiwar teach-ins, followed by an even larger one at the University of California, Berkeley, in May. Friedman remembers seeing groups like Students for a Democratic Society and antiwar activists on campus, especially in the student center. But like many American college students at the time, he viewed them with little sympathy. While antiwar momentum would later grow on college campuses, at this stage the movement remained quite small.

Academically, Friedman did not perform as well as he had hoped. If he felt interested in either a subject or a faculty member, he had the ability to get As and Bs, but some subjects, like economics, seemed to stump him. By the end of the third semester he was on academic probation.

Friedman knew that without a student deferment, he would be drafted. As a result, he tried to enlist in the National Guard, Air Force, and Navy Reserve. Of course, many young men had a similar idea, and these branches of the military had long wait lists. Rather than matriculate back at school for a fourth semester, Friedman took a job.

To this day, he believes that his economics professor, a faculty adviser for Kingsborough's branch of Students for a Democratic Society, turned him in to the draft board.

We didn't get along. I was the resident John Wayne enthusiast.

In May 1967, Friedman received notification that he had been reclassified as 1-A for the draft and the following week his induction notice arrived. He went down to Fort Hamilton in Brooklyn for his physical and was soon taken by bus to Whitehall Street in Manhattan for his swearing in.

I really didn't care. Though I wasn't prepared to enlist, I didn't lose any sleep when I got a draft notice, either. I bought the political philosophy that we were going to have to fight in Vietnam to keep them from fighting on the beaches of California and save the world from Communism. I didn't know a lot about it back in those days, but I bought the line; I bought the political story.

His mother was extremely nervous. Friedman says that every day he was in Vietnam was a living hell for her. She had nightmares about it, and he says it aged her a lot. His father had been 4-F during World War II, serving in New York as an air-raid warden when there was concern about possible Nazi raids on the Port of New York. His father didn't have much to say about Vietnam.

Immediately after being sworn in, Friedman was put on a train to Fort Jackson, South Carolina, for reception, then to Fort Gordon, Georgia, for basic training. Despite being invited to apply for officer candidate training, Friedman says: *I declined because my father never had a nice thing to say about an officer.*

He also did not want to give the military the extra year necessary. Eventually, Friedman went to Fort Knox, Kentucky, for Advanced Individual Training (AIT) as an armored reconnaissance scout. After a few months at Fort Knox he left for Vietnam in November 1967.

The trip was long, with a layover at Clark Air Base in the Philippines. Upon arrival at the Tan Son Nhut Air Base, the pilot made a rapid descent, and everyone on board was hustled out quickly.

Everybody was still a little woozy from drinking and everything, and I remember saying to the stewardesses, "Don't let them take us; don't let them take us; hide us—hide us," you know. [Laughs.] And she was looking at me like, "Get the hell off my plane," you know. [Laughs.]

Friedman was assigned to the D Troop, Seventeenth Armored Cavalry, 199th Light Infantry. He was soon educated in the intricacies of the Vietnamese black market. Soldiers would buy items from the American PX and sell them to Vietnamese cabdrivers. When they had enough money, they would go to the city of Bien Hoa for a big steak dinner and some entertainment, which they enjoyed while the other newly arrived replacements went about their business on base, assigned to routine duties.

We had intense action not [on] a daily basis but, I would say, on a weekly basis. We were having combat operations, I'd say, in the period between the end of January and the middle of May on a pretty much regular basis.

Basically, this was still like a lark for me. This was like an extension of playing soldier in the neighborhood; it was just like doing it for real; it's kind of cool, you know. You get to wear a uniform; the guns are real. Somebody says there's bad guys out in that area, we will fire our guns out there, you know. Maybe we got somebody and maybe we don't; we don't know.

On January 30, 1968, an estimated eighty thousand members of the Vietcong and North Vietnamese Army launched attacks on thirty-six of forty-four South Vietnamese provincial capitals and more than a hundred towns and cities in total. Caught by surprise, U.S. and South Vietnamese forces recovered and counterattacked. While the military situation in South Vietnam was quickly stabilized, the boldness of the Tet Offensive demonstrated that years of graduated escalation, bombing, and body counts had failed to secure military victory for the United States and the government of the Republic of South Vietnam. For a range of reasons—military, economic, and political—it seemed the limit of American intervention in Vietnam had been reached.

Friedman now says that, for him, *Tet changed everything.*

In the dry season after Tet, on February 25, 1968, Friedman and his unit were out on operation in some rice paddies when a rocket hit one of the vehicles in his troop. As the rocket exploded, it killed everyone inside, including James Thornton from Philadelphia. Thornton was a friend and the first man Friedman had ever smoked pot with in Vietnam.

Immediately, Friedman and the other troopers were ordered to dismount from their tracked vehicles as their commander called in an air strike. The strikes were aimed at the area just in front of Friedman. Assuming nothing could survive after such an air strike, Friedman and his unit began firing into spider holes and dropping grenades, not believing any real danger existed. Then, he recalls, "all hell broke loose." From deep within their holes, the Vietcong emerged, firing away.

I hit the ground, and I don't know [why, but] I'm not even wearing a shirt; I'm wearing a flak vest but no shirt underneath, and I remember hearing the rounds go over my head. I remember hugging the ground, and I remember there being a lot of red ants on the ground that were knocked out of the trees from the air strikes and they were very angry red ants. And they were eating me and I couldn't move.

Finally, I see off to my side there's like a muddy canal, and I crawl over to the [combat photographer] and said we're going to roll over into the canal, which we did, and it felt good just to get wet and get the mud. Some other guys we could hear were pinned down sort of like on the other side of this [brush], and I said let's work over to them. Let's work over in that area.

So [we were] slowly moving in a crouched position through this canal with this photographer who now [had] his M16 in his hand. And we turn—it's like a bend in the canal, and there's three VC there. And they look at me and I look at them and then they fall dead. I had my hand on my trigger; I don't remember firing. But I emptied a magazine into them. And—and I look back at the [photographer]. He had his camera in his hand. He was behind me.

And I flipped out; first of all, then I realized there was no way he could have shot them. And I saw my hand on my trigger, and I realized it was still depressed; the trigger was still depressed. I guess automatically I ejected my magazine and put in a new magazine, locked in a round, and then I turned around to him and I just went at him. I didn't hit him, but I kind of like started to scream in his face: "What the fuck are you doing taking pictures? We could have been killed! You've got an M16 and you better fucking use it or I'll kill you—you son of a bitch." I was just like flipping out.

Within the same few weeks we had a very similar operation. This time it was only one guy was killed and the lieutenant and a couple guys were wounded.

In that second incident, Friedman's unit took small-arms fire as he worked to make himself as small as possible behind his gun and shield. A grenade hit the shield of his machine gun, and a round exploded in the machine gun's chamber and blew up the weapon's bolt. Shrapnel hurled itself into Friedman's hand. The medic patched him up.

After May 1968, the action around Friedman's unit tapered off. By September of that year, the plan was for Friedman to rotate back to the United States in November. A request went out for volunteers to join a security force for the base at Long Binh. Friedman, who was up for promotion to sergeant at the time, was acting track commander and therefore in charge of an armored personnel carrier and didn't want to leave the field. However, he was "volunteered" for the job and assigned to perimeter duty at Long Binh, where he was wounded a second time.

In a friendly-fire incident, a single, isolated shot hit Friedman in the neck. It was almost as if someone were specifically aiming at him—or got lucky. Apparently, there was little significant damage because within a few days, even though the bullet was still in his body and located near his spine, Friedman was sewn up and sent back to his unit.

Friedman's mother, distraught over his assignment to Vietnam in the first place, found out that he had been returned to service with a bullet still lodged in his body. She was working as a bookkeeper in a synagogue at the time and complained to her rabbi that the Army was not treating Friedman properly. The rabbi got in touch with the New York senator Jacob Javits, who contacted the Army. Shortly thereafter, Friedman was called into the troop commander's office to answer questions about a congressional inquiry and asked to sign a letter indicating that he did not want the bullet removed.

I was embarrassed by the whole thing; I was very anxious to sign it and say I was okay. And I basically was kind of in limbo for a couple of months until I rotated stateside.

Home on leave in 1968, Friedman went in uniform to visit friends at Hunter College. Hunter, and other New York City colleges, hosted significant antiwar activity in the late 1960s. While he was there, friends pointed out some students handing out peace-related petitions and information and suggested to Friedman that he go "teach them a lesson."

I walked out there, and they looked like some cute girls, you know? I look at the literature and said, "How can you do this? You're betraying your country. Don't you know what we're fighting for?"

In retrospect, Friedman realized that he was simply repeating information he had been taught in high school, basic training, and AIT.

At some point I just froze up and realized that what I was saying was what I was told before Vietnam and totally contradictory to what I had experienced in Vietnam.

The incident caused him to shut down for the next six months. He recalls not wanting to talk to anyone about Vietnam. He needed to evaluate what he thought he knew and compare it with what he had experienced himself.

[I] drank a lot of beer, went to some parties . . . and made believe Vietnam had never happened.

Friedman was finally discharged in 1969. Once home, he became slowly radicalized. A number of events pushed him toward an antiwar position. He attended Woodstock, worked summers in the Catskill Mountains, and went back to school. By the spring of 1970, he was working on Wall Street, around the time the Hard Hat Riot took place. On May 8, 1970, some two hundred construction workers, led by the New York State AFL-CIO union, took to the streets and confronted a thousand college students and protesters who had gathered to demonstrate against the Kent State shootings, the invasion of Cambodia, and the Vietnam War. Newspapers reported that seventy persons were injured in the disturbance and six were arrested.[2] One day in roughly the same period of time—Friedman does not recall the date exactly—he found himself in a fistfight with a construction worker.

I'm wearing a Wall Street smock with my ID, and I'm wearing a tie and everything, and I had a little bushy mustache. My hair was starting to get bushy. This guy was talking about the draft-card burners and the Communists and this and that, and I was saying, "Oh, man, you know, that ain't the way it is, you know. Vietnam is fucked-up."

And the guy attacks me and said, "What the fuck do you know, you draft-card-burning hippie?" I said, "What the fuck do you know? I just came back from Vietnam a few months ago." And they started whacking on me. The cops—it was like a high-ranking police officer there, and I said, "Are you going to let them do this?" And he just turned his back. And I said okay; I said I know where the fucking cops are at on this. That's why the students got all their asses kicked over by Pace College and everything.

Friedman soon learned about the growing Vietnam Veterans Against the War movement through another Vietnam veteran, a high school friend who had become publicly vocal about his views. Not ready to act, Friedman filed the information about the organization away until the spring of 1971. After a Miami vacation, he was on his way back home when he heard on the news that Vietnam veterans in Washington, D.C., were throwing their medals over a hurricane fence on the steps of the U.S. Congress.

As soon as I got home, I called the VVAW office at 156 Fifth Avenue. They said they weren't protesting the war so much as they were protesting the way the veterans were being treated, and I went down there, said I'm a Vietnam vet, and said I want to do stuff with you guys.

By the time the Republican National Convention took place in August 1972, Friedman was deeply involved in the antiwar movement, heading to the convention in Miami with a group of Vietnam veterans to demonstrate there.

We had about three days of actions, basically running battles with the state police: tear gas, people getting fucked-up, bad. We had one march where we had three guys in wheelchairs out front—Ron Kovic, Bobby Muller, and Bill Wieman. They attacked us, and they tried to arrest Kovic. Did you see Born on the Fourth of July? *I was actually one of the guys portrayed as breaking him away from the cops. We got him out of there.*

At the end of the demonstration, the group agreed that everyone needed to get out of Miami as quickly as possible. Unfortunately, a few of the cars in their convoy needed gasoline. When those cars stopped at the next exit on Florida's Turnpike, the passengers were arrested immediately. Friedman's car made it all the way to Gainesville without incident.

The Nixon administration bombed and mined Haiphong Harbor in May 1972, and antiwar demonstrations erupted anew. Vietnam veterans took part in many of these demonstrations, at the Miami convention and elsewhere. There were two takeovers of the Statue of Liberty, a demonstration at the United Nations, and several actions at Veterans Administration facilities around Manhattan. These were episodes of guerrilla theater intended not to injure anyone but rather to raise the visibility of the antiwar position and to direct attention to the VA's lack of dedication to Vietnam veterans.

They were not doing anything for employment; they were not helping people get their disability claims; there was just general disdain for Vietnam veterans inherent in the VA at the time.

The Nixon administration attempted to make the case that Vietnam Veterans Against the War was a minority group with violent tendencies. Friedman rejects that characterization and affirms the organization's legitimacy. He had taken a bullet in Vietnam and received two Purple Hearts. He understands the nature of violence in a way only combat veterans can. He has also been on the wrong end of a police club on several occasions, and he knows the difference between violence and protest.

Vietnam Veterans Against the War was taken over by a Maoist group known as the Revolutionary Union in the mid-1970s. Friedman, like many other VVAW members, lost interest in the organization.[3] His goal was to wake the American people up to the injustices of the war itself and to make them aware of the struggles Vietnam veterans faced here in the United States.

Friedman felt that confrontational but nonviolent events provided the best opportunity to do this. He understood, too, that democracy and the confrontations it can spark come with a price. On one VVAW march, he watched while an automobile struck a fellow veteran. He believes the woman hit the man on purpose.

Despite this, Friedman insists that he never plotted the violent overthrow of anything. He just wanted, he says, to end the war. And to that end, he believes that the VVAW gave the peace movement credibility. Once the political agendas of other groups such as the Black Panthers and the Communist Party began to creep into organizational efforts, he left. What he discovered, however, is that he liked community development and support work.

I liked working with people . . . we set up the Brooklyn chapter at the storefront in Red Hook, and I lived in a little room in the back. We did health testing, you know; that's when John Hamill got involved and everything, and that's when we planned out the Prospect Park [demonstration]. We would go around, and we were doing TB testing and we were doing diabetes testing, you know; we had some nurses who worked with us. Not just for veterans, just to be involved. It was like a community health center, something that veterans did in the community. We were also fighting against the gentrification of Park Slope, the takeover by Methodist Hospital when they were expanding and buying up houses and stuff.

After Friedman left VVAW, he became involved with the less political and more veteran-oriented Vietnam Veterans of America (VVA).

We did a lot of good things. We initiated programs that are still going on today, like the [Christmas party at the Brooklyn VA hospital]. I started that. We used to come there once a month with a six-foot hero and canteen books. Christmastime we'd bring Santa Claus, we'd bring a band, we'd have music. That's kind of what I liked about VVA.

The VA Christmas parties continue as a VVA Chapter 72 tradition. In 2011, Friedman played Santa Claus again, bringing canteen coupon books and other supplies to men stuck in the hospital over the holiday.

By the 1980s, Friedman was working as a New York State veterans counselor and, with others, began to focus his work on veterans at the VA hospital in Brooklyn. Friedman participated in the establishment of a multiservice center within the hospital, on the fifth floor, bringing in representatives from Social Security, the Department of Labor, the New York City Human Resources Administration, and others. Friedman became increasingly involved with assisting veterans in their efforts to file claims with the Veterans Administration.

Everybody who failed somewhere else was coming to me. Everything else was just walk-in—a couple, three people a day; I had lines outside my office all day long. You know, widows whose husbands had just died in the hospital would come in and the same day even sometimes just, you know, crying and stuff.

And, Friedman found, he was good at it.

I tell the veteran, I says, "Tell me your story; what did you do in Vietnam? What significant incidents do you remember?" And then I'll help him rewrite it into a form that will fit into a claim, into a format that the VA [can understand]. For PTSD in particular you have to first show that the person served in a situation where he would have been faced with stressors—[a] combat situation. If they didn't have a CIB [Combat Infantryman Badge] or Purple Heart or whatever, if they weren't infantry, you had to show, you know, that they did convoys in hostile territories or their bases were subject to attacks . . . The Joint Services Environmental Task Force maintained an archive of morning reports, all from the units. So we got morning reports from units, and we were able to show that these units came under attack these days and that this guy was there certain days, through these morning reports.

And we were able to get them, because the VA was supposed to get them but they never would. So we got them in advance of when we presented them with a claim. When I put in a claim, it was a well-documented claim that the VA didn't have to do a lot of developmental on; everything was spelled out for them in a simple language of one syllable or less, you know, like this is a PTSD claim; you will grant it. Yes, master. [Laughs.]

One particular story illustrates Friedman's transformation from outside activist to one working within the system. In 1972, George H. W. Bush was serving as the U.S. ambassador to the United Nations. He was scheduled to speak at the Riverdale Country School in the Bronx, and the VVAW decided to engage in an act of street theater. Friedman and four others filled balloons with stage blood. Students from Riverdale smuggled the activists into the kitchen under the noses of the New York City Police Department. During the early portion of the event, Friedman and the others burst in, shouting, "The blood of the Vietnamese people is on your hands!" and threw the balloons up into the air. When they burst, blood was all over everyone. Friedman distinctly recalls hearing a woman scream, "Oh, my mink coat!" The group escaped, scrambled down the hill to their car, and headed back to Manhattan.[4]

Fast-forward to 2001: Friedman was working for the U.S. Department of Labor's Veterans' Employment and Training Service. He and a number of other veterans were invited to an event at the National Guard Armory on Park Avenue in Manhattan. In attendance at the event were Mayor Rudolph Giuliani, Mayor-elect Michael Bloomberg, and George H. W. Bush's son President George W. Bush. As he was introduced to the president, Friedman said, *"I had the pleasure of meeting your father when he was ambassador to the United Nations."*

To this day, Friedman sees himself as someone who defends all people and their right to live in peace. His status as a veteran, he believes, gives him special insight into the realities of war and the wrongs it can inflict. He says he uses this knowledge to help veterans defend themselves against injustice, standing up to power when necessary. Currently, he is an assistant director for the U.S. Department of Labor's

Veterans' Employment and Training Service, working to meet the needs of a new generation of returning veterans.

I wasn't really interested in arguing politics; I just wanted to help those who wanted to make the statement be effective. I was good at logistics—getting things done. I was never one to be into rhetoric. I didn't accept it on a religious level, and I didn't accept it on a political level. I enjoyed doing things on a human level.

Fred Louis did not participate in the Vietnam Veterans Against the War movement. While his antiwar activism came later than Friedman's, it was also inspired by what he had seen and experienced in Vietnam.

Louis, the son of an assistant civil engineer, lived on a farm in Orange County, New York, until the age of four. In the summer, the guesthouse bungalow would host relatives who would come up from Brooklyn for the fresh air. The family moved to the Midwood/Flatbush section of Brooklyn when his father's job at the Rondout Reservoir in the Catskill Mountains ended.

The area was heavily populated with Italian and Jewish families. While his last name does not give immediate clues to an ethnic identity, his mother's maiden name was Moscowitz and his father's family name was Losser. As he would learn later from a relative, the Lossers moved from Germany to France. To avoid the French anti-Semitism prevalent at the time, the family changed its name to Louis.

A shy young man, Louis attended P.S. 99 on East Tenth Street in Brooklyn and stayed there through the eighth grade, when he passed the entrance exam for the highly prestigious Brooklyn Tech High School. As he puts it, school was *a source of approval. I learned how to play the game. I learned how to give teachers what they wanted. I learned to be able to read that really well.*

A number of his friends' families were affiliated, in some way or other, with the Communist Party. While it was not obvious at the time, he realized it later.

I just happened to end up with this whole group of red diaper babies, just surrounded by them, as it turned out.

While Communism as an influence did not stick—at all—the social environment did introduce him to folk music and especially to Pete Seeger. He remains close to a group of folk musicians, and music is still a big part of his life.

I remember having box seats in Carnegie Hall for my first hootenanny, hosted by Pete, and I think Lead Belly was there. It was the first New York appearance of Joan Baez, and my reaction was, why is she wasting that incredible voice on this music?

Lead Belly (Huddie William Ledbetter) wasn't there, having died in 1949, but Louis may well have seen another one of the many blues musicians traveling on the folk circuit in the early 1960s. Anyway, Joan Baez was the one who made the impression on Louis that evening.

Louis had an aptitude for math and believed he might follow his father's path into engineering. After his graduation from Brooklyn Tech High School in 1964, he applied to MIT and Cornell University, eventually enrolling at Cornell, where he lasted two years. He did not like it at all.

I love[d] physics to the point where I'd spend hours and hours and hours doing physics problems and not doing much of anything else. So first semester I went on probation, second semester I got off probation, third semester I got back on probation, fourth semester they kicked me out for a year. At that point I got drafted.

It was early 1967. His close friends from the neighborhood were also getting drafted. He felt isolated, as though he had screwed up his life and disappointed his parents. He tried to resist induction into the Army.

I did get my induction date delayed by writing to everybody I could think of, including President Johnson. My draft board, I'm sure, got letters. They had no idea what was going on. And I had doctor's notes, but you had to be basically dead not to get in, you know. At that point they were pretty desperate. I started working at the ACLU, which was interesting, and got to see at least one very prominent CO [conscientious objector] case and read a whole bunch of the briefs and stuff and [thought], "I'm going; I don't have a prayer for CO status." And I wasn't about to go to Canada, although I did think about it. And I wasn't about to go to jail. So that didn't leave a lot of options.

Still, Louis tried to control his fate by volunteering for early induction in exchange for the opportunity to select his job in the Army—his military occupational specialty, or MOS.

I went to the local recruiter on Flatbush Avenue, and I plunked myself very cockily and said, "What can you offer me?" and he looked at me like I was crazy and said, "Well, I'll send you to Fort Hamilton for tests."

When I got the results, I walked in and I put them down on his desk and he looked at them and he shook his head and the phone rang and he's on the phone talking to somebody and he's looking at them and he's shaking his head and he gets off the phone and he's looking at them and he's shaking his head and he looks over at me and he says, "Are you a college graduate?" And I said no, and he says, "You're a high school graduate?" And I say yeah, and I finally said, "What's going on?"

He says, "Well, I've had PhDs in here who don't have scores anywhere near as high as yours," at which point he gave me the book, you know, every job you could have in the military; here's the book, pick something. So I'm there and I'm thumbing through all this stuff, and he's doing his business. [Later] that day, then I got on the phone with [a friend] who is in Fort Hood, Texas, and is arming up, preparing to go. And he started screaming at me: "Are you crazy? I can put a hundred guys on the phone right now who got screwed out of their MOS. Don't do it."

He knew that if he enlisted in the Army, he would be expected to serve for three years, and he might end up in Vietnam even if he requested a noncombat MOS. If he was drafted, he would serve for only two.

So I went back to the guy and I said, "You can't guarantee me any of this, can you?" And to his credit he said, "No, I can't, but I figure you're smart enough, once you get in you'll, you know . . ." But little did I know that Catch-22 is right on and PFC Wintergreens run the Army. Company clerks run the Army. But I said, "No thanks."

Louis decided to take his chances with the draft and accepted induction into the Army on July 25, 1967, his parents' wedding anniversary. In basic training he ended up with an "alternative" crowd.

Somebody in this little cadre had a copy of Lawrence Ferlinghetti's Coney Island of the Mind, *which is still one of my favorite books, and after evening chow they gave us a little smoke break at the parade ground, and there would be five or six or seven or eight of us sitting around, reading Ferlinghetti poems out loud.*

Offered a spot in Officer Candidate School on the basis of his test scores, Louis declined, opting instead to try to escape—he went absent without leave (AWOL). As he recalls, he *just took the bus into town, went across the state line to catch a plane to New York from Columbia, South Carolina. And then was totally freaked. Here I am, shaved head, the whole bit, figuring that any minute now they're just gonna cuff me and take me away. I was one of probably hundreds of thousands.*

Finally, I stayed at a friend's house and basically wasn't home very much and was pretty much terrified whenever I was out in public and turned myself in about three weeks later. So I report back to [Fort] Polk [and] I missed my training cycle. They didn't even dock me for the time, actually; they were supposed to, but they didn't.

After additional training in Fort Lewis, Washington, he was sent as part of a complete company to join a battalion in Vietnam. Arrival, for Louis, was memorable.

Our welcome to Vietnam was a .30-caliber round. The guy was a good shot. We were glidepathing into Chu Lai, and this guy shot dead center right through the middle of the plane. Hit the pile of packs, luckily. Put a hole in somebody's canteen; that was about it.

Arriving in the first week of February 1968, he served with the Twenty-Third Infantry Division (American) until early February 1969. Thinking back, Louis recalls his attitude when he entered Vietnam:

The attitude was "Don't volunteer for anything and be as invisible as possible, for obvious reasons."

When asked how he managed the rigors of combat duty, he replied:

Oh, God—well, I still sort of have a perspective that it really didn't have much effect on me, which I also know is bullshit. I'm sure you've heard this from everybody. You definitely just kind of numb out.

He tried to distance himself emotionally from what was going on. Still, he recalls his experience of Vietnam as a combination of 99 percent boredom and 1 percent sheer terror. On one occasion he recalls being attacked by American artillery, with big chunks of dirt falling on him while he and two others were on listening-post duty.

Body counts, used to measure progress against a stubborn and often invisible enemy, were, for Louis, a reflection of the chaotic and ultimately illegitimate nature of the war in Vietnam. In one incident, he recalls:

We're up on top of this ridge, full company, [and] down in the valley we spot some black pajamas walking on this trail, and everybody just lined up and started shooting. And I suppose that's when I found out that the CO's [commanding officer's] policy was "no prisoners." Apparently, it had been from an experience—sending these guys back for interrogation and then running into them again. I was carrying a grenade launcher, so they were way out of my range. The guy next to me offered to let me shoot his rifle, and I said, "No, that's okay, no thanks." And they sent a patrol down to see what had happened, and they found what they estimated to be an eight-year-old kid with a belly wound and just left him. I heard the CO on the radio call in three VC kills. I guess that was my first experience with what bullshit the body count stuff was.

Later that night, Louis again experienced friendly fire:

We were on the other part of the ridge and setting up camp for the night, and there was this chopper circling around, circling around, circling around, and he circles around and he must have been up there for ten minutes. And he opens fire on us. Luckily, it didn't hurt anybody and probably got [him] into a little bit of hot water. [Laughs.] So another friendly-fire incident. [There were] lots of them. And that's just totally terrifying.

In retrospect, the war Louis experienced was already spinning out of control by 1968. These were very young men, trying to stay alive while making the best of a difficult situation. He recalls one incident that took place while his unit was stationed near Chu Lai:

It had been three weeks since we had a hot meal. I mean, generally when we were out in the field, they would fly us in a meal at least once a day. It was either lunch or dinner. They'd come out with containers and stuff, but it had been three weeks since that had happened. It had been three weeks since we had clean clothes, and it had been close to that since I had even washed, you know. [We had] fatigues that were white with dried sweat. Actually, we wore T-shirts more than anything.

So we decided to set up right there, and they flew us in food and clothes, they paid us, they brought us mail, you know, and we had been under, you know, an awful lot of stress. And we set up for the night, some people dug foxholes and set up Claymore [mines] and trip wires and flares and the whole bit around the perimeter and stuff, but it was, I don't know—we let down our guard, let's put it that way.

I'd set up my little tent, and in the middle of the night all hell broke loose. I mean, there was firebombs from everywhere, trip wires were going off, explosions everywhere, and I remember crawling around on the ground trying to find my weapon, which I don't think I ever did. It's dark and then one of the guys from my squad off to my right was screaming he was hit or was blind or something. Actually, what had happened was he had opened fire and they fired back, and what happened was that sand got kicked up in his face, and it ended up he was all right, but at the time he couldn't see.

*Somehow somebody pulled me over or somebody called me or something, and so I slipped down into this hole, and as I'm going down the hole, I'm going feetfirst, I'm going down this hole, there's this big flash of light in front of my face. I think probably this guy that's got sand in his eyes was there before me and after me came this gunner who was rather nervous. [*Laughs.*]*

And so this guy goes, "I can't see, I can't see." Well, I'm looking around and it's black and stuff and I'm feeling my chest and I'm feeling this dripping down my chest, you know, and I can't see a thing and this guy won't keep his mouth shut. All they had to do was throw a bomb or grenade down the hole and we all would have been dead, you know, so I'm trying to get him to shut up so they don't know where the hell we are. And anyway, all hell's breaking loose; you hear people screaming and explosions.

[The enemy] knew where everything was, they undoubtedly, you

know, just sat around and watched us all day; knew where all the trip wires was; knew where all the defenses were and came up with a good plan to get around everything. We had three killed and thirty-nine wounded. Oh yeah, it was a bad night.

Louis freely admits that his antiwar position today has to do with what he saw in Vietnam.

A lot of guys come back with survivor's guilt. Friend of mine got wounded in an ambush, and his two best buddies lay on top of him to keep him from harm and they both were killed, so that's what he lives with. [I have] another friend who stepped on a mine and lost his leg and wonders how many people he took with him and stuff. I kind of figured out that mine is participatory guilt. I knew better; I shouldn't have been there, and somewhere along the line I should have just said no, I ain't doing this shit anymore. As I say, little My Lais happened every day.

As a student at Cornell University, he had gone down south to work for voters' rights. He learned a lot about the war and had participated in an antiwar demonstration in March 1967, where protesters marched from Central Park down to the United Nations. One year later, he was on the ground, fighting in Vietnam. He blames himself for not doing more to stop the war.

His return home was a classic New York story.

I landed at Kennedy. It's probably late evening, ten or eleven o'clock, something like that. Full-dress uniform, all the bells and whistles, all the ribbons, you know, everything, full-dress greens. Get my stuff, go out to the cab line, throw my stuff in the back, get in the cab, tell the cabdriver where I want to go. He says, "I ain't going."

My parents lived in Flatbush in the middle of Brooklyn. East Thirteenth Street between J and K. He ain't going there at eleven o'clock at night, because he ain't picking up no fare there, you know; he wants to go to mid-Manhattan, you know, or at least somewhere where he's going to get a fare. So I'm a little more alert than I usually am. [Laughs.] I say, "I know the law; I'm sitting in your cab; you're going to take me." He says, "I can sit here as long as you can." I said, "I'll give you $10 over the meter." He said, "Okay." That's my hero's welcome.

Once he was back in New York, Louis contacted his childhood

friend Bob Greene, who had returned from Vietnam just a few months before him.

He was there, and we spent, as I remember it, three days straight with a meal here and there and a little bit of sleep here and there, just trading stories . . . That was one of the tragedies of Vietnam vets, you know, not having any decompression . . . These guys in the Second World War came back on troop carriers, you know, they were at sea for a month or more, you know. With us, you know, one day in the jungle; the next day in civilization and—bye. So, happily, that was my debriefing, and we literally spent three days just trading stories.

Louis credits those days with Greene with allowing him to avoid some of the worst difficulties that many veterans experienced upon their return. It is tempting to speculate how other veterans would have fared if they had been fortunate enough to find that kind of relationship.

Apart from his relationship with Greene, Louis says he essentially stayed "in the closet" as a Vietnam vet until the 1980s.

In the early 1990s, Louis was participating in Buddhist meditation groups, and through one of them he met Claude AnShin Thomas, a Vietnam veteran and an ordained Buddhist. As part of his Buddhist practice, Thomas helps veterans understand the place that service in Vietnam should hold in their lives.

Louis became actively involved, traveling with Pastors for Peace in a 1993 caravan carrying humanitarian aid to El Salvador. He and seventy-five others drove thirty-four vehicles across Mexico into Central America to deliver supplies to the poor. A year and a half later, Louis participated in another Pastors for Peace aid caravan, this time to Cuba to help break the U.S. blockade of that country. As the first Gulf War began, he was a founding member of a chapter of Veterans for Peace in the Hudson River Valley, officially chartered in March 1991.

Retired now after a career as a union electrician, Louis has learned to speak out about his own experiences. He has put some distance between himself and the guilt he feels about what he saw and did in Vietnam. It has not been easy. Today, he speaks comfortably and effectively, often appearing as a spokesperson for Vets for Peace. The group has grown to more than 125 chapters nationwide and in Vietnam and continues its efforts to "abolish war as an instrument of national policy."[5]

In a 2006 interview with Louis about the global war on terror, posted on YouTube, he says, *It was like, Oh, man, they are doing this crap again. We cannot keep our mouths shut anymore.*

He has this to say about the global war on terror and our presence in Iraq and Afghanistan:

Like almost any war I can think of, with the exception of true wars of national liberation, our insanity is based on lies, no matter how you look at it. We are in there because a lot of corporations are making a lot of money and there are some crazy people way high up who believe that we should control the world.

He tells the interviewer:

These guys that are over there now . . . are losing their souls because of what they see and what they have to do. And it is criminal.[6]

10

BECOMING VETERANS: EDELMAN, GERMAN, AND PAS

In May 2005, at a small ceremony on a cold, blustery day, the former New York City mayor Edward I. Koch recalled the dedication twenty years earlier of the New York City Vietnam Veterans Memorial and the parade of twenty-five thousand Vietnam veterans across the Brooklyn Bridge and down New York City's famed Canyon of Heroes. Witnessed by an estimated one million people, the 1985 parade was led by the wheelchair-bound Long Island assemblyman John L. Behan; at the time, it was said to be the largest ticker-tape parade in the city's history. These events, Koch recalled, were a tipping point in the city's relationship with its Vietnam veterans. Ten years after the war ended, the veterans were finally, really, welcomed home.

The memorial at 55 Water Street in lower Manhattan is a wall of glass blocks inscribed with portions of eighty-three letters, poems, clips from *The New York Times*, and words from American presidents and other leading figures. The memorial and parade played an important part in the emergence of a community of Vietnam veterans in New York City. Vietnam veterans themselves kindled a new relationship with the city as they worked to change public perceptions and to help veterans in need.

The memorial and parade were also reactions to specific events. On January 30, 1981, New York City hosted a parade for the returning hostages who had been held in the American embassy in Iran. A reported 1,250 tons of confetti greeted them as they traveled the Canyon of Heroes. Amid all the hoopla, some Vietnam veterans became resentful. Bobby Muller, a Marine lieutenant who lost both legs in Vietnam in 1969, told *The New York Times*, "That's what probably would have been for us, if we had won." He went on, "A lot of guys paid a heavy price, and for many of them there is no sense of appreciation or recognition of what they went through."[1] The wish for a parade that would honor returned Vietnam veterans grew out of that experience.[2]

The political needs of Mayor Koch mattered, too. A sergeant during World War II, he understood the significance of military service. He was also a divisive figure in New York City politics. Honoring New York City's veterans, many of them working-class white ethnics and a critical component of his political base, was both politically savvy and a matter of personal conscience.

In 1981, Mayor Koch appointed twenty-seven citizens to begin planning a memorial that would acknowledge the service of those New Yorkers who served in the Vietnam War. This group gravitated toward two ideas: a physical memorial to New York City's Vietnam veterans and a "living memorial" to assist those veterans who had needs that were not being met by agencies of the government. In 1982, the twenty-seven were transformed into the Vietnam Veterans Memorial Commission, which had a hundred members, the inner core of whom were Vietnam veterans. This group built the memorial, created the assistance program, and gave shape to a powerful restatement of the Vietnam experience.

Bernard Edelman was among the veterans subsequently appointed by the mayor to the New York Vietnam Veterans Memorial Commission. He explains how he got involved:

My ten-month tour of duty [in Vietnam] in 1970 shaped me, for better or for worse. I was a broadcast specialist/correspondent, assigned to the United States Army Vietnam–Information Office. While I was not caught up in combat, I saw my share of its aftermath. I lost friends; I made lifelong friends there, too. Vietnam became, and remains, an integral facet of my frame of reference, as it is, I believe, for most veterans who served in a combat zone.

Four months after I was released from active duty, I went to Washington as a participant/chronicler of Operation Dewey Canyon III, the first major demonstration by veterans since the Bonus March some forty years before. Some of my photographs were part of the first art show, in St. Paul, Minnesota, of the works of Vietnam veterans. And one year after that, on Veterans Day 1981, we brought an expanded version of this show to New York City, to the old birdhouse in the Central Park Zoo. Some 1,500 people—veterans, their families, friends—came to opening night; some 650 people a day viewed the show during its monthlong run. Then Vietnam came back into my life full force. I was named by Mayor Koch as one of a hundred citizens who would comprise the New York Vietnam Veterans Memorial Commission.

A central goal of the art show Edelman curated, and of the New York City memorial, was to allow men and women to develop pride in their status as veterans.

There are a lot of people who—they just put their veteran-ness, their veteran's identity, in their pocket someplace, or in a closet someplace, and there it stays. When we did the Vietnam art show, Jerry Balcom was a court officer; he's in private business now. And I used something of his, and it was only later that he told me he'd been a Marine, very proud of it, but he said he only literally came out of the closet around like 1979, 1980, because this wasn't something you necessarily put on your résumé. If you were a veteran, particularly if you were a combat veteran, there was this assumption that you were somehow fucked-up.

As a member of the commission, he, like the others, worked to recast the meaning of service in Vietnam.

As the commission defined its mission, it decided to create a monument that celebrated the lives of those who had died but also of those who had survived. The members wanted to "acknowledge the service and sacrifice of all veterans from New York City who did their individual and collective best under trying and unusual circumstances," to "evoke reconciliation and an awareness of the enduring human values reflected in the conflicting experiences," and finally to show "the contradictory yet universally shared experiences of war and peace, danger and relief, weakness and strength, isolation and comradeship." The veterans on the commission demanded a "living memorial," a project that would help needy Vietnam veterans make the transition to successful civilian careers.

The monument's design was selected in a juried competition, as had been the Vietnam wall in Washington, D.C. A panel composed of veterans and architectural experts judged approximately 572 entries from forty-six countries. The architects William Fellows and Peter Wormser, together with the Vietnam veteran Joseph Ferrandino, submitted the winning design, and their plans became the basis for the memorial.[3] The memorial's centerpiece, a wall, is set back from the street itself by approximately a hundred yards. It is sixteen feet high and sixty-six feet long, and there are two door-sized passages through it. At chest height, there are two silver shelves, on which people can leave photographs, flowers, and other mementos; the idea was derived from the practice of leaving items at the Vietnam Veterans Memorial in Washington, D.C. Ferrandino, who came up with the original conception of the memorial, described it as "a window through which to view the Vietnam experience. The experience must be provided by the people whose lives were touched by Vietnam . . . We are not looking for great literature, flowery prose or correct grammar. We are looking for the truth from many different points of view."[4] For that reason, many of the written texts inscribed into the wall were drawn from the more than three thousand pieces of correspondence sent to the commission in response to a call for letters. In 2001, the names of the 1,741 New York City dead were installed on a walkway leading from the street to the wall itself.

The parade was important, too, and the commission understood it would be so. The veterans' parade poster said: "If you are a Vietnam veteran, you're invited to take part in a very special parade. It will mark the 10th anniversary of the end of the war . . . We urge you not to miss this special celebration. After all, it's being held in your honor."

The multiday celebration of the new memorial began May 6 with the dedication of the wall at an event on the USS *Intrepid*, a World War II aircraft carrier anchored in the Hudson River, where Donald Trump handed the commission a check for $1 million. The celebration concluded with a ceremony at the wall attended by an estimated twelve thousand people and a display of fireworks over the East River.

On May 7, 1975, President Ford had issued a proclamation declaring that day "the last day of the Vietnam era," and so the seventh was chosen as the date of the "Welcome Home" Parade. John Hamill, the medic and Brooklyn-born brother of the New York *Daily News* columnist Denis Hamill, remarks:

> For me the most special part of that day . . . was when we passed Pace University. And from the windows appeared all these secretaries, and students, women 10 and 15 years younger than us, a generation removed, who waved and blew us kisses. That moved me. Unlike a lot of places around the country, in the neighborhoods of Brooklyn I never saw anyone spit on Vietnam vets when they came home. In our neighborhood there was a lot of individual support. But this was the first time strangers had embraced us as a group. It meant a lot. Twenty years later, it still does.[5]

The themes of reconnection and mutual acknowledgment echoed throughout the festivities. As one veteran quoted in *The New York Times* said, "Anybody who's been in 'Nam is automatically accepted by anybody else who's been in 'Nam."[6]

As the effort to build the Water Street structure gathered steam, the commission began to consider the other central component of its mission. In order to create a successful "living memorial," the commission needed to understand the problems veterans faced.

Professor Robert Laufer of Brooklyn College prepared a study for the commission that found that Vietnam veterans were more densely concentrated in low-paying jobs than Vietnam-era counterparts. He also found that Vietnam veterans appeared to experience more difficulty in holding on to prestigious, high-paying jobs than did other members of their age cohort; that 25 percent of heavy-combat veterans had some PTSD symptoms; that 43 percent of heavy-combat veterans reported drinking regularly, weekly, for at least four months in the last year; that heavy-combat veterans were significantly more likely to smoke marijuana; and that the proportion of veterans using hard drugs was very low.

At this point, the commission's efforts connected with the work of other entities operating veterans' initiatives in the city and nationally. A number of Wall Street employees had joined together as the New York Vietnam Veterans Group in 1981, at least in part because of their view that the returning Iranian hostages received better treatment than Vietnam veterans had. According to one Wall Streeter, Eugene Gitelson, "Those of us who were successful hadn't had anything to do with our vet identity for almost 15 years. We decided it was time we did something with our expertise to help those who weren't as fortunate."[7] Gitelson himself had been a rifle platoon leader in Vietnam. After the war he worked in marketing research for the Seagram Company and directed a drug prevention program in the South Bronx. Later he earned an MBA from New York University, worked at Chase Manhattan Bank, and then became a corporate consultant.

In 1981, Thomas Pauken, the director of ACTION, a federal umbrella agency for volunteer activities, created a program designed to tap the leadership potential of Vietnam-era servicemen and servicewomen. The idea was that veterans could provide various kinds of mentoring and assistance to their peers who were doing less well. President Ronald Reagan provided a commitment of federal funds for the program, called the Vietnam Veterans Leadership Program (VVLP). Edward Timberlake, at one time a national director of the VVLP, described his task this way: "Our job was really twofold. We had to address the problems of underemployment and unemployment among Vietnam Veterans and also the problem of a false stereotype of the Vietnam veteran as victim and loser. We really couldn't impact on the former without also working on the latter . . . I came on board the leadership program because I wanted to do everything I could to change the image." The program engaged in a campaign to combat stereotypes in the media. For example, the VVLP reported that in some locations it "made direct contact with key local media personnel to insure that any news event potentially damaging to the image of Vietnam veterans is also analyzed with the intent of objectively seeking rational explanations for the behavior involved." It also organized "recognition events," including "parades and proclamations designating Vietnam veterans 'day' or 'week,' luncheons, banquets, and memorial services."[8] The VVLP had enormous reach. The historian Patrick Hagopian has documented the VVLP's role in vetting Hollywood feature-film scripts to determine which ones deserved the Pentagon's financial and logistical support. For example, the first of the Rambo films, *First Blood*, was turned down because it portrayed the central character as a "psycho."[9]

The VVLP office at 25 Broadway opened in 1982 in space donated by the brokerage firm Drexel Burnham Lambert. The objective was to help veterans relate their military skills to the job market. The VVLP eschewed any interest in issues such as Agent Orange or "whether the Vietnam War was won or lost, and by whom." Indeed, it asserted it only cared about "harnessing the unused or underused energies of a remarkable pool of men and women who still have a lot to contribute to their country." The VVLP was convinced that these individuals would do whatever it took to get themselves out of the welfare system and into meaningful careers. Its central argument was that "we haven't mothballed our experience . . . It is still working for America."[10]

Ed German was one of the first volunteers for the New York VVLP He remembers:

Gene Gitelson contacted me and told me about what he was proposing to do, and once we got started with it, the whole effort to put together an organization of Vietnam veterans seemed to help to validate our experience, which was never validated before, you know . . . Everything was just negative. A lot of it came from the media and the movies. A lot of movies came out, not Vietnam movies, but just general regular movies that somewhere in the script would be a sniper or somebody and then he would be identified in the film as a Vietnam veteran and that all Vietnam veterans were crazy. The whole thing about losers was because a lot of veterans came home and dropped out of society and were on drugs and stuff like that. We weren't seen as heroes when we came home. There was nobody there to welcome us, we had no parades, and there were no organizations that were helping us do anything. Nobody. There was a fear in the general public if you mentioned Vietnam. A lot of people shunned it and didn't want you to be involved with what they were doing because they felt like you weren't stable. The Vietnam vets were portrayed as being people who had been through something so horrific and crazy that it was going to affect them and that the war itself wasn't successful.

The whole thing about VVLP was vets helping vets. One of the strategies of the program was to identify successful Vietnam veterans. Veterans who had come back and had some success in their careers and businesses. Veterans who might be able to, in some way, offer a hand to help those veterans who had not been so successful. Identifying those successful veterans also helped to validate our experience because there was a general notion that Vietnam veterans were losers.

Corporate assistance was critical to the effort. Manufacturers Hanover provided money to create a database of prospective employers and job candidates.[11] The VVLP asked other major corporations for help, too. A solicitation letter to IBM echoed the national leadership's goal of restoring the image of the Vietnam veteran. It asserted a connection between employment, a veteran's identity, and the idea that Vietnam veterans could see themselves differently. "For too long," the letter said, "veterans have been seen as victims and unfortunately have accepted that role to some extent. We do not believe this is so. We believe that veterans are resources that are sorely needed in this community and the only way we can make that happen is for veterans to take that responsibility on themselves with our guidance." The organization claimed that "those who did well after they returned from the service were, until recently, reluctant to step forward and use their experience and door-opening ability to help their fellow veterans." The VVLP therefore was an opportunity for well-placed veterans to acknowledge their veteran status and help others, who got a "second and perhaps last opportunity to reenter the mainstream."[12]

The New York VVLP believed it deserved corporate support because of the way the war had disrupted the lives of New York City's young men. The rhetoric mirrored very closely that of the memorial commission in 1985. It asserted that "at the young age of 19, they went off to war and came back to an indifferent if not hostile homecoming. Many vets feel that the world and certainly technology has passed them by." As a result of the war, according to the VVLP, a disruption occurred in the identities of young soldiers, preventing them from claiming their rightful place in the "American economic mainstream." By missing out on civilian experience for the duration of their military service, these young men found themselves in a position in which they could not catch up with their age cohort. Military service somehow, inexplicably, seemed to render Vietnam veterans unable to use new technology. More important, the VVLP wrote, "experts in the field of Vietnam Veterans have clearly stated that a veteran's identity hinges on his work. By not having a viable career, his manhood is stripped and there is a loss of self-esteem." The VVLP therefore aimed to restore the manhood of Vietnam veterans by providing access to meaningful labor.[13] The image of the emasculated veteran is a striking one, running counter to the usual rhetoric about military service making a young boy into a "man."

The city's VVLP chapter—one of a number of chapters around the country—contracted with the memorial commission to run the Living Memorial Program in 1985. Quickly, tensions developed over the program, specifically because it appeared that very few veterans were in fact taking advantage of VVLP services. Memorial commission files demonstrate that the practice of what Gitelson called "triage"— accepting only some Vietnam veterans into the program, in particular those who could be placed—was standard operating procedure.[14] Indeed, by June 30, 1986, the commission noted that the New York VVLP had placed exactly—and only—twelve veterans in jobs. Despite growing bitterness between the VVLP leadership and the memorial commission, the contract for the Living Memorial was renewed for two years in October 1986.[15]

The problem was that the pool of veterans who might have been most helped by a living memorial were "hard-core," as one memorial commission member put it. He asserted that these veterans were not used to having jobs. They had serious gaps in their work history, and they often had fifth- or sixth-grade education levels and "junkie attitudes."

Ed German recalls:

We would service any veteran, but one of the things that would disqualify a veteran is if he were not clean and sober. At least sober enough to go to work. If anyone came in with alcohol on their breath, they were automatically [out]. If anyone came into our program with alcohol or seemed like they were high or something, we wouldn't, we couldn't service them. We would not send them out to represent us. No way.

As the program evolved, all kinds of different services came into the program. The Living Memorial was one of them. Our staff increased, just from the VISTA volunteers who were doing job development, the staff increased, and we had all kinds of people who came on board as we began to raise funds and were able to hire professionals, and then we were able to hire psychologists and therapists and people who could help vets with some of their psychological issues and things like that.

In 1989, it cost the program approximately $20,000 to put someone in a career-track job, and there was little follow-up to see if he or she would stay. The commission was increasingly concerned that it was difficult to tell how many veterans had actually been helped, despite the $1.3 million it had spent on the Living Memorial. The commission member Robert Santos argued that an eight-week jobs program was a "shot in the arm," not really a jobs program at all. It could not deal with the most difficult cases, including those with drug and alcohol problems. In October 1989, the memorial commission decided to close down its relationship with VVLP.

Still, there were real successes. Wenny Pas was exactly the kind of man the program aimed to help, and help him it did. A trim man when I met him, Pas could still wear his thirty-five-year-old Marine Corps dress uniform. By 1980 he was having trouble. He opened a photography business with a loan from the Small Business Administration. He was taking wedding photographs and beginning to incorporate emerging video technologies into his business when things fell apart. His marriage failed, and in an effort to keep his children fed, he took a variety of low-wage jobs. Depression and anxiety followed, later diagnosed as a result of post-traumatic stress. Pas says:

I looked around for help in the veterans' community, and what I did find was a program in the Wall Street area set up by some professional corporate Vietnam veterans.

I walked in as a client because I was in need. The guy said, "We could help you find a place, but would you like to come and volunteer and we'll give you a stipend?" I said, "Okay, listen, some money is better than no money." That happened to be right around the time that the City of New York was just picking up on what Washington, D.C., had done in '82, and that was the dedication of the Washington Vietnam Veterans Memorial, so now there was a big sympathetic move to help Vietnam veterans . . .

I found a place that I could go where there were other veterans, and I found a place that was now listening to veterans in the corporate area. So I basically worked for them, and I actually did find employment. I embarked into a whole new career when the National Puerto Rican Forum, a 501(c)(3)-type not-for-profit, got granted money to establish their own job-developing program. At the time it was said that the majority of the Vietnam veterans, especially here in New York City, were minorities— black and Hispanic. So the National Puerto Rican Forum said, "Well, we're a Hispanic organization; we will help all veterans, but you know, primarily, a lot of our veterans will be Hispanic." But they were bilingual, and so they put out a request to hire. I went for the interview, and I got the job.

So now I was a job developer counselor of social services.

The Vietnam Veterans Memorial Commission project had done for Pas precisely what it aimed to do for many of New York City's Vietnam veterans. It had restored a sense of pride and eased his transition to full-time civilian employment. He found a career as a job developer and counselor. Eventually, he was able to go to work for the federally funded Emergency Assistance Rehousing Program. Pas's position was not permanent, as he was subject to the whims of funding agencies, but the VVLP had done its job for him, activating his sense of "veteran-ness" around the themes of self-help and personal agency. Pas continued to work until the events of September 11 triggered a severe episode of post-traumatic stress and he stopped working. Today he runs a free-lance photography business.

The memorial commission and parade had an impact that reached beyond the city's boundaries. They were the genesis of the book *Dear America: Letters Home from Vietnam*. Published in 1985 to coincide with the dedication of the memorial and in print almost continuously for more than twenty-five years, *Dear America* is a collection culled from the several thousand letters sent to the commission for possible inclusion on the memorial.

At the invitation of the commission, Bernard Edelman conceptualized and organized the volume, wrote a preface and chapter intros, selected thematic photographs, and received a lot of assistance from other members of the commission, all in ten weeks, with another six or seven weeks, he recalls, of "fine-tuning." It has since been excerpted in scores of high school history and literature texts, not only in this country, but in Finland, Japan, Germany, and Great Britain.

The book was then made into a film of the same name, directed by Bill Couturié and presented on HBO in 1987. It also had a theatrical release in the United States, Europe, and Asia. Letters drawn from the book were read by voices familiar to film and television audiences of the decade, like Michael J. Fox, Tom Berenger, Willem Dafoe, Robert De Niro, and Ellen Burstyn. Edelman recalls:

I did a lot of work for the film as associate producer. It's extremely well done, I think. The film and the book serve kind of an unsaid mission of the commission: to educate people on what the war was about. To me, it talks about the human landscape of the war. It's about the boys, the young men and women who served in Vietnam. It's not political. It does show the footage from the POWs, which was NVA footage, we know that, and it's acknowledged there because when we had one of the screenings, one of the guys got up and said, "You're using propaganda." And I said, "We're not using propaganda if it's properly labeled." I made sure that it was thus labeled. The punch line is at the end when the POWs are returned, were repatriated, and there's Springsteen singing "Born in the U.S.A."

I like to think that books and films like Dear America *open eyes and minds a bit, just like* Saving Private Ryan *did in a very big way. And it's taken the wars in Iraq and Afghanistan (where, whether or not we agree with them, we embrace those who have served under the Stars and Stripes when they come home) to "rehabilitate" the Vietnam vets.*

Maybe America has grown up; unfortunately, it's taken two more wars for that to happen.

11

WAR AND NORMALCY: ROBERT PTACHIK

Even the luckier returning Vietnam veterans who seemed to have an easier time reintegrating into the civilian world of New York City in the 1970s and 1980s eventually realized that the war would never be completely behind them.

The return of the hostages from Iran in 1981, the construction of the national Vietnam Veterans Memorial on the Mall in Washington, D.C., and the presidency of Ronald Reagan, who made a special effort to single out Vietnam veterans for praise, all contributed to a reevaluation of the significance of Vietnam and Vietnam veterans in American life. So too did the construction of the New York City memorial in 1985. This can easily be seen in the life of a single veteran, Dr. Robert Ptachik.

One of Ptachik's letters home appears on the memorial. The letter reads:

4 Apr 67
Dear Family,

. . . I got a shrapnel wound in my shoulder and one in my knee.
There is some good in this though. Within a few weeks I will

*probably be back in the States . . . I'm really getting lazy. All I do
all day is lay around and heal. It's hard work . . .*

*Love,
Bobby*

Seriously wounded in Vietnam, Ptachik had written the letter to his
family while recuperating in Japan. Finding the good in the bad, making his family comfortable with the fact that he was wounded but
"okay," Ptachik expresses his drive for "normalcy." If we read between
the lines, he may have wanted to reassure his family that he would not
be a burden. Once he returned, he would make it; he would fit in.

Ptachik arrived in Vietnam in early January 1967. He had been in-
country only three months before being wounded by a booby trap near
Cu Chi on March 27.

*I remember—some of this I remember clearly as if it happened
yesterday—we were in an area of dry paddies, [a] rather open area. One
of the things that you try to never do is to walk on the dikes. That was
always very appealing because the dikes were flat, the paddies were lumpy
and bumpy and you'd sprain an ankle. And Sergeant Davis for some
reason was walking ahead of me on the dike. And he tripped a booby trap.
And I just remember, I still have this memory of feeling like the world was
a spring that had been compressed to an inch wide and then let go and
the whole world was reverberating. I guess it was the pressure in my ears.*

*I was actually blown back quite a bit from where I was, and I was
fortunate in that I didn't really feel any pain. The first thing I saw was
that my left hand was all bloody because I had a minor wound there, and
it turned out, though, that a piece of shrapnel went in my right shoulder
and came out my back and bled quite a bit. It damaged the nerves; I
never really felt anything. And it also turned out I had shrapnel in my
right knee, but I didn't know that until the next day.*

*Sergeant Davis got much more seriously wounded than I did. A cou-
ple of the medics, one came to him and one came to me and put the
dressings on my shoulder, front and back.*

Someone had just been shot by a sniper a few minutes before, and there was a medevac chopper that had just picked them up and that chopper came back, so I was medevaced out on the chopper within ten minutes. I was able to walk to the chopper. Davis was a mess. He got the shrapnel, I guess, on his right side, and he wound up losing an eye and a lot of his hand, and he was in bad shape; he was screaming the whole way back.

The helicopter flew to the Twelfth Evacuation Hospital at Cu Chi, the same hospital where the nurse Sue O'Neill would be stationed in 1969. At the time, Ptachik thought he was all right. Indeed, he helped carry the stretcher with Davis on it into the hospital. Quickly, the medical staff insisted he lie down flat on a stretcher.

Within a relatively short time they took me into the prep room and started cutting my clothes off. The last [thing I] remember, basically, was one of the doctors saying to me, "Did you get wounded in the leg, too?" And I said no. And he said okay, and then the next thing I remember it was the next day.

I woke up in a hospital bed, and I had my arm in a sling and my right leg in a splint. My left hand was wrapped up from my thumb injury. But the thing that I think is the most striking to me: We had been out in the field for almost a month, and I'm sure [you know] from speaking to other people you get filthy. And when I woke up the next day and I got to look at my body, they had washed and shaved, I'd say, from here over, and the rest of the other side was all still black. [Laughs.] And I'm wondering, couldn't they wash all of it? But I was not in pain; I was very fortunate, because of the nerve damage.

Looking back, he calls it a "million-dollar wound," serious enough to get him out of the war. In fact, it seemed not to hurt at all, though he remembers that the doctors were blunt, telling him that if he recovered the use of his arm, it would take a long time. Apparently, they believed that a primary nerve had been cut. In the end, it had only been bruised, and Ptachik recovered the use of his arm more quickly than anticipated.

After a foul-up with his personnel records, he was sent from Japan to Walter Reed Army Medical Center in Washington, D.C., and then to St. Albans Naval Hospital just southeast of Jamaica, Queens, where he stayed until November, when he was discharged from the Army with a permanent 40 percent disability rating.

As a wounded but ambulatory soldier assigned to St. Albans Naval Hospital for medical care, he had duty obligations at the hospital but was able to spend the night at his own home, in his own bed, on Avenue P and East Fourteenth Street in Brooklyn. Although he had to take a train and a bus to and from St. Albans every day, a two-hour round-trip, it was worth it. It was good to be home.

In retrospect, he believes his reentry into civilian life was made easier by the buffer of the duty he did at St. Albans. It gave him time to adjust, functioning somewhere between the status of a soldier and a civilian.

Today, Ptachik is senior university dean for the executive office and enrollment at the City University of New York (CUNY). Brooklyn College, where I teach, is part of this university. Meeting him was a bit like meeting the executive vice president at your corporation. I was somewhat nervous about the impression I would make. I am more comfortable now. I have interviewed him three times in his office, and we've met on a number of other occasions. He has also been a guest in my course on the history of the American war in Vietnam.

Still, he remains a formidable presence as he sits behind his rather large desk facing the door of his office. He is a pleasant-looking man, in his mid-sixties now, with thinning short gray hair. During our interviews he wore a business suit, usually with his jacket off and tie on, ready to attend the next meeting, often with the CUNY chancellor. While he understood the objective of the research interview and cooperated willingly, he resisted the quasi-therapeutic dynamic that can often emerge during oral history interviews. Despite this, Ptachik reminisced easily, peppering our conversation with references to some of the literature we have both enjoyed, such as Michael Herr's *Dispatches* and Tim O'Brien's *The Things They Carried*.

Ptachik was born in 1946 in Brighton Beach, Brooklyn. His father was a World War II veteran, and after the war he ran an Army-Navy store in the Yorkville neighborhood of Manhattan, on Third Avenue between Eighty-Seventh and Eighty-Eighth Streets. He operated the store with one of his brothers. Ptachik's father did not see combat, and spoke infrequently about his service to his children, so Ptachik had learned relatively little about the Army from him.

He jokes that his background sounds as though it might come out of a Philip Roth novel, and in some ways that is so. When he was a middle-class Jewish kid growing up in postwar Brooklyn, his family valued patriotism, fitting in, and social and economic success. One measure of success was academic, and at first Ptachik seemed primed to go to college and succeed. When he was in the sixth grade, the family moved to the Midwood section of Brooklyn, and he attended James Madison High School, where, by his own admission, he started out doing well and then did *progressively worse each year.* By the time he was in his senior year, he spent more time in the poolroom than with the books.

Lest the mention of a poolroom conjure up images of teenage delinquency, Ptachik's memories of street life in 1960s Brooklyn contrast sharply with those of veterans who grew up in tougher neighborhoods.

We were basically pretty well-behaved Jewish kids, and some Italian kids. The terrorists of the time were the Fanelli gang; there was Charlie Fanelli and his cousins, who were from Avenue U. You'd be playing in the park and they'd come and they'd push you off the basketball court or take your ball and there would be a couple of fights—in retrospect, nothing terrible. But these were the gangsters of the time. Well, I get to basic training, and not in my platoon but in my company there is Charlie Fanelli and his cousins, okay, and now everyone's head is shaved and they're all wearing the same stuff. These are the guys who are just like us; they're not any tougher; they're not any worse.

But Ptachik was smart. He did so well in elementary school that he skipped eighth grade, and despite his waning interest in his schoolbooks he graduated from high school at the age of sixteen. He gained admission to Brooklyn College, a prestigious school within the CUNY system, enrolling in 1963. He didn't like it, though, and in the fall semester of his junior year, he dropped out. He wasn't thinking about the possibility of being drafted: *I just thought, well, I would drop out and nothing would happen to me—everything would be okay.*

By dropping out, however, he lost his deferment from the Coney Island draft board. When his draft notice arrived, he had enrolled at the State University of New York, Stony Brook, for the spring semester.

He went to the draft board and applied for reinstatement of his draft deferment, but the board refused. He was drafted in August 1966.

I was inducted into the Army on August 16, 1966; January 6, 1967, I arrived in Vietnam. So it was eight weeks of basic training, eight weeks of Advanced Infantry Training, about ten days' leave at home, and then over to Vietnam.

Ptachik had tried to avoid being assigned to an infantry MOS. He was offered a slot in Officer Candidate School but turned it down because he thought it might increase his chances of landing in Vietnam. He applied instead for quartermaster training.

I still have this memory. On the day, I guess, that we were all supposed to go to our next assignments after basic training, we were all standing out in front of the barracks, and they were calling names and saying, all right, you go here and you go here. At the end of the run through the platoon, there were three of us left standing there, and it turned out there was two other guys who either had graduated from college or had some college like I did, and the sergeant says, "All three of your orders have been changed. You're going to infantry training." So I have no idea whether that was just random or punishment or, you know, just my luck ran out, but I stayed at Fort Jackson and got my infantry training there and then from there [went] to Vietnam.

Even though few of his peers did military service, Ptachik does not recall even a moment when he thought that avoiding service was an option once he was drafted. Like many others, he looked at it as a rite of passage.

I just assumed that if you're asked, you go. Maybe it was my upbringing; I was too sheltered, or it was just not something that I—I even considered. You know, I would just as likely [have] said "Well, I'll go to the moon" than go to Canada. I didn't see any other options.

At the time, large-scale efforts to resist the draft were only just getting under way. In any case, Ptachik had no personal experience with the antiwar movement and gave himself up to his fate.

Up to this point, Ptachik's life seems to parallel that of many Vietnam veterans. Swept up in the draft, he went to Vietnam simply to do his duty, and no more.

When he got out of the Army in November 1967, Ptachik tried to put Vietnam behind him.

I sort of blocked the war out when I came back. I would never watch the news on TV. I was aware of the protests, but, you know, I neither participated in them nor objected to them.

It was quite common for wounded soldiers like Ptachik to experience periods of depression. He remembers focusing on himself, simply trying to keep himself functional. He went back to college, attending classes at night while working. He told no one about his Vietnam experience.

At Stony Brook, there was one professor who I had who I did tell that I was in Vietnam, and he really encouraged me to do things with it and to talk to people and so on, and I just refused. I think I probably dropped his class to avoid having to do that. This is something that will prevail right through when the Iranian hostages came home, which was a tipping point for me in how I dealt with Vietnam.

After finishing college, Ptachik got a job working for CUNY in the University Application Processing Center, which handled document processing for the entire university system. His mother had worked there, and the head of the department was a World War II veteran, sympathetic to Ptachik's war experience. Ptachik wound up staying at the processing center for twenty years, eventually rising to become its deputy director.

After the election of Ronald Reagan and the return of the Iranian hostages, Ptachik and many other Vietnam veterans found themselves feeling a deep resentment. This was directed not at the hostages themselves but at the way the American public embraced them so easily. How could the hostages be treated so well, many wondered, when the men who had fought, been wounded, and died in Vietnam were seemingly forgotten? The return of the hostages turned out to be a trigger.

In late 1981 or early 1982, Ptachik became aware of the existence of the Vietnam Veterans of America and went to a chapter meeting in Queens. Recognizing that there was no VVA chapter in Brooklyn, he decided to establish one. He reached out to other CUNY veterans, particularly to Mike Gold of Brooklyn, who was at that time working in the Office of Admissions Services at CUNY. Other activists included Ed Daniels, who currently runs the Incarcerated Veterans Consortium; Joe Reiter; and Tom Coughlin, for whom the Brooklyn chapter of the VVA is named. Ptachik was elected the first chapter president.

After the dedication of the Vietnam Veterans Memorial in Washington, D.C., in November 1982, Ptachik began to meet other veterans who had been to college or who had successful careers. This connection with other veterans helped him to realize his own capabilities and interests. He became ambitious. Fitting in was no longer limited to working a comfortable job and raising a family. Maybe he could do more, he thought. Soon, others would recognize his capabilities as well.

In late 1984, he became involved with the New York City Vietnam Veterans Memorial Commission. The commission was charged with the responsibility of raising half a million dollars: $250,000 to build the physical memorial in New York City and $250,000 for the jobs program. The group wound up raising over $5 million, exceeding its goal tenfold. Looking back, Ptachik recalls:

We just did much more than anyone thought was possible. I was not an isolate in the sense that there were people who had been to Vietnam who weren't crazed vets. There were other people like me; I wasn't doing the greatest of anyone in my generation, but I was certainly doing okay. I had a college degree, I had a job, I had a reasonably good life, and then I saw other people who were like this and people who were even much more successful.

I met people like Robert Santos and Jim Noonan or Frank Havlicek and others, [and] it did a couple of things to me. One, it showed me here are guys who did the same thing I did, went through Vietnam, and look how successful they are, look how polished they are, look how comfortable they are in this other world, and, you know, through them I think I started to realize there are other things I could do. I also saw that other people, World War II vets, respected us and [we] respected them, which was different because you didn't have that respect from the older vets right [before]. So that was a real turning point for me.

One of the other veterans working on the memorial commission persuaded Ptachik that he might benefit enormously by getting a doctorate. He did so, completing his degree in public administration at the Robert F. Wagner Graduate School of Public Service at New York University. Getting his PhD was something that would never have occurred to him before his involvement with the memorial commission.

While working on the commission, Ptachik also began to think more deeply about the meaning of service and the impact it can have on veterans.

One thing I realized—and I realized this for myself in some way, too—for almost everyone the time in Vietnam was the most exciting and the most alive time of your life . . . I mean, if you're a cop or a fireman or you know . . . you can re-create it, but for a lot of guys it's a peak, and for an unfortunate proportion of people who were in Vietnam, it's a peak they never got back to, and the rest of their lives could never be as interesting or as important.

He did not want to look back on his life and be forced to remember Vietnam as the most important thing he ever did. The commission allowed him to acknowledge his ambition to achieve more. Meanwhile, by embedding himself within a wider network of Vietnam veterans during the 1980s, he came to see that his views and experiences, singular though they were, were not entirely unique.

Vietnam remains a touchstone in his life.

I still have this little trick that I would say. I [don't] do it every night, but when I lie down and go to sleep, if there's something bothering me, I say, "You're warm, you're dry, and there is no one shooting at you."

12

TWONESS: HERBERT SWEAT

In his book *The Souls of Black Folk*, W.E.B. Du Bois wrote, "One ever feels his twoness,—an American, a Negro; two souls, two thoughts, two unreconciled strivings; two warring ideals in one dark body, whose dogged strength alone keeps it from being torn asunder."[1] Herbert Sweat is the intellectual child of W.E.B. Du Bois; his world is a working out of "twoness." He is a black man in a white man's world, a soldier in a world of civilians, a child of the ghetto in a world of riches out of his reach.

Most of my meetings with Sweat took place at Black Veterans for Social Justice (BVSJ), a private social service agency where he serves on the board of directors. I was asked to meet with several members of the staff before I could talk to him. Sweat and others at BVSJ were wary. Finally, Sweat agreed to come visit me at my office in Washington Heights, in northern Manhattan. He was early, arriving a good hour before our appointment. He reported that he spent the time walking around the neighborhood, preparing himself for our conversation.

Herbert Sweat grew up in Bedford-Stuyvesant, in central Brooklyn. The area was originally populated with Canarsie Indians and "bought" from them by the Dutch West India Company in the seventeenth century. The Dutch settled there and renamed it Bedford. Improvements in transportation and infrastructure made the area accessible to both downtown Brooklyn and Manhattan; therefore, the wealthier classes were lured to Bedford-Stuyvesant in the middle and late nineteenth century. At the same time, the region remained one of the only places in New York where free blacks could buy homes and land.

By the 1950s, Bedford-Stuyvesant was one of the largest black settlements in New York City. However, the housing stock deteriorated with time as landlords failed to invest in repair and upkeep, and by the 1960s the neighborhood was identified as a slum district. This is the Bed-Stuy where Sweat grew up.

He describes his background as essentially working-class. The family lived in a brownstone with a backyard, a birdbath, and a rose garden. His father was a veteran of the Korean War and lost a leg in the service. His father and his uncles belonged to the Masonic Lodge, and lodge meetings were held in the basement of the brownstone. Sweat remembers it as a mixed neighborhood—Italians, Germans, and African Americans living side by side. He acknowledges that the neighborhood was at the time considered a ghetto. But as a child he did not see it that way.

We understood and was raised by almost each and every neighbor and it—it was a beautiful thing to observe or to be part of [a place] that was pictured to be the worst, but yet there is the beauty. Why? Over my years I've understood that was the tree that grew in Brooklyn; that was the life . . . And one would never believe the unity of that block . . .

Everything was in place; it was a mother and a father, and they were providing for the children and themselves, and the relatives would come on all the holidays, and we would go downtown to Robert Hall on Flatbush Avenue and get our Easter suits and coats, and we would find Easter eggs in the backyard and throughout the cellar and all over the house. The holidays were celebrated like in any other home on the block.

Like so many others from his generation, Sweat fondly remembers life on the streets as a kid, playing stickball and stoopball and all of the street games with a diverse population of kids. There was order in his life, even if just a few blocks away things could be profoundly different. He is not blind to the realities of Bedford-Stuyvesant in the 1950s and 1960s. He knows that there were gangs and drugs and gambling and prostitution. But in his recollection, that kind of activity was happening on the main thoroughfares. The side streets were different: islands of respect, mutual care, and order.

Once he was forced to leave his block, life got harder and he changed. By the time he was in fourth grade, he was being bused from his neighborhood school to P.S. 221, a mostly white school on Empire Boulevard in East Flatbush.

Going to school on the bus was a beautiful ride, but getting off the bus was traumatizing, now that I look at it.

The only thing that I could truly remember is that when we lined up in the park, there was only three of us—three black children on these lines—and the girl who was next to me, on her line, was Alice. The other black child's name was Tyrone. We became immediately attracted to each other; we were always trying to understand, you know, like, why—why me, you know what I mean? Why do we have to come here?

He vividly remembers the Bedford-Stuyvesant riot of 1964, started by a police shooting of an African American youth in Manhattan, and the damage it did to his neighborhood.

To walk down what we call Broadway in Brooklyn, you would think you were on the Broadway in Manhattan, when I grew up. So to watch it one night be burned down and tore down because of the riots and then couldn't go . . . my family wouldn't allow none of [us] to go down to Broadway; that's where our movies and clothing stores and things were, and then to have seen it—these were traumatic experiences.

And that's another thing about coming up through my era. You were either with it or against it. You were either for the war or against the war. You were either black or you were white.

Those years changed him. By the time he reached junior high school, by his own admission he got *a little roughness with me. And I tell any of my people, you got to have a little roughness in order to survive. You had our fathers and teachers and leaders telling us to be peaceful, but when we got to get off that school bus or to get on that school bus, it's not peaceful at all. We don't understand how to [act] like we were taught in our churches.*

He attended Franklin K. Lane High School, graduated in 1965, and then, like many of his relatives, went into the service in April 1966. Though he enlisted, he didn't think much about the Vietnam War or American social problems. Rather, military service was simply understood as a rite of passage for young males in his family. His father, his uncles, his cousins, and his brothers all had military service in their backgrounds. They had been in World War II and Korea and deployed to the Dominican Republic. He felt that if he was to earn his lineage, he would have to be part of that tradition.

All his family members who served had been paratroopers: members of the 82nd Airborne, the 101st Airborne, and the 555th—the Triple Nickels. Sweat recalls: *Now, my mind wasn't set on whether or not I was scared or worried; my mind was to get my wings.*

The Parachutist Badge, also known as Jump Wings, is a badge of honor, a symbol of an elite status in the U.S. military. Earning it would be his way of asserting his equality. He was both African and American. He wanted to be part of a larger American history *because of Paul Revere, because of George Washington, because of the teachings, because of the understandings of what we were standing for.*

Sweat wanted me to acknowledge the *hurt but yet the endurance that I must have possessed. You see, when you go into the service, I told you I was doing it as an honorable thing, a man's chore.*

He anticipated that he would be treated fairly because there were so many other black soldiers. And perhaps the personal consequences of enlisting would have been less traumatic, less injurious, if he had experienced the equal treatment he expected. His life going forward would've gone better; he would have been proud, in the end, of his "gallantry." But he doesn't feel that he was treated fairly.

And it was such a crucial part of my individual life, as well as, now that I think about it, it had to be that with many of my brothers.

He went into the service thinking he might become a noncommissioned officer or even an officer. He had high hopes and aspirations. As he put it, citing a gospel song, *I got my eye on the sparrow.* What he didn't foresee was the racism he would meet with in the military.

So going into basic training and Advanced Infantry Training, it was like me going full force but always bumping into a wall. The wall being the system that was in order at the time, and that system was as always—to hold the blacks back.

He met men from Wisconsin and Texas, as he recalls, who had literally never seen a black person before. Likewise, when he went to Jump School at Fort Benning in Georgia, he encountered the first segregated bathrooms he had ever seen, in the bus station. Having grown up as a leader in his neighborhood, physically stronger than almost everyone and better able to deal with difficult situations, Sweat believed he would and should be granted a leadership opportunity within the Army. He was not. He felt singled out because of his race.

After getting his Jump Wings, Sweat was sent to Vietnam to serve with the 173rd Airborne Brigade. It was October 1967. His account of moving into the jungle echoes the theme of twoness. He felt as though he traveled the distance between civilian and savage, between normal and not normal, regular person and killer.

Other soldiers quickly taught Sweat how to behave in the field. His sergeant, a black man named Abner, also from Brooklyn, instructed him to go through his rucksack and leave any unnecessary items, including underwear and books, that would be useless in the field. Sweat shed his civilian life, buried it in a foxhole.

So then, naturally, I became a Herdsman—173rd Airborne Brigade. Read your history books; we were at that particular time General Westmoreland's strike unit. We were just what they wanted—men who would die.

Life becomes the other side, the side that I don't give a damn whether I get back to New York or not. All I want to do is kill. I was what they called a boonie rat, and maybe someone in your interviews explained very deeply what a boonie rat is. And all you have to do is relax yourself enough to understand what a rat is and what and how a rat lives and then put it in what the word "boonie" means, and you have a human being running around in the jungles, eating, killing, very rarely sleeping, very rarely bathing, very rarely getting our mail properly, very rarely getting clean clothes, fresh water.

As he recalls it, the unit was pushed from place to place as the ultimate backstop, made out of bodies.

Vietnam retains a powerful hold on Sweat and many other African American soldiers, in part because the racial divisions of American life were sometimes forgotten. For once, "twoness" didn't necessarily define Sweat's existence. He could feel a sense of common humanity with fellow Americans at the very moment they were asked to engage in that most inhumane act of all, organized killing.

The trick of this is to understand that as we go through this jungle depending on each other, anything that happens, everything that happens, we're all one there. Like I said, there wasn't no color problem; there wasn't anything—especially after the firefight when you really see the true tears and the true understanding . . . This little group of men out in the middle of this jungle is really glad to be alive themselves but hurt because their best pal was dead. And to witness this and live like this and to live with the harmony of each other as well as the sacrifice of death, it was a beautiful way to live. That's why they say in war it's also love. And I found that love there for my comrades. That's when there's no color . . .

When he returned to the United States in the fall of 1968, Sweat began to experience—again—what he believed to be racism within the American military. He accumulated Article 15s, often listed as "minor" disciplinary charges. Even though he felt entitled to a discharge from the U.S. military, he was shipped to an armored unit. He telephoned his wife, and she wired him money to return directly to New York. He went AWOL. Four hundred thirty-two days later he wound up in the stockade at Fort Dix. He became, simply put, rebellious.

In 1970, the Pentagon listed 65,643 American soldiers as either AWOL or deserters.[2] Herbert Sweat's decision to go AWOL began a trajectory that would lead him into serious trouble with the Army and alienate him from government institutions. Something like this had been foreseen by African American community leaders. In 1966, Whitney M. Young Jr., the civil rights activist and president of the National Urban League (NUL), used the pages of the *New York Amsterdam News* to describe the problems that African American veterans were likely to face and to describe the efforts of the Urban League to meet those challenges. The NUL established the Veterans Affairs Department, which was "designed to contact the G.I. shortly before he is to be discharged, to see if we can help him in his readjustment to civilian life." The plan was to find out specifically what skills the soldier had and if any of them, through retraining, could be adapted for civilian use. Further, the NUL wanted to help soldiers return to school and find adequate housing. But Young understood the dramatic problems African American veterans were going to face. "Nobody gave a tinker's damn," he wrote about this group of ex-GIs, "what they hoped to do, or even how they were feeling when they returned home, except his family and close friends." The result was that thousands of them returned to the same old communities, Young asserted, "to the same old discriminatory conditions, to the same or worse nondescript little-paying jobs and to the same old depressing, dismal and hopeless second-class citizenship status that they have left." Young concluded, "With all the trouble currently besetting the country, here at home, these Vietnam vets will be a force the nation can ill afford to have embittered."[3]

In 1970 and 1971, Sweat was suffering from PTSD and he was angry, too. He got out of the Army on October 7, 1970. And then, he says, *I was back in jail for murder in '71.*

He and another man were playing chess for money. Sweat won, and the man refused to pay. A fight followed, and the man pulled a knife. Using a pearl-handled .38-caliber pistol he had acquired while in Vietnam, Sweat fired. The bullet struck the man's collarbone, and something, a bone or a bullet fragment, penetrated his heart, and he died. Sweat was arrested and charged with first-degree murder. He went through the justice system and was sentenced to probation when the charge against him was reduced from murder to manslaughter. It was ruled that the man he shot had reached for a weapon first. Thinking about it now, he says, *It's not hard to pull the trigger. It's hard to live with it. In fact, I don't live with it. I suffer with it.*

Three marriages came and went. So did a number of jobs. He began to have flashbacks to a particular incident in Vietnam. In the fall of 1967, his unit was on a search-and-destroy mission when it took sniper fire from a village. Someone was hit. Assigned to carry the M79 grenade launcher, which fired an explosive 40-millimeter round, Sweat fired on one of the huts. After the firing stopped, Sweat's company moved through the village, and he entered the hut where his rounds had landed, 45-millimeter pistol at the ready. Sweat discovered the bodies of a number of individuals who looked like civilians, including an old man, two females, two or three younger children, and two men clad in "black pajamas," identified as the uniform of the Vietcong. He is certain that he killed them.

It has haunted me to the point where I felt it was an omen. That's why I couldn't keep a family—because I destroyed one.

After breaking up with his third wife in 1993, he became homeless, living at the Borden Avenue Veterans Shelter in Long Island City, Queens.

Homelessness among Vietnam veterans became a major public issue in the 1980s, though there had been homeless Vietnam veterans living on the streets of New York City since the 1960s. As the problem gained national visibility, the New York City Office of the Comptroller published *Soldiers of Misfortune: Homeless Veterans in New York City* in 1982. The report found that as of that year there were as many as ten thousand veterans living on New York City streets, accounting for an estimated one-third of the city's homeless population. On average they were in their late thirties. The causes varied, of course, but the report pointed to both unemployment and underemployment and a lack of low-cost housing. Another explanation offered was that veterans were less likely to have completed their education than their peers. The report also cited stepped-up discharges from mental hospitals as a contributing factor. In 1982 unemployment in the city was running at 9.5 percent, while 11 percent of Vietnam-era veterans were out of work. The picture was much worse among minority veterans, who were suffering an unemployment rate of almost 25 percent. The housing market in the city changed dramatically between 1970 and 1981, too; the report estimated that 321,000 apartments had disappeared, mostly in low-rent buildings.[4]

Partly as a result of public pressure created by this report and the opening of Vietnam memorials in Washington, D.C., and later New York City, in 1987 New York City opened the shelter on Borden Avenue, the country's first for homeless veterans. The community fought the shelter unsuccessfully. Located in an industrial building near the Queens-side entrance to the Midtown Tunnel, the shelter would house some of the estimated twenty-seven hundred homeless veterans already in the New York City shelter system. It was never a particularly welcoming place. It was originally designed for 275 occupants, but its population quickly ballooned to over 400. The city initially promised that veterans would receive both health care and job training on-site, but those services did not materialize for some time.

In February 1988, Bernard Edelman, then director of the Office of Veterans' Affairs for Mayor Edward I. Koch, reported that among the 400 residents at the Borden Avenue shelter, 80 percent were black, 15 percent Hispanic, and 5 percent white. Fifty percent were Vietnam-era veterans, and 20 percent "ex-offenders."[5] In 1988, the Veterans Administration additionally opened a drop-in center on Ryerson Street in Williamsburg, Brooklyn, which contained an examination room, a lounge, and a kitchen.[6]

The effort was only partly successful, as estimates of the number of homeless Vietnam-era veterans continued to climb. The press frequently cited statistics asserting that one-quarter to one-third of America's homeless were veterans, and as late as 1991 some estimated that the proportion of Vietnam-era veterans among the homeless ran as high as 50 percent.[7] Sweat was among them.

On August 7, 1993, Steven Zadarala, a forty-two-year-old homeless veteran sleeping on the cot next to Sweat's at the shelter, was stabbed in the chest.[8]

I seen him and he was changing colors. I saw him going into shock now because he couldn't even talk, you see. I had to get him to the floor so he wouldn't run. I finally flipped him down to the floor. I truly didn't really, really think that this guy was going to make it, [but] I started giving him mouth-to-mouth and trying to stop the bleeding and all of this at the same time. Once I got up to take a breather myself, and my man, who we called him Sarge, he jumped down there and he told me, "Sweat, he needs mouth-to-mouth again"; that's all I remember. And then when I went back down to give him mouth-to-mouth the second time, we got his pulse back, but it was real faint. So then, naturally, we're waiting and waiting on this ambulance. I didn't know that much time elapsed, but it was something like fifty-something minutes before this ambulance came.

Why did it take all this time? Because it was a shelter? You understand, it's nobody important, just a bunch of veterans; you understand me—they're drug addicts and misfits and everything else. We wasn't real people. We wasn't nothin'. So they didn't get there for about fifty-four minutes.

Zadarala died. Police arrested Milton Vasquez, another Borden Avenue shelter resident, for the murder. Sweat recalls: *He ran and tried to flush a knife eight inches long down the commode. The police got the knife, got everything.*

The incident brought Sweat to a mental breakdown.

I started flashing back. All I could think about was how I killed these people. That just kept piling in my mind as I was trying to get his blood off of me. They had me in the shower. Then the police came in and told me they were going to take me to the hospital. So they took me. And in a way that was the best thing that ever happened to me because they took me from there to people who I feel helped me. They put me in the VA on Twenty-Third Street, and they left me there for five months and twenty-three days. That was a lot of time to be locked up—not knowing what to do in there. Finally, that's when they sent me to Lyons, New Jersey, and then from there they sent me to Martinsburg, West Virginia, which is a long-term hospital. And that's why I thought I would never get back to New York.

While Sweat was living at the Martinsburg VA Medical Center, a residential care facility, a friend told him about Black Veterans for Social Justice, an organization that offers treatment and social assistance for veterans from all wars. Founded in 1979, BVSJ aims to fill in the gaps left by the Veterans Administration.

One important service the organization provides is supportive housing for veterans. Sweat himself now lives in a BVSJ-owned building.

That's why I belong to the Black Vets for Social Justice, because this is the only place that has said these words—that we have served too. We have these problems of war sickness, of socializing, of our behavioral pat-

terns; we have problems and you shouldn't just look at us as just guys in the ghetto. You should look at these soldiers of war as collateral damage.

Sweat had no desire to remain permanently at a Veterans Administration facility. Instead, he wanted to live as independently as he could. In BVSJ, he found a group that would help him move from dependence to independence by stressing the twin values of mutual aid and self-help.

I came to this organization because of what it stood for. And what it stands for is to unite blacks and other veterans, all veterans, in a united way to give us the benefits which we've never really received as being veterans. "Yes, we served too." That's our motto.

Within Black Veterans for Social Justice, that's the key word: "justice." We need justice. As you know, in our society of America, the black man and woman do not receive justice. So yes, there are organizations that must be formed to [fix] the injustices that have happened to us over the generations being here in America.

As a participant at BVSJ, Sweat has run the organization's Veterans Action Group for many years. He describes it as *a group which was formed by veterans for veterans. It exists today at 665 Willoughby and also 22 East 119th Street, where veterans come together and we relate to each other all kinds of situations that may approach us as veterans. To receive veterans' benefits . . . to just enlighten each other and hearten each other in our tribulations. It's a group that all veterans are welcome to come to, not just blacks. Not just [men], but all people can come to it. We open our doors to everyone.*

Here I am—sixty-two years old and left the war when I was nineteen years old, taken care of by Uncle Sam for eleven, almost twelve, years. So from that time that goes to show you that for all the other years, I was out here suffering; that's what I'm trying to do now—to slow the suffering down of other veterans, and move right on.

Sweat was elected chair of the board of directors at BVSJ in 2010. In that capacity he pushes forward the organization's aim of aiding people like himself. And he struggles every day with the impact of Vietnam on his life. In his mind, life since then has been a kind of cosmic payback for what he did as a "boonie rat," a soldier in the bush, for twelve months nearly forty-five years ago.

Once you commit the murder of war, you can never forget that. War is that, murder. Someone will die. I was so young that I did not understand what I was doing. I didn't only destroy human life and destroy villages, but I also destroyed myself. I suffer now from post-traumatic stress disorder and the situations, the missions, the air assaults, just the killing fields itself, remain vivid and in me forever. It's not a day that goes by that I don't think of or have a flashback or a thought about Vietnam, about the incidences, about the missions, or about just the simple smell.

It's the truth that I want to explain. It's what holds me back from being a whole man. It's—it's the guilt—it's the killing, it's the not caring about human beings at that one little time, that year, that just keeps coming back and back.

13

LONG ROAD HOME: NEIL KENNY

It's long been recognized that combat can have profound psychological consequences for soldiers. The psychiatrist Jonathan Shay has argued that the problem can be traced as far back as the *Iliad*, where the wrath of Achilles follows the death of his beloved Patroclus. In the nineteenth century, soldiers affected by combat were said to have "soldier's heart." In the aftermath of World War I, their condition was identified as "shell shock," and during World War II as "combat fatigue." Until fairly recently, these conditions were considered to be short-term; the assumption was that symptoms showed up immediately and faded relatively quickly.

In 1988 the journal *Science* reported that fifteen to twenty years after the end of their service in Vietnam, veterans of that war were more than twice as likely to suffer "serious psychological problems"—alcohol abuse, major depression, and anxiety—as soldiers who did not serve in Vietnam.[1] The recognition of post-traumatic stress disorder by the American Psychological Association in 1980 was, by the mid-1980s, provoking what the writer Leslie Roberts called a "seemingly intractable debate on how to prevent it," as well as a discussion of "which veterans should be compensated."

The Centers for Disease Control spent four years and $23 million conducting analytic interviews with some fifteen thousand veterans.

In all, the health of about seven thousand Army veterans who served in Vietnam between 1965 and 1971 was compared with that of about seven thousand Vietnam-era noncombat veterans. The study concluded that about 14 percent of Vietnam veterans were having problems with alcohol abuse or dependence, as opposed to 9 percent of noncombat Vietnam-era veterans.

The New York City resident and Vietnam veteran Neil Kenny was eventually diagnosed with PTSD in 1995, twenty-six years after he left the Marine Corps.

Kenny speaks with what New Yorkers would recognize as a Lower East Side accent. A commanding presence, he is only about five feet eight inches tall and by his own admission sixty pounds heavier than he would like to be. His rigid bearing still contains traces of his military background. At sixty-three years old, his hair remains full and dark, and his face has retained a boyish appearance.

A self-described survivor, Kenny lived through a difficult childhood, thirteen months of service in Vietnam, and years of alcoholism, drug abuse, and depression. He was eventually diagnosed with disabling post-traumatic stress disorder, and his story is one example of how the symptoms of the syndrome can shape a life without destroying it.

He remains vigorously active and is ebullient, witty, and engaged as he communicates. While his symptoms have alienated some, including other veterans, he works hard to maintain his equilibrium. Some days, he says, he wakes up in a homicidal mood and it is best not to cross him. Overall, it's best to become a member of his squad, or as Alice, whom he calls his *bride of twenty-five years*, puts it, to be "inside the wire." If Kenny considers you a "friendly," you will be all right.

Not that there isn't plenty of venom to go around. In recent years, Kenny has begun to joke, *I don't have PTSD. I just have an anger problem.*

Neil Joseph Kenny was born on March 13, 1949, and grew up in the Governor Alfred E. Smith Houses, a New York City public housing project built in the shadow of the Brooklyn Bridge. Proposed by Mayor La Guardia in 1943, the project housed 1,780 apartments with room for

6,850 persons.[2] Designed by the architectural firm Eggers & Higgins, which, coincidentally, was owned by the father of his fellow veteran Richard Eggers,[3] it was a remarkably safe place to grow up, Kenny recalls.

I had Chinatown. I grew up with blacks, grew up with Hispanics; it was a mixed neighborhood, which I didn't think was really a bad thing. It really wasn't. I grew up in a time when people could leave their doors open, when you lived in a project and things really weren't happening. We all got along; we all got along on the Lower East Side. I'm a kid from the Lower East Side. I have fond memories of living in the projects.

Even as a child, Kenny dreamed of being a soldier.

One of the things that I've always had memories of, and sometimes it comes out to me in dreams, is I always had—I always played soldiers, always. I was always—it was an always thing.

While he remembers the Lower East Side projects as being safe, there are also memories of deprivation, violence, and even death. The family was poor, and Kenny can recall times when there was nothing to eat. Sometimes the family couldn't pay the rent because of his father's drinking. There was a lot of alcoholism in Kenny's family, and drinking would become part of his story, too.

I always felt in many ways that my childhood was training for Vietnam. I did very well in Vietnam because I was trained for that and having a sixth sense about things. I think [it gave me] street knowledge; I think deprivation . . . that there's a sense of survival about it.

He was sickly as a child, and until fifth grade he was very, very small for his age, but as he remembers, *My mouth was never very small.* Fights were common between the kids from the Smith projects and another nearby project, Knickerbocker Village. Despite his small stature, he could afford to be cheeky. For one thing, he had a big brother he could rely on. Also, kids in the neighborhood knew his uncle Frank, the toughest police officer in the Fifth Precinct. Kenny had the power to walk down the street, approach the meanest kids on the street, and tell them to move. Kids would be quick to admonish Kenny's victim, "Don't hit him. His uncle will beat you up."

Violence seemed part of the natural order of things. He says, *When*

I was about five or six, I was very young, and I remember seeing a dead guy right in front of my building. Someone had slashed this big black man, cutting him from his neck to his stomach in the parking lot.

By the seventh grade Kenny was getting into trouble in school for not doing his homework and mouthing off. His poor academic performance may have been due, in part, to circumstances at home. One night his father came home in a rage and began a physical confrontation with Kenny's mother, breaking her leg in two places.

I can remember the sound when her leg broke. I said, "Holy shit."

It was a turning point in the Kennys' lives. Their mother and father never really lived together again. After his father left, his mother was in bed for two and a half days, and Kenny stayed home to help. When he emerged after a few days, he ran into Uncle Frank, the police officer, who asked where he had been. Kenny told him about his mother. When his uncle came to Kenny's apartment, he took one look at his sister and called for an ambulance. She was in danger of losing her leg because gangrene was starting to set in. At the hospital, doctors wanted to amputate her leg, but Kenny recalls her protesting, telling them to let her die instead. She kept the leg.

The Kenny family moved out of the Smith Houses into a small apartment in Bay Ridge to live with Kenny's mother's family. There were already a lot of people living there. Now, with five additional bodies, including four kids, it was stressful. Nevertheless, Kenny, his brother, and his sister would get up every morning and take the train into Manhattan to go to St. James School. The train rides were educational in and of themselves. Kenny recalls sitting on the train one morning and seeing a man in a business suit leaning against the door, grabbing his chest and making noises of distress. He slid down onto the floor. At the Canal Street stop people dragged him off, propped him up against the wall along with his bag, and got back on the subway. No one stayed with him. No one made an effort to contact the police or bring him any kind of aid.

I realize today he was having a heart attack. But as a kid what I thought was really weird was to observe the guy slide against the door and he was lying there with people stepping over him to get on and off the train.

Kenny's father found a one-bedroom apartment in Bay Ridge on Eighty-Fourth Street and Third Avenue. His mother took a place around the corner on Eighty-Third Street, the very street she had lived on as a three-year-old. As a poor kid from the Lower East Side, Kenny never felt that he fit in with the Bay Ridge "rich kids." He just didn't have the same breadth of cultural knowledge. They used to play football in front of Fort Hamilton High School, at the southern tip of Brooklyn. One day Kenny got into an argument with another kid. Kenny recalls saying, *"Listen, there's one thing I want to know before I kick your ass. Are you a nigger, or are you a spic?"*

The boy told him he was Lebanese. Kenny vividly recalls feeling embarrassed. He had never heard the word "Lebanese" before and had no idea what the kid was talking about.

Sports became an arena where he could vent some of his frustration, although the release wasn't always appropriate. Once, Kenny recalls, during a football game he noticed a "ringer" on the opposing team. He was sure he knew the kid, a fifteen-year-old, who was playing against twelve-year-olds. He insisted that his coach speak to the other coach, but his coach refused. So Kenny took matters into his own hands. Marching across the field, he got into the face of the opposing coach and remembers saying: *"You've got to get that fucking Greek out of here. You're cheating."*

The coach responded by threatening to slap Kenny in the face. Kenny made a derogatory remark, and when the coach began to swing at him, Kenny hit the coach in the side of the head with his helmet. Kenny's family backed him up, but he was thrown out of the game anyway. He was told to leave the field, but he refused, standing on the sidelines to watch the rest of the game.

Eventually, Kenny decided to walk away from school. *At the bright age of sixteen, I set out to go to Wall Street to make my millions.*

He got a job making $60 a week at the Wall Street law firm of Winthrop, Stimson, Putnam & Roberts, imagining that he would become a great lawyer. He got a suit, a briefcase, a pipe, and special tobacco and made his way from Bay Ridge to work each morning. The job did not last long, though how or why it ended is lost to the mists of memory.

In 1966, Kenny's brother George joined the Air Force. Meanwhile, Kenny recalls hanging out at the candy store across the street from his apartment, smoking cigarettes and reading the newspaper, while the other kids his age went to school. In the evening, he would hang out in front of the Hinsch ice cream parlor at Eighty-Sixth Street and Fifth Avenue in Brooklyn.

In the spring of 1967, the soldier in him emerged as he read in the New York *Daily News* about a battle at Hill 881 in the northern section of South Vietnam, where 155 Marines were killed. This was history in the making; this was real. Suddenly he realized that he wanted to be part of it, he wanted the experience that his father's generation had. When Kenny's brother came home on leave and told the family that he was headed to Fort Belvoir, Virginia, to learn how to make maps for aerial reconnaissance, Kenny was worried that his older brother would be killed. At the same time, Kenny was eager to enlist and serve in Vietnam. As it turns out, he would become intimately familiar with Hill 881 as a part of the Khe Sanh battlefield. In fact, his life would be marked by it.

I had this great plan. I said, "Well, I'll join the Marine Corps," because I figured I was going to get drafted anyway. So I said, "Well, if I'm going to get drafted, I want to go with the best that I can," and so I joined the Marine Corps. And lo and behold, as I'm going away to the Marine Corps, my brother is getting out of the Air Force.

When I enlisted in the Marine Corps and I went to Fort Hamilton for the physical, the guy did the physical and he said, "All right, you're 4-F." I said, "What?" He said, "Yeah, that elbow. I'm not taking a chance on that." I said, "What do you mean, 4-F?" I said, "I want to go." He said, "You want to go?" I said, "Yeah." He said, "One-A." Because, apparently, I mean [my elbow] curves because I broke it. They weren't going to take me. I actually could have avoided military service. [Laughs.]

Kenny graduated from boot camp on August 29, 1967, and from there went to infantry training at Camp Geiger, which was part of

Camp Lejeune in North Carolina. Then he headed home for ten days on leave. While home, his beloved grandfather told him that when he came back from the war, "you and me are going down to [the] bar and have a beer and a steak together." There was no "if"; no doubt. His grandfather was the only member of the family who expressed such confidence.

When he reached Vietnam, he loved it. *I was home*, he says.

Arriving in Vietnam in January 1968, Kenny was assigned to Lima Company, Third Battalion, Twenty-Sixth Marine Regiment. Within a few days, the siege of Khe Sanh would begin. In the late autumn of 1967, the U.S. military, led by General William Westmoreland, had become convinced that the North Vietnamese were preparing a major assault, although they did not know its timing or objectives. Westmoreland believed that the NVA wanted to replicate its success against the French in 1954 at the Battle of Dien Bien Phu. North Vietnamese troops had surrounded and laid siege to the French outpost. Defeated, the French lost their hold on Vietnam as a colonial possession.

General Westmoreland and President Lyndon B. Johnson insisted that no such defeat be inflicted on U.S. Marines in Vietnam. As a result, in the days and weeks leading up to the North Vietnamese Tet Offensive, reinforcements were added to the key base at Khe Sanh. Kenny was one of those added during the buildup. He would serve in I Corps in the northern part of South Vietnam through the spring, summer, and into the fall of that year.

Despite the passage of so many years, Kenny can still recall his first artillery barrage.

I remember the first time they hit the place. I was sleeping in the bunk. By this time we were living underground, you know. We had dug in and we had this bunker and everything, and Skip comes in and he says, "Get up, get up, get up." I said, "Fuck you; I did my watch. Get the fuck out of here. Let the fucking lieutenant get me." He was like, "Get up." I said, "I'm not getting up." He said, "I'll fucking shoot you; get up." And then I said, "Then shoot me, motherfucker, because I'm not getting up." And he's like—he just said, "Oh, fuck you." That's all he said. He didn't, he wasn't yelling anymore and it's like—one thing I learned, like—when somebody is yelling and screaming, you're usually pretty safe. You can duck this. But when all the emotion is gone and they say, "You just want to sit down," and you've got to really lean forward to listen, there's no emotion, you know you're cooked.

Something said to me, "You better get up," you know, and I got up and I grabbed my weapon and I went out and we were running down the trench line and he was in front of me and I said, "Skip, Skip, Skip." And he stopped and turned around and he said, "What the fuck is . . . ?" I said, "What's that fucking noise?" you know, and I pointed up. And he looked at me and he said, "It's incoming." And I was like, "Oh." But he was like—it was like shocking to him that I didn't know what this was, but to me it was like, well, why would I? I had never heard that before. You know [a] 120 rocket [is] coming in; it's kind of like a freight train and a fire engine and a siren, and it's all screaming and like Mach 2, and you just hope it don't hit you, you know. It's not personal; it really isn't—it's not personal.

He had his "adventures," as he calls them, at Khe Sanh, doing things to alleviate the boredom and fear. He recalls that he and his friends *stole the place blind*, with raids on the commissary for food and water. He played pranks on other Marines, and he made friends.

With the lifting of the siege of Khe Sanh, the Third Battalion, Twenty-Sixth Marines carried out a maneuver on April 14. Dubbed the "Great Easter Egg Hunt" by the grunts, it was an effort to take Hill 881 North. According to the historians John Prados and Ray Stubbe, "more than five thousand rockets had been fired during the course of the siege" from that hill. The troops assembled on Hill 881 South, having moved there during the night. Despite concerns about the condition of the Marines who had fought through the siege, they were raring to go. By midafternoon the operation was over, and they had retaken the hill. Six Marines had been killed, nineteen wounded. As for the NVA, 106 bodies were recovered from 881 North, with their total losses estimated to be three times that number.[4]

In some ways, Kenny's war had not yet begun. He made his first confirmed kill, a North Vietnamese soldier, on July 4, 1968. He tells the story.

Killing is holding a thunder stick, as a novel would call the weapon, and having the power of God. I decide if you're going to live or you're going to die; I'm making that decision.

It's an amazing thing. It's not hard to explain, but it takes some time to explain. It's a nanosecond of feeling every possible emotion that you could possibly feel, and it's something that you just do. And after you do it, you tend to live with it forever. I don't think that I live with it like, "Oh, what a horrible thing I've done." I also don't live with it as, like, "Oh, what a wonderful thing I've done." I have to put it in the context of what the situation was.

The events of that day stay with him in ways that he can't always articulate. Sometimes the anniversary sneaks up on him. For example, July 4, 2005, Kenny recalls, was *just a nasty motherfucker—something was just going on. I really couldn't even put a pin on it, and then it occurred to me, because I spoke with Phineas and he said, "Yeah, you know, it is the Fourth." That's the day a guy named Franklin Delano Ratliff got killed. A big black kid. I recall him physically. It's also the day I got my definite first confirmed kill.*

January to July is almost six months; Kenny acknowledges he may well have killed prior to July 4.

When you see a guy and you fire and ten other people are firing and the guy gets dead, the question is, Did you get him? I got him? Who got him?

He doesn't know. But July 4, 1968, was different.[5]

On that particular day, while the platoon waited in position, the lieutenant sent out a patrol. They heard shots, and then—nothing. Soon they got word that a medevac was needed. Members of his squad came struggling back into the perimeter carrying a soldier by the name of Ratliff. He had been hit in the chest. Based on what Kenny was told, *I'm sure he was dead before he hit the fucking ground.*

Tensions were running high. They had no idea what they had run into: a random soldier sitting on a trail, a listening post for an entire regiment—they just didn't know.

They tightened up the perimeter. Right outside, there was a steep drop-off into a ravine, so the platoon did something slightly unorthodox: they placed the machine gun outside the perimeter, to cover that ravine. Just inside the perimeter, a young Marine sat reading. An NVA sniper must have spotted him with his back to the perimeter line, and without warning a bullet split the back of his head. Now two Marines were dead, and they still didn't know what they were dealing with.

Kenny and his gun partner, Ronnie Marsala, were covering the ravine. Marsala decided to go take a look around. Kenny was left with the machine gun to cover the area.

I'm sitting there and I looked down the ravine, and then I see a helmet pop up from behind a rock. And I'm looking at this. I can't really tell who this is, friend or foe. Is this one of our guys who went out and is trying to see if somebody is right in front of the position, or is it the guy who was doing the shooting? I don't know.

The man stepped out from behind a boulder.

He's got shorts on, and he's got Ho Chi Minh sandals on. Now I know exactly what he is. As it turns out, he's looking right at me. I don't believe he saw me, but he stepped out in front, and I saw that he had his AK-47. And he stood directly in front of me, and my comment was "Goodbye, motherfucker." That's exactly what I said. And I cranked off—I hit that fucking thing. I had a starter belt with either fifty or eighty rounds on it. I was right on this motherfucker.

And—and—an eternity—an eternity went by. I just let the whole burst go with the starter belt.

Kenny simply kept firing. But while doing so, he remembers that he focused on much more than just his trigger, his ammunition supply, and his target. He felt as if he were aware of everything else that was going on around him. His visual recall of the killing remains especially vivid.

And it was as if he stood and accepted each round. It was as if he waited to accept them. And I was watching each round go into him, and I was watching each round come out of him, and I was watching, you know, the blood and whatever else [as he was] getting blown away. This guy was taking a serious motherfucking shellacking. And it seemed to go on forever. But in fact it was seconds, and he fell out of my sight.

As quickly as it began, it stopped. Kenny grabbed a weapon and ran forward to find out what had happened and to secure the ground in front of the gun. Suddenly something landed next to his knee, and it was smoking.

I reached down to grab it. I almost had it in my hands, and I said, "Gas!" Thornton, who had moved down parallel to me, was real close; he said, "It's a fucking Chicom!"—which is a Chinese Communist grenade. It was on the little bamboo stick, and I was like, "Shit." I just tried to crawl inside my helmet, and I pulled back my hand and the fucking thing went off. . . Thank God for quality control. If it was one of our grenades, we are not having this conversation, as sure as there is a God. I got dirt and ringing in my ears. So I said, "Well, fuck this," and I started throwing grenades down, and we threw in about eight grenades, and it was pretty fucking horrific. You just kind of hug the ground, but we were above it. After that when I was able to get down there, and you're picking up AK-47s, it looked like . . . Did you ever work in a butcher shop and see what a pound of steak looks like when it goes through a grinder? That's what it looked like; these guys were fucking mangled—fucked-up mangled. Which one I shot, I can't tell you; we weren't taking names.

Kenny then tried to make peace with his God.

One of the things which makes me the person I am today, I have a sense of my own spirituality. I don't know if that's the word. My own soul, a sense of my own soul, like, what I had done. I had killed another human being; I had killed this guy. There was no question about it. It was my kill. There was no denial of the ownership of who killed this guy. There were three or four of them down there, and maybe I killed all of them, or some of them, but I knew for certain that the one confirmed was the guy that I had laced into with that machine gun. There was no fucking way that this guy was walking away. I mean, he must've taken twenty-five, thirty fucking hits.

And when I got down there, I kneeled down—I actually, literally knelt down—and I said the Lord's Prayer, and I said an act of contrition, and I was asking God to forgive me for what I have done, because there is a realization; you just took another human being. You have taken another life; you—you have done that, there's no question now, my friend, that you've crossed this threshold. There's just no question about it; it's done.

Kenny relates what took place in therapy when he tried to explain his behavior that day, getting angry even as he does so.

When I shared that in the group therapy, some of them mocked me about that, and they would say, "Oh yeah, are you going to say a prayer for him? Ha-ha-ha." It bothered me on one level, but on another level it didn't bother me, because the bottom line was, I can bare my soul and I can be at peace. The fucking demons inside your head, they own you. If you can't understand that you took somebody's life—that there's a price to go with it—then I don't even know if you're fucking human anymore.

It's not so easy to kill a human being. It's not so easy to kill somebody looking them in the eye. So we have redcoats and rebels and Tories and gooks and Nazis to hide this; we have whatever the fuck we want to have, because it's not killing a person. But killing somebody, I can tell you, is leaving a part of your fucking heart and soul there, if you're a human being.

So killing somebody is something that I can talk about. I can talk about it openly and honestly. It takes something from your heart and from your soul, from your spiritual condition, to do that when you own it one-on-one. Killing from above, dropping bombs, is different; you may know it, but you don't have the ownership of it.

It's very easy to be the Rumsfeld of "Kill them all"—and I'm not picking on Donald Rumsfeld; I'm just using him as an image—[or] John Lennon, "Don't kill anybody," or . . . Gandhi. Those are the extremes; the reality is, you're the nineteen-year-old kid looking at a nineteen-year-old kid and you just whacked this motherfucker, and I'm going to tell you something: he would have fucking killed me if I didn't kill him. And if you don't believe me, go ask that guy who was reading the book that day, and go ask Franklin Delano Ratliff. Oh, that's right—you can't have that conversation.

Kenny will tell anyone who asks that he has killed people but is quick to add that he has never murdered anyone. He says he tries to find words to express the feelings the incident left him with, but sometimes *the feelings can't be expressed.* Many veterans would understand this. Those veterans who don't, like the men in group therapy who mocked Kenny for his act of contrition, well, he says: *I wonder whose soul is in disarray. I don't think it's mine, but I'm not here to save the fucking world.*

In October 1968, Kenny was slated to attend a ceremony for his promotion to corporal. He had arrived in-country as a private first class, and the promotion represented an acknowledgment of his skill and service. Ordered to clean himself up as best he could, he was to present himself to the company captain at 1400 hours—2:00 p.m.—the next afternoon. He found his *cleanest dirty shirt,* walked down to the river to scrub it out, and placed it on a bunker to dry. As he waited, he heard the radio inside the command bunker, "Be advised, Kilo, November, Juliet, 1649. There is a jeep coming and it will meet him on the road. It will be there right away." It took Kenny a couple of moments to figure out what he had heard, because the words sounded somewhat familiar but didn't make sense. "Kilo, November, Juliet" stood for "Kenny, Neil Joseph," and 1649 were the last four digits of his service number.

A moment later, someone came out of the command bunker and told him that Lieutenant Meegan, his platoon commander, wanted him to gather his gear and get on the road. Kenny's mind raced. He had recently sent his brother back home *a box of the finest Vietnamese herbs* that he could find. He recalls enclosing a note saying, "Save some for me!" He says: *I thought somebody had grabbed the box of herbal medicine.*

He was terrified that he had just been busted for shipping home marijuana. Kenny climbed into the jeep and asked the driver what was going on. The jeep driver had no idea. The tension mounted when they arrived at their destination. Kenny recalls: *I never saw so many generals. You could see the sun shining off all their emblems, and they were having some big-ass powwow. And the jeep came in, and this guy came over to me. He says, "Corporal Kenny?" I said, "Yeah." And he says, "Come with me."*

Kenny saw his former company commander, Captain Bennett, give a little shake of his head, and Kenny thought he was in serious trouble. He was walked over to a landing zone, and the lieutenant there asked him to unload his shotgun, seemingly fearful of what Kenny might do when he heard the news. It was then that he learned that his grandfather—listed as his closest male relative, or "in loco parentis," on his personnel forms—had died. His one anchor at home was gone.

I remember Captain Bennett came up to me and he said, "Neil," and that's when I knew they wanted to get my attention—when they used my first name. [Emotionally laughs.] He said, "Neil, I'm really sorry, but they are sending you home." He said, "You must have—you lived with your grandparents?" I said, "Yeah; yeah, I did." He said, "I hate to see you go home this way, but go home. Your war is over. You've been a great Marine."

Even the battalion colonel, J.W.P. Robertson, approached and told him very much the same thing. His war was over, and he was going home. Kenny recalls the moment with both shock and anguish. He wanted to go home, make no mistake. But he never imagined it would happen this way—due to emergency leave.

The only problem was that Kenny, like all Marines, was slated to serve a thirteen-month tour of duty in Vietnam. So far, he had served approximately nine and a half months. As he rode in the helicopter that afternoon, he felt certain that he would be coming back to both Lima Company and Vietnam. He knew in his bones, he says, that his war was, in fact, not over.

Others in the Marine Corps knew it too. As he was being processed for his leave, a lieutenant gave Kenny the date he was due back in Vietnam. Kenny told him that his commanders in the field had said he was headed home for good. He recalls the lieutenant saying, "Well, the regulation states that if you have 90 days or less on your tour, you do not return to Vietnam. You have 107 days left for a full thirteen-month tour." Kenny argued back.

"Wait a minute. I think I can answer this. I may have been a high school dropout, but I know this much; 90 days or less and I don't come back here. You're giving me 15 days emergency leave. Ninety plus 15, even when I went to school, was 105. So for forty-eight motherfucking hours you're bringing me back here after the colonel and the captain told me I was going home?"

A sympathetic first sergeant standing nearby intervened. He insisted that the lieutenant sign the orders for Kenny's emergency leave while at the same time convincing Kenny to keep his cool. Soon, Kenny was on his way home but with the understanding that he would have to return.

After a long trip from Da Nang, with stops in Okinawa, Alaska, and then South Carolina, Kenny finally arrived at McGuire Air Force Base in New Jersey. Twenty-four hours after leaving the field in Vietnam, he was at his grandmother's apartment on Eighty-Sixth Street in Bay Ridge. He hadn't showered or changed. He was bloody, dirty, and smelled bad. After a shower and a shave, he put on a dress blue Marine Corps uniform a neighbor had arranged for him to borrow from someone stationed in the Brooklyn Navy Yard. It would be the first and only time in his life Kenny would wear a dress uniform.

His recollections of his leave recall the issues many New York soldiers faced when they returned home from Vietnam for good.

Conflict with family members began almost immediately. One uncle offered Kenny a drink, which he understood as an acknowledgment of his maturity and a gesture of respect toward his military service. An aunt immediately objected, claiming that the last time family members came home from a war, World War II in this case, "the boys" drank and "went crazy." After all he had been through, Kenny saw this remark as an affront. He stormed out, walked to a nearby watering hole, and began to drink. His trip from Vietnam to the corner bar took just over twenty-four hours and began a pattern of drinking that would last until Kenny was thirty-two years old.

The funeral service took place at McLaughlin Funeral Home on Ninety-Seventh Street and Third Avenue in Bay Ridge. Kenny says: *This is where my story starts, because it's the beginning of the end, in many ways.*

As he sat smoking a cigarette in the funeral home, Kenny listened to the conversations around him. A family member who had made money in the stock market, "Uncle Bill," a man Kenny describes as a "captain of industry," began to offer his opinions on the war in Vietnam.

Then Bobby Looney, a great name, said, "Oh, Uncle Bill, I don't know, Uncle Bill. If I was going to try to figure out what to do in Vietnam, I'd ask Aunt Regina's son; he's sitting over there. He just came back." And I heard this—I was in earshot and I heard this, and I kind of looked at him and I was kind of like, Well, that was cool. There was some recognition from Bobby. And Uncle Bill goes [mimics puffing on cigar], "What the fuck does he know? He's only a fucking kid."

I'm telling you something, I will never forget that: What the fuck do I know? I'm only a kid. You made a million fucking dollars while this kid was fighting. This kid went and fought that fucking war because growing up and listening to you at Thanksgiving, the Christmas parties, the weddings, and the wakes, you always told us what the right thing to do was. You were just part of the whole bandwagon, "Do the right thing." You were hot dogs, apple pie, and Mom; you were everything—you were Yankee Doodle fucking Dandy. And now I go and I do your dirty work, and then you're going to come back and tell me I'm just a fucking kid; I don't matter for much. To me that was just total devastation . . . that I'm sitting there . . . my grandfather never would have said that; I know that.

He returned to Vietnam ten days later to complete his tour. He was convinced, he remembers, that God had sent him home to make peace with his family. In contrast to his first trip to Vietnam and the sense of adventure it had, he felt this trip would be the end. As it turns out, he was just in time to be part of Operation Meade River.

The official U.S. Marine Corps history of operations in Vietnam states that Meade River "was to be a cordon and search operation under the First Marines, like many which had been conducted previously, but on a much grander scale. Rather than surround and search single hamlets or villages, the division planned a cordon around 36 km² in the Dodge City area, south of Da Nang." The Dodge City area was so named because of its Wild West gunslinging atmosphere. Between November 20, 1968, and December 9, 1968, Marines from the First Marine Division, supported by tactical air, artillery, and helicopter gunships, killed a reported 841 enemy soldiers, capturing 164 weapons. In the twenty-day operation, 106 Marines were killed and 523 wounded.[6]

Whatever the reports say, Kenny has his own interpretation. *It was horrific*, he recalls. *We got our asses kicked.*

According to the official report, veterans of earlier wars who were present stated that it "was the fiercest fighting they had ever seen."[7]

The Marines took heavy casualties, but Kenny distinguished himself, earning the Navy Commendation Medal for his actions on November 23. The first platoon of Lima Company had gotten into trouble; three machine gunners had been shot by North Vietnamese troops, and one machine gun was lost. Despite the presence of a higher-ranking officer, Kenny took charge of the situation.

I took the machine gun, and we took like two thousand rounds of ammo—it was like ten cans of ammo. I said, "You, come with me," and the fucking guy did; there was no question. I went into the middle of this rice paddy with this guy. They still had at that point fire superiority to us.

The lieutenant said, "What are we going to do?" And I said, "Here," and I opened up all the ammo and I said, "Link these rounds." The water was like—like to mid-thigh, the water we were in. He was kind of lying on the bank with half his ass in the water, and he looked at me. It was probably his baptism of fire, so to say. And he was with a guy who didn't give a fuck. It was like, "I'm a dead man; it doesn't matter anymore. I'm already dead."

In his seminal work on Vietnam veterans and PTSD, the psychiatrist Jonathan Shay identifies a state of mind he calls "the berserker state," an emotional condition that combines rage with a complete disregard for personal safety. It would seem to be an apt description of Kenny's state of mind at that moment.

And I looked at the guy and I said, "If I get fucking killed, pick up this gun and keep firing." And I stepped out from behind where we were, and I just fired two thousand fucking rounds; I never stopped firing. And as soon as I fired, almost instantaneously you heard bababoom, bababoom, and all three guns started opening up and it was perfect. It lasted all of like maybe a minute or two minutes, and then we were out of ammo. We went back up, and the Marines had gained control; they were able to get the guys with the maps and the dead and the wounded.

According to the medal citation, Kenny acted "when the lead platoon was pinned down by a heavy volume of fire from a well-entrenched North Vietnamese Army force. Rapidly assessing the situation, Corporal Kenny boldly maneuvered his squad across the fire-swept terrain to a position from which to deliver accurate suppressing fire upon the hostile unit. Ignoring the enemy rounds impacting near him, he skillfully supervised his men in placing their machine guns and, boldly directing their fire upon the enemy soldiers, enabled the Marines to gain fire superiority over the hostile force and evacuate their injured comrades. His bold initiative and resolute determination inspire all who observed him and contributed significantly to the accomplishment of his unit's mission."

As the operation continued, Kenny recalls, he didn't have much time to focus on anything other than the two gun teams under his operational command. But he does remember being concerned about food. As Thanksgiving approached, Kenny remembers making up stories about his mother's cooking, all of which, he concedes, were lies. *My mother couldn't boil water.* But the closer they got to Thanksgiving, the more he looked forward to his turkey dinner. Turkey came in a can. Kenny had stored his away even while, as he puts it, *guys were eating toothpaste on leaves for food.* His group of friends included Phineas, Corporal Richard Dale James, from Shelbyville, Indiana, and maybe two others.

We hadn't eaten in about two or three days. And I said, "Look, man, it's Thanksgiving; we've got to have a feast." And they said, "Who the fuck has got food?" And I said, "Hey, my man," and I whipped out this can of [turkey]. And they say, "Oh, man, you got fucking turkey." I said, "I got turkey. What do you got?" Well, you know, Phin turned out—I think he had like a can of jelly. I said, "Jelly, that's cranberry sauce." I said, "What do you got?" [Another guy] said, "I got bread." I said, "Stuffing, yeah; we got stuffing."

And we had a meal. Between the five of us, we each brought a can of something to that—to that circle—and we cooked it all up, and it's bizarre because we're standing there in this little circle: perfect targets. By then we were arrogant. And we're sitting and everybody took the first fork and it went around—I think it went around four or five or twenty times, I don't know. But we were totally stuffed, and it was like three ounces or four ounces of product, for God's sake.

I can always remember the theology of the fish and the loaves, and we were so fed.

I've always said that the irony of war is that the most inhumane thing known to man, that which we call war, is where we learned our humanity. That's where our humanity comes to us. And it's just the paradox of it.

Sadly, one of the young men who shared that Thanksgiving meal, the kid from Indiana, never made it home to share the story.

I remember James. When [the food] went around, he said, "Wow, I can't believe that." I said, "What—what—what can't you believe? Speak, ass, what are you talking about?" And he said, "I just took the turkey from, you know, from Phin." I was like, "Yeah, so . . ."; it didn't register . . . what does that mean? And he said, "Nobody at home will ever believe me when I tell them that a black man handed me that spoon, I didn't rinse it, and I didn't clean it or throw it away, and I took the food and put it in my mouth, and it went from his mouth to my mouth." And everybody was like, "Yeah, duh. Well, you know." And, you know—but it just struck him—I guess the irony.

I watched him die, too. He never got home. He never got home to tell that.

On December 8, Kenny and his platoon were leaning up against a rice paddy dike when a Marine named Bailey got separated from his squad. Another member of Bailey's squad, David Ned Moore, was stuck on Kenny's side of the dike. With incoming fire passing over their heads, Kenny's squad waited and had cigarettes. Kenny watched as a Marine stood up to throw a hand grenade over the dike and was shot through the hand. Moore came over to complain to Kenny about the situation and asked for a cigarette, which Kenny handed him.

I wasn't looking directly at him and I hear uhhggg, *like that. He had raised his weapon and he started to come up and he got hit right above [the] right eyebrow, and as he fell over, he landed in the dirt. But as he landed, it was like a fire hydrant. [The blood] was gushing, and it was* like, "Oh, man." *I was just covered with fucking blood. I looked and the fucking cigarette was still between his lips and it was like, you know, that's smoke curling up. And the blood just kept going. It was all over.*

And then Bailey said, "Moore, Moore." I said, "Forget it, Bailey; he's hit. Moore is hit." He said, "I'm coming over." I said, "Moore is hit; take over the squad." He said, "I'm coming over. I'm coming over." I said, "Wait, wait, wait." We're screaming. I said, "Before you come over, who's next in command for that squad?" He said, "Why?" I said, "Because when you come over that wall, you're going to be dead like Moore." He never came over. He was sobbing, crying. I felt bad for him. I just knew he—he just lost a part of himself, and he was gone.

By the time the unit returned to base, Kenny was unmanageably angry. He walked back into the tent he had shared with other members of his unit only to find their places already taken by new Marines; there was new gear spread out all over the boxes and bunks once used by men who had been killed and wounded. Kenny reacted by throwing their equipment on the floor and chasing those new men out of the tent, going so far as to throw a knife at one of them who had the temerity to speak up.

Finally, Captain Bennett, who had been his company commander for a significant portion of his tour, approached Kenny. Bennett, by now promoted to major, offered Kenny a promotion to sergeant. At first, not understanding the implications, Kenny accepted. Major Bennett explained that in order to take the stripe and promotion, Kenny would have to stay in Vietnam until the end of his enlistment in June 1969. Kenny responded: *"I can't do that, Skipper. It was pretty bad out there. It was the worst. Skipper, my war's over. I can never go to war again. They can keep their stripe." And he said to me, "You know, Neil, I knew you were going to say that, but I had to ask you."*

When he returned to the United States in January 1969, Kenny felt a strong compulsion to talk about what he had seen. Some members of his family, though, couldn't take what Kenny had to tell them, especially those who had not been in combat. The combat vets, by contrast, were willing to listen. *I always wanted to talk about it,* he says; *everybody told me not to.* In addition, antiwar sentiment was making many

Vietnam veterans feel as though they should be wearing a shroud of shame for their participation in the war. This left Kenny feeling marginalized also. Despite having done what he thought was right, Kenny felt the world believed him to be a bad person for serving there. Jonathan Shay describes the destruction of self-image as one of the central elements of post-traumatic stress disorder. It hit Kenny hard.

Assaults to his dignity began early, starting with his arrival at El Toro Air Force Base in California. Some reservists wanted the returning Vietnam veterans to clean the barracks for an incoming reserve unit. They confronted Kenny and some other Marines. In the end, the staff sergeant making the request found himself thrown out of the barracks, physically, by Kenny and his crew, *ass over teakettle. You're not back seventy-two hours, and people are fucking with you. What is that about?*

By the time he got back to New York for good, his attitude was, *My name is Buck and I don't give a fuck. I did sex, drugs, and rock and roll almost until the age of thirty-two. I drank my way out of more good jobs than most people will ever have the opportunity to have.*

Most likely, he had post-traumatic stress disorder but didn't know it. According to the National Institute of Mental Health, PTSD symptoms can be grouped into three categories: reexperiencing symptoms, avoidance symptoms, and hyperarousal symptoms. Reexperiencing symptoms include bad dreams, flashbacks, and frightening thoughts that cause problems in a person's everyday life. Avoidance symptoms may include staying away from reminders of the original traumatic event, depression, worry, and even a tendency to forget the dangerous event itself. Hyperarousal symptoms include being easily startled, tension, trouble sleeping, and anger management issues. Kenny's PTSD principally seems to take the form of flashes of anger.

One day, his younger brother, Gary, and some friends invited Kenny to join in a stickball game outside the family residence in Bay Ridge. Some kind of dispute began between Gary and one of the other kids. Kenny taunted his younger brother to stand up for himself and fight, telling him, he recalls, *If you don't stand up for yourself, I will kill you.* Apparently, Gary took Kenny at his word and began to fight. At some point, an older boy intervened. Kenny recalls picking up the stickball bat and hitting the older child in the back.

When that bat hit him right in the small of the back, he was, like, frozen. And he just doubled in half backward, like I severed his spine. He went to the ground, and he couldn't even breathe; I took his breath away.

Someone threatened to get the boy's father. Kenny replied: "*You bring your father. I'll kill your father. I'll kill him in front of you and fuck your mother in your house.*"

I should have gone to jail for it. It was criminal assault. That kid was hurt.

Kenny now understands that his early life experiences may have predisposed him to PTSD. Kenny thinks that his father, a World War II veteran who served as a stretcher bearer at the Battle of the Bulge in 1944–45, very likely suffered from his own undiagnosed post-traumatic stress disorder, which also took the form of drinking and violence.

Drinking became a significant element in Kenny's life too. After he returned, his father took him to a Veterans of Foreign Wars post where, Kenny recalls, one of the older World War II members told him that Vietnam was "not a real war." Kenny believes this was a turning point, a social declaration of what his family was already telling him—that he did not matter. His experiences were not relevant, his thoughts not wanted, his presence not welcome. At this point, Kenny began to grow his hair long. Family members began telling him that he had, indeed, died in Vietnam.

Also contributing to his tumultuous return was how difficult it was for veterans to find work in the early 1970s. A study written for the Joint Economic Committee of the U.S. Congress in 1975 concluded that New York City experienced a net population loss between 1960 and 1973 of 1.7 percent. At the same time, private-sector employment appeared to dry up. The report notes that while total private-sector employment grew 7.4 percent nationally, New York City's private-sector employment fell by 6.2 percent. Only Philadelphia and Detroit fared worse.[8]

Kenny had dropped out of high school. Returning home from the Marine Corps in 1969 with his one Purple Heart and a Navy Commendation Medal, he had difficulty finding work. What he did find were low-paying, dead-end-seeming jobs. Without a high school diploma, he felt he didn't have the grounds to object.

Issues related to PTSD began to get in Kenny's way, most especially the drinking. Excess became a theme in his life. Sex, drugs, and alcohol were all available in abundant quantities, and he used them to distance himself from the trauma of his recent past and the people, places, and institutions that he believed were rejecting him. Uncle Frankie, his mother's brother, would see him on the street and walk right past.

Kenny reconnected with his Marine Corps buddy Phineas, who was in California, and decided to visit him. He arrived in San Francisco in the summer of 1969, having left the Marine Corps in January. He remembers seeing Jim Morrison and the Doors perform at the Cow Palace, as well as the Grateful Dead and Janis Joplin and Big Brother and the Holding Company. Somehow, he got mixed up with LSD. As he thinks of it now, drugs were an effort to make the pain go away. *We had this code of good drugs and bad drugs. I was kind of going over to the side where I shouldn't go.*

After about four years of this kind of life, he took steps toward pulling himself together. By 1973 he was a married father of two and twenty-two years old. His father-in-law got him a job with Union Local 3, where he would make good money as an apprentice electrician. But he had to get a haircut for the job. He refused. Kenny faced a host of pressures, *and I think underneath all of that was probably this incredible pain and anger of what I experienced from my eighteenth to my nineteenth year, in the war.*

He had applied to the New York City Police Department when he got out of the Marine Corps but was never called, probably because of the dire financial situation the city found itself in. But in 1974, just as the department was about to close his file, a member of the staff realized that Kenny had relatives on the force. His file was reactivated and a background investigation begun. Kenny recalls that he was smoking marijuana in his house when the background investigator arrived. He took the oath and was sworn in to the police department on February 4, 1974. It didn't work out.

This would trigger a truly bad time in his life. More drinking and more drugs, mostly marijuana, followed.

I was going to hell in a handbasket, and I didn't even necessarily see it. It's always, "Well, it's not my fault; it's her fault." Everything was outside myself, like I wasn't the problem.

As things deteriorated, serious financial need set in, and he had to take a job as a private security officer at the Breezy Point community where he lived. He felt utterly humiliated, working in what he calls a *rinky-dink* job for an ex–police officer.

The New York State Police offered a way out. Kenny became a New York state trooper in 1977 and found the state police force more congenial. Many members of his State Police Academy class had served in the military; they were the first group hired after the end of the hiring freeze of 1975. His wife and children continued to live in the Queens neighborhood of Breezy Point with his in-laws while he commuted to Albany to attend the academy, driving home on weekends. One of the members of his graduating class at the academy had been a childhood friend of William C. Wray, a member of Kenny's squad killed in Vietnam.[9] Finding out about this connection to Billy Wray painfully reminded him of all he had experienced in Vietnam.

I went out that night and got fucking obliterated—I mean obliterated. I came back and I was a mess and I was crying and couldn't believe it.

Despite the troop handler's explanation that drinking could get him terminated, Kenny didn't care. He managed to graduate and made friends in the state police barracks in Peekskill. Many of the other troopers there were roughly his age, even though they had been on the job for a few years and had not been in the service. Drinking, women, and running around became common. He recalls that on one of the first nights out with his new colleagues, they told him to take off his wedding band.

Soon stationed at a different barracks, with older officers, Kenny felt as though he fit right in. But, as he says, *my drinking was off the charts.* He would do a shift from 7:00 a.m. until 3:00 p.m. and by 3:15 would be at the Fishkill Inn, drinking. Sometimes he couldn't even drive back to the station house and would need to phone for a lift.

I was living this wonderful life. I had a wife with three kids at one place. I was working somewhere else. I had all the booze I wanted. If I wanted drugs, I could get all the drugs I wanted. Nobody would ask any questions.

But it wasn't enough.

There was this fucking huge emptiness inside of me. There was a hole where my soul and my heart should be and it was just gone.

Eventually, Kenny began to run into trouble on the job because of his drinking. Civilians complained of abuse. On one occasion, he attended the St. Patrick's Day Parade in Manhattan and then a Patrolmen's Benevolent Association party. Apparently, the alcohol flowed freely, and Kenny pulled his weapon on a New York City police officer.

In another incident he got into an argument with a man at a bar, pulled out a revolver, and stuck it in the man's mouth.

I have a trigger cocked, and I had a hammer back; I mean, if somebody had said "Don't," it could have gone off. I said, "I'll blow your fucking brains out if you don't shut the fuck up." And he just stood there like that, and I just put it away. It wasn't necessarily the case that it was my intent, but there wasn't a control to realize, you know, you can deal with this with words. And I guess, really I was drunk, but that's not an excuse, because the drink or the drug or whatever the fuck it was, was something you choose to do.

His substance abuse had damaged his reputation on the job, and his anger problem had earned him no real friends. He began to lose his will to live.

I was just empty; I was totally empty. I thought, "Well, I fucked everything else up." I had fucked the marriage. People don't like us, because we went to war. Whatever you did that was right was wrong—it didn't matter.

At one point, he devised a plan to kill himself while pretending to be in pursuit of another automobile, thereby providing his wife and children with substantial insurance money. On another occasion, he thought about using a service revolver.

One morning, instead of committing suicide, he decided to leave a note on his lieutenant's desk: *I just want to advise you that I can no longer be responsible for what I'm doing and I need some help.*

Kenny left the note at 7:15 a.m., and by 9:30 a.m. troopers had tracked him down and brought him back to the barracks. Because he could not be placed into an inpatient treatment center until Sunday, Kenny asked to work with a fellow Vietnam veteran during his weekend shift. He felt comfortable in a fellow veteran's presence, as though someone who knew what he had been through would be able to help him over the ensuing thirty-six hours. By the time the state police offered him two weeks of inpatient therapy, he had begun to persuade himself that things were not really so bad. He took the offer of inpatient therapy, conning himself, as he says now, into thinking that *maybe the fucking heat will pass, you know, and I'll stay away for two weeks and I'll be okay. I can get my breath and go forward again.*

On September 14, 1980, a fellow officer took Kenny to Villa Veritas, an inpatient drug and alcohol addiction treatment program in the Catskills town of Kerhonkson, New York. Later one of the counselors there told him that in the first two weeks of his residence, the staff had serious doubts about his ability to successfully recover from his alcoholism. He was told, "We really thought you belonged in the insane asylum."

Originally scheduled to stay only two weeks, Kenny was persuaded to stay for three. He participated in group meetings, where the members went around the circle and introduced themselves as alcoholics. In the third week, Kenny suddenly felt differently about doing so.

That was devastating. I remember that moment because that was the acceptance of what I am.

Soon, his wife served him with divorce papers. That very same day one of his fellow troopers delivered the paperwork containing the charges and specifications that had been filed against Kenny by the New York State police force. Disciplinary proceedings followed, but Kenny knew the job was gone before the hearing. He recalls an older woman at Villa Veritas saying: *If God didn't want you to stay there, no force in the universe can keep you there. There's a reason and purpose.*

He understood.

Eventually, he would learn that the state police thought he had been involved with the murder of a drug dealer in Breezy Point, and had even tested his service revolver to see if they could identify a ballistic connection. They failed to demonstrate any connection between Kenny and the killing.

In the end, Kenny had no money and nowhere to go. He asked the staff if he could stay at Villa Veritas. They agreed.

He had arrived in September 1980 as a New York state trooper. He would leave in January 1981 with no job, no family, no home, and no bank account. Nothing.

But I was sober, and probably for the first time in my life I was like, you know, it's going to be okay.

He ended up in Jersey City for a while, staying with his sister and attending meetings of Alcoholics Anonymous. He slowly began to rebuild his life. Tom Dillon, first deputy commissioner of the New York City Fire Department, learned about Kenny's predicament and got him a job with the department as a confidential investigator, a CI-2, with the Internal Affairs Division. Soon he had an apartment on Eighty-Sixth Street in Bensonhurst and sole custody of his children.

I had a living room and one bedroom and bathroom, and there was nobody above us and just the store below us. We made a go of it there.

After completing a bachelor's degree in sociology at Brooklyn College in 1985, Kenny left the fire department, taking a job as a high school teacher in the New York City public school system. He retired in 1995 after another explosion of rage forced him to consult a Veterans Administration psychiatrist. He now receives a PTSD-related disability pension from the VA.

With the passage of time, Kenny feels that he has gained a perspective on PTSD that he now willingly shares, especially with fellow Marines. Reflecting on his experiences in Alcoholics Anonymous and the nature of post-traumatic stress disorder, he explains what he calls "the triangle of life." For him, life is made up of a mental/emotional component, a physical component, and a spiritual component, the three sides of the triangle. *All of those things were damaged by PTSD and by life.*

In 2005 he heard a story about Jason Dunham, a Marine who

sacrificed himself in Iraq by throwing his body onto a live grenade to save fellow Marines. Dunham had lingered for a few days, making it to the Walter Reed National Military Medical Center, where his parents managed to see him before he died. Kenny and a number of volunteers have set up a foundation in his memory, the Jason L. Dunham Scholarship Foundation, which raises money to pay for the education of young returning Marines.

In 2006, I traveled with Kenny to a Khe Sanh veterans reunion in Washington, D.C. We spent the weekend visiting the brand-new National Museum of the Marine Corps and the Vietnam Veterans Memorial and seeing some of his old friends. On the Sunday afternoon before our return to New York City, we stopped at the bookstore in Marine Corps Base Quantico, across the river from D.C., in Virginia. There, we met a young Marine, Jeremiah Workman, who had served in Fallujah in 2004 as a part of Operation Phantom Fury, the Second Battle of Fallujah in the Iraq War.

On December 23, 2004, Workman had led his mortar platoon into a building three times in order to rescue isolated Marines who had been trapped by an ambush. At least twenty-four insurgents were killed in the fight.[10] Later, Workman was awarded the Navy Cross for his action. Kenny and Workman fell into conversation, and we invited Workman and his wife to join us for dinner. Over steaks, Kenny and Workman began to share their experiences with post-traumatic stress. To this day he and Workman are in constant contact. This young veteran has become part of the fabric of his life.

For Kenny, this represents the passing of a torch. A new generation of Marines and other veterans is returning from Iraq and Afghanistan, and soon there will be many more who need and deserve the kind of help Vietnam veterans did not receive forty-odd years ago.

Vietnam is never very far away for many of these veterans. One counselor told Kenny, "You have an awful lot of grieving to do. You're not done grieving." Kenny replied: *"I don't know if I ever will be."*

14

LEADERSHIP: VINCE McGOWAN

As Neil Kenny's story demonstrates, returning Vietnam veterans would in some cases be rebuffed by the very institutions meant to support them—like the Veterans of Foreign Wars. Many men I interviewed echoed Kenny's sentiments and experiences. *The New York Times* ran a story on October 14, 1974, about the sense of rejection that many veterans felt. According to the article, at three o'clock in the morning, thirty-five veterans huddled around a fire in an open trash can, drinking coffee, sleeping, and sharing sandwiches in front of a veterans assistance center in downtown Brooklyn. The men had been waiting over fifteen hours in hopes of meeting with a caseworker. A twenty-four-year-old veteran from the Bronx told the papers, "I fought in the war for two years and no one gives a damn." According to statistics cited in the story, about 25,000 of the 330,000 Vietnam veterans living in New York City were unemployed, with 7,000 of them on welfare. "It seems like we are still fighting, except this time it's for our dignity," said one veteran, wrapping himself in a sleeping bag.[1]

The lawyer, author, and Vietnam veteran Eric Dean disputes the "abandoned and abused veteran" theme in veterans' narratives, asserting that Vietnam veterans were in fact welcomed home no less warmly than veterans of earlier wars.[2] The difficult issue, however, is not the behavior of the majority of the American population, although there was probably greater variation in attitudes than Dean allows. As the Bacolos' story made clear, the real issue is that many veterans *believed*, and continue to believe, that they were not treated well. As Bernard Edelman put it: *We were not welcomed home into the arms of a grateful nation.*

That perception is more important than any number of "welcome home" parades or the dollar amount of veterans' benefits received.

Eventually, some veterans realized they would have to fight for the recognition and services they believed their due. It was a relatively young generation of men who would come forward to serve as leaders of the emerging veterans' community, especially in New York City. One veteran who stands out in this regard is Vince McGowan, the founding president of the resurrected New York City United War Veterans Council. For McGowan, leadership was a natural outgrowth of his military experience. He describes himself this way:

I can figure it out, I can actually make it happen; it is a situation, and I will deal with it, right? I would never ask somebody to do something I won't do, and that includes work today or any of the jobs that I have had.

Born in 1945, at St. Clare's Hospital in Manhattan, McGowan grew up with his family on Forty-Ninth Street and Ninth Avenue, in the neighborhood known as Hell's Kitchen. His mother ran a tearoom on Sixty-Fifth Street in the area now dominated by Lincoln Center. (At the time the neighborhood was called San Juan Hill.) Later the family moved to 143rd Street and Broadway, an area heavily populated by German Jews. He attended All Hallows and Cathedral High Schools before ending up at Lincoln High School. He joined the Marine Corps at age seventeen.

McGowan says he joined, in part, because of the Kennedy assassination. *That really pissed me off,* he says. Kennedy was killed November 22, 1963. McGowan was in Parris Island for U.S. Marine Corps Recruit Training by January 1964. He admits, however, that the Kennedy assassination was also something of an excuse. At the time, he remembers feeling as though he lacked purpose in his life, *spending more time getting out of trouble than doing anything that's good.*

He broke out of that by joining the Marine Corps. As a fairly independent young man, McGowan had spent his summers wandering the beaches at the Jersey shore or the Rockaways in Queens, finding unoccupied bungalows to sneak into and spend the night. Because of this independent streak, he feels that his parents couldn't have stopped him from joining the military; he was about to leave home anyway, one way or another.

McGowan took his tough New York City attitude into the Marine Corps and did very well there, earning the Dress Blue Award for the outstanding new Marine in his platoon. He loved it. He found it rigorous, but the discipline was good for him. Because of the award, McGowan had his choice of duty stations. He chose sea duty, ending up on the USS *Little Rock*, a guided-missile cruiser. He traveled all over the world, above the Arctic Circle, across the equator, and through European waters. McGowan says: *I saw parts of the world that I would have never seen otherwise.*

He has chipped ice off a ship's mast in the Arctic, experienced hurricanes out at sea, and had other *life-altering experiences that every young man and woman should have the opportunity to experience.*

Promoted to sergeant, McGowan ended up in Vietnam in 1966. *You know, all you had to do was say, "Yeah, I'll go,"* he says. While his decision to go to Vietnam seems to lack drama, his arrival there certainly didn't.

First assigned to replacement duties, McGowan was sent to the outpost at Ban Me Thuot, the capital of Dak Lak province. He recalls the arrival by helicopter.

They were being overrun, and I was in the number two helicopter. The first helicopter coming in got shot down, and I'll never forget watching that. I'm in the door and I'm in charge of about fifteen guys, and that thing gets hit and just disintegrates.

From the air, he could see the battlefield and the Special Forces camp. It had a concrete bunker on the top of a knoll with clear fields of fire. There was barbed wire around the perimeter. As they came in, they could see the battle. His unit landed on one side of the hill as the enemy was coming up the other side. It would turn out to be one very long day and night, but the lessons learned would stay with him for life.

We got filled in on the line with the Special Forces guys and the indigenous soldiers that they had, and we held for the night until relief came the next day. That was my first experience with actually having to live-fire against a very determined enemy. It teaches you a lesson. Never assume that what you're doing is going to work. Always act as if it is on the brink of failure, because it is. And be prepared to have to adjust as you're going down.

Perhaps fine-tuned by his New York City upbringing, he learned quickly to trust his instincts for survival. As fierce as the firefights were, McGowan also came away from Vietnam incredibly impressed with the spectacular beauty of the landscape.

I recall one time we were lost. In order to figure out what we wanted to do, me and another guy climbed to the top of the tree. [We got] to the top of this tree and got to the top of the canopy and just looked out across this unbelievably beautiful valley to try to figure out where the hell we were. You had to get up to something high, because when you're down there, it's like being in a basement with no lights on. Like I said, it was beautiful, but it was dangerous. I'll never forget the water coming down from the top of a mountain. We were crossing streams that had boulders moving on the bottom of them. The force of the water was so terrific that [there were] boulders underwater, around your feet.

But he also remembers the physical labor involved in just getting around the countryside.

It would rain hard up there, and all of a sudden you'd get flash floods, but the easiest place to travel was down at the bottom of this ravine. You always ended up at the bottom of this goddamn thing because gravity is taking you down it and it's easier [to walk down hills than up]. You keep on pushing up and you're whacked and your arms are getting tired and you're pulling yourself up on these vines and the ants are running down your arms, leeches . . . [and it's] hot—hot—suffocatingly hot, and you're all dressed up in your bulletproof vest, and you're carrying your seventy pounds of stuff, grenades and rifles and M79s . . .

McGowan's family had emigrated from Ireland within living memory. He had heard the stories of how difficult rural farm life was. He understood, in a way many American soldiers did not, the Vietnamese villagers.

My family are farmers, you know; I remember a story my grand-mother told me about the Black and Tans [paramilitary forces that worked to repress Irish nationalists] coming to take the young men. [Families] used to hide them out in the fields. I arrived in Ireland as a military guy, the one time I met them, and that brought up stories. We'd sit around at night and talk about it. So you know, then I go to Vietnam and I'm looking at these people, and they are dirt-poor. Whatever they are eating they just grew or caught; there's no electricity, no refrigera-tion, there's none of that stuff. So, I'm not that far [away from it]. There's no disconnect for me.

As a result, McGowan identified intensely with his next assign-ment. Before American combat involvement in the war, the Vietnam-ese government had tried implementing local defense initiatives. One such attempt was known as the Strategic Hamlet Program, in which Vietnamese farmers would be moved off their land, out of their homes, and into a centralized location. The thinking was that it would be eas-ier to defend these centralized communities and keep the population safe, rather than trying to protect scattered individual hamlets.

The Vietnamese Communists made propaganda out of the initia-tive, charging that South Vietnamese civilians were being rounded up and put into the equivalent of concentration camps. The Strategic Ham-let Program gave way to another plan: squads of Marines called Com-bined Action Platoons (CAPs) would be sent out to the villages, where they could have access to elected officials or village representatives. The job of the Marine Corps was to develop an indigenous national guard, a ready defense force.

McGowan's CAP unit was assigned to protect a small hamlet that was just outside another, somewhat larger, town that was being guarded by a second unit of Marines. At one point, McGowan likely saved the lives of the men in the second unit.

I was out on patrol with my platoon, and we set up in an ambush position, and I could hear these guys coming. All of a sudden there were like fifteen guys coming down the trail. There must have been thirty of us in an L-shaped ambush position.

But McGowan's instincts told him something was wrong, and he refused to allow his squad leader to begin the ambush. They would soon discover that the men coming down the trail were not Vietcong; they were a patrol of American soldiers from nearby Fort Page. As a result of the incident, McGowan's squad leaders reported to the captain that McGowan was afraid. He had failed to carry out his order to ambush anyone coming down the trail. Because he was a relatively new guy, the question became, who had been in the wrong place at the wrong time—McGowan's squad or the men coming out of Fort Page? In the end, they learned that the men coming out of Fort Page had patrolled the wrong pattern. To prove it, McGowan had to take the captain and his officers back to the position of the ambush.

We walked across these sand dunes; it's five miles. This is not a walk in the park. And those sand dunes are big, and you've got to have strong legs to plow through them. But you have to prove your point. I mean, you can't take these things lying down.

Being proven right helped McGowan advance. *The result is that I became the commanding officer of a Combined Action Platoon as a sergeant.*

McGowan is enormously proud of his service in the Combined Action Platoon. He had the men he needed, the necessary weapons, and the authority to use them. And as a New Yorker, he wasn't going to mess around. The success of his unit is documented in Bing West's book *The Village*. It is a history of how small-unit tactics worked in Vietnam.

We were the first successful CAP unit. We took the territory. We had elections. We got rid of the corrupt officials. The regional defense forces that we developed, the 350 guys, were able to protect themselves. They were able to hold the line and put up a fight, account for their weapons, instill discipline in their ranks from leaders who were not susceptible to corruption. That's how we define success. People wanted us.

I actually burned the police chief's house down. He wasn't getting the message. Here was a guy who, every time we would bring in either the load of cement to fix the school or whatever, he would fix his well, build his house, buy a second herd of ducks, with the American money. When he finally lost his house, he got the idea that we were very serious about that. And it gets to that level; I mean, it always gets back to the street area, you know, how things happen in the toe-to-toe world.

At twenty-one years old, McGowan had three stripes and was in charge of 350 men. He had no education for the job, just street smarts and his experience as a Golden Gloves boxer in New York City.

I think I got a lot of it from living in New York. It's one of the reasons that I chose to raise my sons here. I think that this environment can give you a lot of tools, if you're willing to engage, if you're willing to extend yourself.

After leaving the Marine Corps, he worked first for the Rand Corporation, in Guatemala and southern Mexico. (McGowan declined to tell me more about this period of his life.) Later he returned to the United States and operated a bar in Southern California, which, according to McGowan, was a lot of fun in the early 1970s. A social guy, he found he liked operating nightclubs and bars. By 1973, he had returned to New York. He owned and ran a place called McGowan's Alley on the West Side of Manhattan.

I put an after-hours club in there that was the hottest after-hours club in the city. We had a lot of fun. I actually had Bruce Willis as a bartender for a while in one of the clubs that I had.

Despite being social, there were moments he felt alone.

Everyone I know who went to Vietnam either came back all screwed up and I didn't really want to know him or was killing himself, a slow suicide with drugs and alcohol.

As veterans began to find one another, McGowan became instrumental in the process. The inaugural meeting of New York City's first chapter of the Vietnam Veterans of America took place at the YMCA on Sixty-Third Street in 1983. The YMCA gave them a room, and they put out a call by word of mouth. A small group of men showed up. None of them knew each other at all, but they had one thing in common: they all seemed to be seeking a connection with other veterans who understood what they had been through. McGowan asserts that without other veterans it was too easy to be sad, lonely, and sometimes desperate and fall into bad habits.

You're angry, you're hurt physically, [you were] certainly wounded mentally, even if not physically, and you're listening to the paper every day telling you what a jerk you are.

The sense of loneliness that seemed to become a theme for so many Vietnam veterans came, from McGowan's perspective, because *everybody wanted to be on your side, but nobody wanted to do anything substantive. So you end up very much alone.*

These veterans found one another as a matter of self-preservation. The Vietnam Veterans of America grew out of a desire to create connections between veterans and society at large. For McGowan, what's especially interesting about this particular organization is that it is largely run by enlisted men, without the help of officers.

The officers seemed to just move on; they want to forget about it.

Some men had done well after Vietnam, achieving success to varying degrees, like Robert Ptachik and Richard Eggers. Many, however, were continuing to struggle. Combat veterans in particular seemed to have the most trouble adjusting to civilian life.

McGowan, the founding president of VVA Chapter 126 and leader of the original group, recalls that they all felt *very strongly as combat veterans that we were misunderstood, that we had been maligned, that the system was against us, that our story was not being told. There was a lot of sensationalism but not a lot of facts being represented, and the only stories that were getting out were the horror stories.*

In the very beginning, one of the first obstacles the VVA faced was an internal conflict. The veterans pushing to get a charter from Congress as a veterans' service organization were not combat veterans, but had served in other capacities. McGowan felt that they were looking to use the organization to lobby for veterans' rights and benefits. This was, he thought, a valuable thing to do, *but it doesn't help the individual who needed help at the time.*

In contrast, McGowan and his colleagues wanted the organization to focus on providing services. This was necessary, in his opinion, because the public attitude toward Vietnam veterans was one of *distrust, disregard, and contempt. I've had the experience of being asked to leave American Legion halls because [they said], "You're not really a veteran; you're from Vietnam."*

In the early days the organization would spend ten or fifteen minutes doing business and then head for a local bar. They would spend the evening telling stories and discussing issues that affected them.

By the early 1980s, with unemployment still an issue, knowing how to work with computers had become a marketable job skill. But many veterans didn't possess that skill. The city and its job market shifted profoundly in the 1950s and 1960s. As "white flight" drew mostly older workers to suburban areas, the city's white population declined from 87 percent in 1950 to 67 percent in 1970. African Americans began arriving in larger numbers, while the city also experienced a significant immigration of Puerto Ricans. At the same time, factories like the foundry where Anthony Wallace's father, Ben, had worked were disappearing. In 1950, manufacturing jobs accounted for 33.6 percent of the available employment in New York City. By the time Anthony Wallace returned home with a Purple Heart in 1970, these types of jobs would make up only 23.5 percent of the total jobs available. The manufacturing sector was hit particularly hard between 1969 and 1972, shedding forty-nine thousand such jobs and declining by 8.3 percent in 1971 alone.[3]

By the time New York City's veterans came home, it was extremely difficult to find a blue-collar job, let alone make a living wage.

The marketplace was changing. Guys like myself, and most of the guys who were in this community, had fairly typical 1950s, early-'60s skills. I could fix a carburetor, and I could install windows. I could do a lot of stuff administratively, but all that died while we were away. By the time you come back, the world has changed. I mean, the materials you would use were junk-tiques and you were a junk-tique, you know, and that's real.

In other words, his skills had become junk and antique at the same time. As the decade of the 1970s slipped into the 1980s, a chronic employment problem for veterans became a crisis. As a result, McGowan and others participated in the Vietnam Veterans Leadership Program, where they learned to use computers and upgraded their skills.

At the time of our first interview in 2005, McGowan was deeply involved with encouraging the Marine Corps to continue utilizing the small-unit concept; he believed the Combined Action Platoon he'd served in was a good model for counterinsurgency. In his opinion, putting military men among the ordinary people of Iraq and allowing them to help the people *who want to be helped, and give them the authority and the equipment and the support to get it done,* is an effective tactic. He says that his own son served with the Second Battalion, Seventh Marines, because he believes in that mission, too.

McGowan talked about some of the fluctuations in the organization. In the late 1970s and early 1980s, Vietnam Veterans were in their thirties, seeking like-minded veterans with whom they could share their experiences. Later there was a plateau as these men aged. Then, as they reached their early fifties, there was a rejuvenation, coinciding with the 1990s, the first Gulf War, and the fact that some men began to retire at that age. Currently, interest in the chapter seems to have waned again.

Today, McGowan is the chief operating officer at Battery Park City Parks Conservancy in lower Manhattan, overseeing a staff of more than 150 and a $12 million budget. He is also the president of the United War Veterans Council, the organization that puts on the annual Veterans Day Parade in Manhattan—the nation's largest. He sits on the mayor's Veterans Advisory Board and has received the Outstanding Civilian Service Medal from the secretary of the Army.

Despite taking pride in his efforts over the years, at times McGowan still feels a deep sense of loss.

Some of the best and brightest, in my view, of the Vietnam veterans are long dead, or long incarcerated because society couldn't handle them. They're lost to the world in so many different ways.

15

THE DIVERSITY OF THE VETERAN EXPERIENCE

The long-term consequences of service in Vietnam for veterans are defined by physical and psychological changes, as well as by the ways that veterans approach their public and private worlds. Their minds and bodies changed as a result of service, as did their interactions with friends, families, and the world at large.

Physical changes took a variety of forms, of which wounds are the most obvious. Other physical changes, like heart disease and the variety of illnesses connected to Agent Orange exposure, took longer to become evident.

The discussion of psychological changes brought about by service in Vietnam has been dominated by the literature on post-traumatic stress disorder, and indeed PTSD loomed large in my interviews. The disorder has affected perhaps 30 percent of American Vietnam veterans at one time or another in their lives, leading sometimes to substance abuse, violence, and divorce. But other kinds of changes, including increased self-esteem and pride, have resulted as well.

Finally, interviews with New York City's Vietnam veterans make clear that military service has connected many veterans to their wider communities, providing instruction on citizenship, commitment, and selflessness that has lasted a lifetime.

For some veterans, the long-term significance of Vietnam lies in what it did to their health. Tony Velez, whose father served for four years during World War II, grew up in the Cypress Hills housing project in Brooklyn and vividly recalls the ethnic and racial antagonism directed at him and all the other Puerto Rican kids he went to school with. There was *a pretty hostile environment in the community, in the church, in the public school*, he remembers. Drafted into the military, he served with the Blackhorse Regiment, the Eleventh Armored Cavalry Regiment, as an engineer.

Now a professor of fine arts at Kean University in New Jersey, Velez explains what Agent Orange, one of several defoliants used in Vietnam, did to his health:

I suffer from a residue of Agent Orange exposure in Vietnam, and it's been defined in terms of cancer for me . . . and I've had it now for at least nine years. I had an operation nine years ago when it was detected. I've had radiation last year, and this year it seems that the cancer is still active in my body. Where it is, no one knows. President Clinton, about six months after I had my prostate out nine years ago in 1994—in August, I actually had the operation—about six months later, I noticed that he—in The New York Times—*he had signed the bill allotting benefits and compensation to veterans who had prostate cancer and a whole other slew of cancers that are connected to exposure [to Agent Orange]. Large numbers of veterans are coming down with these kinds of cancers, and early in their lives. I happen to have been forty-six years old when it was detected, and I volunteered, I asked my doctor, actually, to take some blood out of me extra.*

Anyone who knows anything about prostate cancer knows it's a very, very slow-growing cancer. Therefore, to get to a number of nine or ten at age forty-six quite simply means that I had it in my body for some time. I probably had it, I suspect, somewhere in my early forties, maybe my late thirties. No one can really say exactly. And it's still around. It's known that many of these cancers from environmental causes show up twenty, twenty-five years later. I'm right on the money. I'm right in there. I came out at twenty from the United States Army in Vietnam, and I was forty-six when it was discovered at a very high rate, and it's a slow-growing cancer that needed a long time to gain a critical mass to be picked up, and it was picked up, you know, in a sky-high number; then it's been with me for some time. So there's an obvious connection there.

When I interviewed him in 2005, Velez emphasized that the benefits he received from the Veterans Administration were inadequate. At that time they were paying him $81 a month in compensation for the loss of an organ (his prostate). His brothers, both of whom served in the military—one in Germany and the other in Vietnam—received more in the way of financial compensation than he did. He felt fortunate that he had a good insurance policy through his employer, which permitted him to get and pay for the necessary medical treatments, including surgery, radiation, and testing.

At the same time, when we spoke, Velez was doing well. That day, he said, was a good day. As an artist, he works to find ways of dealing with his illness. He teaches, speaks with groups and classes, and more. At this point, cancer has become part of his life, and he has tried to learn how to accept it and live with it.

I get educated. I read a lot about my cancer, about issues related to the war, to the past. I look at the past. I reevaluate it. I think about myself. And being a teacher, it's incorporated into my curriculum because as a photographer, as an artist, there's a big chunk of photography called war photography that has existed from the beginning of the invention of the medium. And, of course, all artists and all art forms have expressed war, and every civilization depicts war through its sculpture, its painting, in one way or the other.

And so I do my part, and I'm able to communicate my own feelings, my own personal experiences, in my own classes when it comes to that area. And I can bring in my own photographs, and I talk in a very personal way about it.

John Hamill, among many others, makes the connection between Agent Orange and the ability to have children. His story, in contrast to many, has a positive outcome. Hamill served as a medic with the 173rd Airborne Brigade in Vietnam and returned in 1968.

My daughter is ten, and it took us fourteen years to have her. That was another Vietnam hangover. I got dosed with Agent Orange. It was a low-grade infection that was exacerbating things like dioxin. [The doctor] was like a genetic detective. He's the only one who ever took a thorough medical history, and it took him all of about three months, and then we were able to do the gift, you know, the in vitro thing. But fourteen years for having kids. So, you know, for me it's like a gift.

Paul DeSaro, who volunteered to serve in the Army in 1966 and served with the 303rd Radio Research Battalion in Vietnam, now has Agent Orange–related type 2 diabetes. *Because of my diabetes and related diseases caused by being exposed to Agent Orange, the Veterans Administration provides the medications to treat me.*

I am taking two types of insulin [fast-acting and long-lasting] to control the spread of this disease. My legs, eyes, and vascular system are slowly deteriorating due to my exposure to Agent Orange, which caused my diabetes. Now that I am retired and have more time on my hands, I am starting to remember events that I had forgotten, or the impact it had on me at the time it happened. For example, ammo sites being blown up very close to where I was camped. I am experiencing how I felt then, instead of just recording the event in my mind.

I am fearful that large crowds make a desirable target [for terrorism], so I avoid any function with large crowds. When I can't, I am always mindful of where the exits are and anyone who gets too close to me. I count the minutes [until] I can leave and feel relieved when I do.

I am very claustrophobic now and just recently needed to take an MRI to detect if there is any cancer in my hip area. I was on the table to go into the MRI (sweating so much the attendant had to wipe my face and head several times), and I panicked to the point where I refused to go any further and had to stop the procedure.

I am thankful that the VA recognizes these problems and is helping me through them.

Other veterans wounded in Vietnam count themselves as lucky. Ray Robertson, from Staten Island, lost a leg in the Cobi Than Tan Valley. I asked him how he felt about being a badly wounded Vietnam veteran, one of 300,000. His reply astonished me.

Badly wounded? Not! I went to [visit] this friend at St. Albans [Naval Hospital, now St. Albans Primary and Extended Care Center, in Queens, New York], who was on the neurology ward. Something similar to mine:

he had been shot in the elbow and the nerve had been severed, but not too badly. They thought they could get it back together, which they did. So I go up to the neurology ward, and he's the only guy in the ward sitting up. Everyone else in the ward is in a fetal position, being fed intravenously, because they have a head wound. I left that fucking ward and I said, "If I hear anybody complaining about anything, I'm going to drag them up to that fucking ward and show them what could have been. That's even worse than being on the wall." Not that there was [a] wall then.

As he thinks of it now, he wonders: *Where are these people now? Are they still hooked up? Are they dead? It really blew my mind. Where did all those head-injury guys go? And that was a little hospital; imagine what the big hospitals had. I don't consider myself as having been badly damaged.*

If already present, PTSD can be triggered by exposure to a new trauma. It's not surprising, perhaps, that a number of New York City police officers and firefighters who are Vietnam veterans retired after 9/11. For other men and women, life since Vietnam has been defined by their experiences coping with PTSD.

Henry Burke, who received a Bronze Star with a *V* for valor for his actions in 1966, remarked in 2004:

My personal opinion is, it seems as the veterans get older, and they start retiring, they have more time to think. I think this is why more people, or more veterans, are coming forward with post-traumatic stress disorder—because they have time on their mind to reflect back, whereas before, most of us were working. Our day was taken up by our occupations and stuff, so you just kind of put it in the back and you forgot about it.

Another reason, I think, is I was never debriefed when I came out of the service, so you kind of took it in stride. Anything that was abnormal you just felt was normal, that this is what happens, right? As we went on and grew older, we found out by associating with other veterans that no, this is not true. I mean, I found out in 2000 that I was suffering from post-traumatic stress.

Lucian Vecchio, who grew up in Queens and, like Hamill, served with the 173rd Airborne Brigade, is now an administrative law judge. He speaks with candor about his struggles:

We all have the PTSD. In my opinion, it's just a matter of degree. I have it to a relatively high degree.

Aggression chases fear. Anger chases sadness. So when you get that whack on the back, and you're stiff, and you're sad, and you say, "What do we do now?" and someone says, "We get payback," that's anger chasing depression. So anger and aggression become important tools. They are cultivated.

We didn't have enough food. We literally didn't have enough food when we were paratroopers in Nam. That's not true now. We really were always hungry. And they'd say, "Keep you lean and mean." Lean and mean. You're hungry, you're angry.

The next time I hear an explosion and a cry, I'm going to run to that as quickly as I can. And I revisit that. And I revisit that. And I revisit that. Why? Because if there's an explosion and a cry, I don't want to be the last one there. It's a pride thing.

That's the aspect of PTSD and the Vietnam experience that is of significance now. Vietnam is gone in one way but remains profoundly present in another.

As New York City's Vietnam veterans evaluate the long-term significance of Vietnam in their lives, the experience becomes something like a kaleidoscope—a single event understood in a vast number of often contradictory ways.

Louis Marcello, who grew up in Brooklyn and served with the Fourth Infantry Division, 1967–68, loved his time in the service and the men with whom he fought, despite his wounds. He felt then and feels now a deep bond with the people in his unit.

I loved Vietnam. That's the only thing that put a damper on it— seeing so many of my, my friends getting wounded. It was the people I was with. I loved the people I was with.

Some veterans, like John Di Sanza, value their experiences in the military highly. Di Sanza, who grew up in the Bronx and now lives in Florida, is an artist and author. He says:

I tell you, you know, it turned out, as strange as it may seem, it turned out to be the best thing I ever did for myself, because I'm at this point right now, with all the suffering and things I've gone through in my life, I would not be where I am. You know, I've got a wonderful family; I've got wonderful children. I've got a wonderful wife. I'm an artist; I'm a writer. I mean, if I didn't go, who only knows what would have happened to me? You know, I might have been dead.

John Flanagan, who served as a combat helicopter pilot in Vietnam with the First Cavalry Division and went on to participate in the development of military training devices, thinks military service was a key element in his life. It, and Vietnam, gave him the opportunity to mature.

I told you about growing up in Brooklyn and didn't think I was ever going to see anything more than New Jersey probably. I wasn't going to be anything more than probably a civil servant someplace just making it through. It's changed me; it's given me confidence; it's given me something to be. Nobody can take away from me the time that I was an Army helicopter pilot . . . not only an Army helicopter pilot: in combat, and in the best damn unit going, bar none.

I know everybody has got fears and stuff like that, but it's how you cope with it, you know, and I'm probably a calmer person because I don't have to show people what I'm doing. I've thought things out. Also, I got pretty good situation awareness. It's about knowing what I'm going to do in any situation. I mean, it gave me confidence; it gave me an education; it gave me a sense of an environment where I could stand up and speak my mind and say this is right and this is wrong. The Army has given me an awful lot.

Others are forced to measure the costs of their service. Speaking of a friend, Frank Arce, a Marine from the Bronx, recalls:

Johnny failed out of school, and the next thing you know, he was driving trucks in the Nam and he ran over a land mine. Whoever it was that was with him got blown up and got killed. When I came back from the Nam, I went to visit Johnny, and Johnny was a vegetable—realistically, he was a vegetable. His kids had been born vegetables—Agent Orange— and we didn't even know what the hell that was back then, you know, in '69 and '70 coming home. We had no idea what the hell is Agent Orange.

I mean, I'm sure we had seen it sprayed or whatever, but who knew your kid was going to be born, you know, with one eye or whatever the case might be or mentally unstable, you know. I guess that was the hardest part to swallow of the war—we lost not only so many guys over there but so many guys over here who came and were able to make it back, and most of them, I bet you if you asked them, they probably will tell you, "I wish I had died back then."

Peter Meloro echoes the feeling of many when he articulates the value of military service.

The one thing the Army taught me . . . you learn . . . in basic training when, you know, they take you as an individual and shave your head and, you know, put everyone in the same clothes so that everyone looks like a twin, you know, for the most part and then started beating you down individually. Not physically, but mentally beating you down in an effort to reduce the individual and create the team. It's an extreme example, [but because of it] I think I've understood the team concept in business. Normally, if you get everybody on the same page, [you are] much more successful . . . I don't think I understood [that] in basic training. These people are nuts, I thought, who were in basic training.

But after a while, you know, afterward as you grow and you move on, you say, "That's the reason." Just to lose the individuality and create the team so that everyone's got everybody's back and everyone is working together for a common goal. That's good in areas of business, so from that perspective . . .

But it is a view that has relevance well beyond the business sphere. In November 2003, Al Singerman, a Brooklyn native and past president of Vietnam Veterans of America Chapter 49 in Westchester County, New York, described to me some of the volunteer work he had been doing since his retirement.

I'm going to tell you something. If you talk to a large enough group of veterans, you will find that . . . they carry this tremendous burden from going to war, whether it's physical suffering [or] mental suffering. You won't hear how they won [the war], or complain about it, or . . . say, "I wouldn't do it again." And, in fact, most of the guys that I know who are members of veterans' organizations like DAV [Disabled American Veter-

ans] or VFW [Veterans of Foreign Wars], because of their service, I mean, in going to war or serving their country, have learned the lesson that there's a responsibility of doing good. That's what their service taught them.

Some men and women seem to have put Vietnam in its place: behind them. Frank DeSantis, who passed away in 2009, told me in 2005 that Vietnam had ceased being part of his everyday life. The war, he thought, was in the past, and he had moved on. In this respect, I suspect DeSantis spoke for many Vietnam veterans when he said:

I don't bother to read books about Vietnam; I don't want to know the history of it. When I'm at a meeting with guys and they know too much, you know, they just know every little bit of information about everything that happened, and it's like, you didn't know that then. You researched it; you went online; you're trying to do every bit of research about the Battle for Hill 227 . . . I don't remember what hill it was, sometimes I remember the name, sometimes I don't, and I kind of remember what was going on, and sometimes I may be a little out of sequence, but I don't want to go on the Internet and look up and know every little thing.

For others, Vietnam is part of every waking moment. Rudy Dent, a helicopter door gunner in Vietnam and a retired New York City firefighter, says:

Someone had asked me about flashbacks, and it's not about a flashback; how about a flash-present? It's there every moment of every day. I don't know how to explain it; it's a feeling that's always there. I'm at a loss for words for it.

It's always there.

It doesn't go away.

16

LIVING MEMORIALS

There are tangible reminders of the Vietnam dead all over the country as well as in the city of New York. The New York City Parks Department maintains twenty-seven parks, playgrounds, and memorials dedicated to New Yorkers who died fighting in Vietnam. Queens has eight; Brooklyn nine. Manhattan and the Bronx have three each, and Staten Island has four.

Although the definitions are slippery, there is a distinction between a memorial and a monument. A monument honors a landmark or physical structure. A memorial, by contrast, is defined by the National Park Service as having "primarily commemorative" purposes.[1] Therefore, a memorial reflects on history in some way. The Vietnam Veterans Memorial at 55 Water Street follows in this tradition, commemorating and honoring those who fought in Vietnam. There are, however, many ways to honor a soldier's service. The idea of a living memorial has been around since at least World War I, and the purpose behind such memorials is to do or produce something useful.[2]

Many veterans do exactly this. Among my interviewees, Danny Friedman, Fred Louis, Neil Kenny, Sue O'Neill, Joan Furey, and many others work to advance public understanding about veterans and their lives. Kenny works with Marines recently returned from Iraq and Afghanistan. Furey has recorded oral histories with other scholars and given interviews. Friedman visits high school classrooms to share his experience. O'Neill continues to write about what Vietnam taught her. Anthony Wallace in his quiet way has adopted this role as my personal tutor.

Such an undertaking is not new for him. Raised in the Cornerstone Baptist Church as a leader, made a noncommissioned officer in the Army, and ordained a church deacon at age twenty-two, Wallace has always been a teacher. He took on this role from virtually the moment he returned to the United States. After being released from the hospital, he recalls:

I sat down and wrote a letter. This is in the summer of 1970. I wrote to President Nixon and told him who I was. I gave him my name, my rank, and I said that I was in Vietnam at such and such a time, point A to point B, and wounded on this day. In other words, trying to give them enough credence to know that, hey, you know, I'm no phony. This is the truth . . . that there were three other people who were in the bunker [and were killed]. And I was able to give two names. Pepe's name—I didn't know his full name. They could not find anything on Pepe. President Nixon, the White House, wrote a letter back and said, "Your request has been referred to the Department of the Army."

I wanted the name and address of the next of kin. I get Thurman Wolfe, and I get William Di Santis; I get their next of kin. I sat down and wrote a letter to the families and told them who I was and that I was with their sons. Wolfe's parents or mother—they were from Robeline, Louisiana. I had pictures of Wolfe, a couple of pictures just like this, and I sent them. And the neighbors advised her don't write [back] to him, he's probably looking at trying to get your insurance money. So she wrote me and said please don't write back.

One day, I get a letter from Aurora, Illinois, and I open the letter and it said, "I prayed to God for somebody like you. You did not put your telephone number in your letter. When you get this letter, you call me, even if you have to call collect." That was Bill Di Santis's mother. And I called her as soon as I finished reading the letter, and she said to me again, "I prayed to God for somebody like you."

She says, "I have to ask you; did my son suffer when he died?" I asked her, "Well, what did the Army tell you?" She replied, "They indicated he was in a bunker that took a direct hit." And I said to her, "That's exactly what happened, and there is no way Bill suffered; it was too fast." And she said, "Thank you." I then said, "Well, I want to come to see you," and she said, "When?" So we set up a time.

I flew out to Chicago, rented a car, and drove to Aurora, based on the directions they had given me. They lived on a semi-farm, and I remember driving up like off this long road and then into their property and the house was like off in a distance. I drove up, stopped the car, and got out, and there was a man on the lawn mower, and he stopped and he looked at me, and I looked at him. He said, "You must be Mr. Wallace." I said, "You must be Mr. Di Santis." We shook hands and we went up on the porch and we talked awhile and we talked about his son. I told him about when you guys were sending the care packages and we would— you'd send the pepperoni and how Bill shared that with us and we got—we talked about those few things, and he then took me inside and I met Bill's mother and his sister, and we talked. And we—they fixed dinner and we talked more and more, and I went to stay two days. I ended up staying four days.

He was an engineer for Burlington Northern, and that next morning he took me to his job, the train yards, and every place we would go, he'd say, "This is Tony Wallace. He's from New York. He was with Bill in Vietnam. He was with Bill in Vietnam." He took me to relatives. He took me to Bill's grandmother. He took me to so many folks, and they all greeted me with warmth; they treated me like a king. Then I have to say that there was no question about me being a brother, Bill being [white] . . . there was no question—no feeling of anything where you'd be afraid or apprehensive of going into this setting. No way.

He took me to the college he [Bill] went to. He even took me to the cemetery to see where he was buried. He took me fishing, and I had really never been fishing, but he took me fishing. And the thing was, we were able to talk, and I was able to share certain experiences that we had over in Vietnam. He thanked me for making this effort to come and see them. He said, "You'll never realize what it meant to the family to do what you did by coming out here."

When I got back home, those guilt feelings began to dissipate.

Wallace has also continued to make peace with his experiences by remaining engaged with them. He speaks to school groups in Brooklyn about his time in Vietnam. He takes part in events aimed at younger veterans at Brooklyn College. He's created a database of the casualties sustained by the First Cavalry Division in Vietnam, his unit, so that he can better understand how the unit worked. In spring 2012 he will become a docent, or "Yellow Hat," a National Park Service volunteer at the Vietnam Veterans Memorial in Washington, D.C. In that role he will help people find names on the black granite wall and share his experiences.

Folks often ask, why do Vietnam veterans say [to each other], "Welcome home"? They don't realize where that came from. The fact is that when you came home, no one said "Welcome home" to you. So we have to do this for ourselves. When a man sees another Nam vet and they greet them and shake hands, they say, "Welcome home." That's the appreciation that they know and have an idea what that person went through and can appreciate who they are. Nobody else can have that. That's their special time, and when they're able to do that, nothing else has to be said. They can keep walking.

Over the years that have elapsed since I began this project, Tony Wallace and I have grown close. We have made many trips together on Veterans Day. In 2008 we spent a cold, drizzly afternoon at the wall in Washington, listening to various speakers tell us of their experiences and about the meaning of the wall. The green of the National Mall lawn was covered with folding chairs and umbrellas as the afternoon wound down. As we were leaving, Tony sought out a homeless veteran he had met at the wall earlier in the year and gave the man a new coat and a new pair of shoes that he had brought from New York just for that purpose. We chatted with him for a while and took photographs as the night gathered.

After we got back to the hotel room we shared and prepared for sleep, from the other side of the room Tony said, *I think it is time for you to see this.* Already in his pajamas, he knelt down and peeled back the pajama top, revealing the deep and ugly scars from the blast that had killed Wolfe, Pepe, and Di Santis. The blast had changed his life forever. There on his knees he exposed his back to me for several moments. It is very hard to describe what I saw. The skin had been torn; it was discolored. There were scars that had not healed properly, and you could see the effects of several skin grafts that had been done to try to close the wounds. Where the skin was not torn, it was peppered with scars where shrapnel had entered his body. Tony rose and rebuttoned his top.

Now you know was all he said.

A NOTE ON METHOD

This book draws on the in-depth oral history interviews I conducted with more than two hundred persons between 2004 and 2010. Interviews varied in length from forty-five minutes to more than thirty hours. Altogether, some six hundred hours of recordings were gathered and transcribed. In conducting and presenting my interviews, I elected to employ a life-story technique so as to comprehend the trajectory of Vietnam veterans' lives.[1] Dan P. McAdams, a clinical psychologist and one of the leading authorities on the life-story model of human identity, defines life stories as narratives "based on biographical facts, but they go considerably beyond the facts as people selectively appropriate aspects of their experience and imaginatively construe both past and future to construct stories that make sense to them and their audiences, that vivify and integrate life and make it more or less meaningful." He adds that an individual's "life stories are psychosocial constructions, coauthored by himself or herself and the cultural context experience within which that person's life is embedded and given meaning."[2] Using McAdams's life-story technique, I asked my interviewees to explain how they became the people they are today. In response, the veterans produced narrative reconstructions of their lives; they selected the bits and pieces of individual memory that seemed most important and arranged them into a meaningful story to be shared with an interviewer—and the general public.[3]

I chose this method in large part because of the peculiar, living, and evolving nature of my source material—living witnesses. Annette Wieviorka's provocative book *The Era of the Witness* records the rise of eyewitness testimony in the twentieth century and reflects on the dangers in using eyewitness testimony, including oral history, uncritically. She argues that historians should not look to autobiographical narratives of this kind for "clarification of precise events, places, dates, and numbers, which are wrong with the regularity of a metronome," but should instead pay attention to oral history for its "extraordinary riches," for "an encounter with the voice of someone who has lived through a piece of history." The genre offers "in oblique fashion, not factual truth, but the more subtle and just as indispensable truth of an epoch and of an experience."[4]

Wieviorka would agree with Alessandro Portelli, who is perhaps the most important living practitioner of the craft of oral history. In Portelli's view, "Oral sources are credible but with a *different* credibility. The importance of oral testimony may lie not in its adherence to fact, but rather in its departure from it, as imagination, symbolism, and desire emerge."[5] Oral histories are therefore texts to be explored for their plot and structure, for imagery, metaphor, irony, archetype, and all of the other devices that narrative analysis may discuss. Oral histories give us access to the subjective experience of historical actors functioning in history and living through historical time. They occupy the liminal space between the psychological realm and the social world of a shared daily reality. Therefore, they cannot be understood as a "transparent form of evidence" granting some kind of magical direct access to past events or experience.[6] Oral histories must be listened to closely and interpreted in order to be valuable.[7]

Just as there are multiple ways of presenting oral history to the public, so are there different theories about the best way to represent orality, people's spoken narratives, in print form. One approach, common among linguists and social scientists, argues that spoken language should be represented on the page precisely as it sounds to the human ear. That is to say, oral historians ought to print every "um," every "er," and every "and." This way of thinking holds that this is the most faithful way of reproducing speech. It hews the closest to the actual historical record and is therefore the most intellectually honest way to proceed.

While I recognize the integrity of that approach, I take a different one. In my view, shared by many practitioners of oral history, the act of transforming spoken language into written text is already a form of translation, and any good translator has dual responsibilities: not only to the veracity of the translation, but also to the end user, the reader. Therefore, I have taken the liberty of excising unnecessary words, such as verbal stumbles and tics, and adding punctuation where appropriate. I have also inserted, where necessary, additional words in an effort to render the text easy to read. Additional words not spoken by the original narrator are always indicated with brackets, thus: [ ]. At no other point have I inserted words the subjects did not actually speak. Throughout the book, the words of my interviewees are represented in italics to distinguish their voices from mine. Because the book is a conscious effort to "share authority" for the telling of the story, I have often used long quotations, allowing veterans to speak for themselves in a relatively unmediated way. Various viewpoints, theirs and mine, have a place in this story.

The memory of war and its consequences is enormously powerful for a variety of physiological and psychological reasons. Psychologists have established that a person's ability to recall a past event is enhanced if adrenaline was present when the event occurred. Therefore combat memories, with all of their associated sights, sounds, and smells, can be powerful and vivid long after the original traumas have drifted into the past. Additionally, narrative researchers have identified the so-called reminiscence bump, a spike in the quantity and quality of memories individuals seem to be able to retain from their late adolescence/early adulthood.[8] Memories from this time of life, which of course matches the age at which most service personnel went to Vietnam, would therefore be especially acute; they would become the figurative text from which veterans would often draw the lessons that guided their life choices later. For these reasons, the Vietnam War has played a powerful role in the lives of the men and women who served in it. That experience shaped the memories, and thus the social identities, of the people who appear in this book, because memory and identity are linked.

Critics of the oral history method complain that the "data" recorded in interviews is soft, that the vagaries of memory make it unreliable. I have heard it said that "the plural of 'anecdote' is not 'data.'" If one is looking for statistical proof of historical claims, then oral history is not a preferred approach. Numerically verifiable information is better obtained through census records, court documents, and other sources—and even when one uses such sources, attaining proof can be hard. In any case, oral history's mission is not the mere accounting and accumulation of data. Instead, it looks for the meaning of events as recalled by informed interviewees: it adds a texture that helps the inquirer find truth. Oral history provides access to what Portelli calls "ways of remembering"; it reveals the shape and structure of individual memories and what those memories share; in the case of this book, it suggests how they have created the sense of what it means to be a veteran in New York City. These are the "truths" that people, veterans, carry with them. Oral history therefore is not a study of historical "facts" as they are often understood in academic discourse—as something grounded in contemporaneously created documentation. It is instead an investigation of the "facts" of memory, the "reality" of perception and recall.

One profound advantage of oral history is that unlike traditional historical writing, it insists that the competing voices of historical actors cannot and will not resolve into a single story with a solitary meaning. History does not work that way anyway. My book shows that the common view of the Vietnam vet as deranged and dangerous is a travesty and that a great many veterans were inspired by their war experience to lead full and successful lives—whether out of loyalty to the war effort or in opposition to it. And yet that too is an interpretation that does not reveal the whole truth. While historians are tempted to construct for themselves narratives with seeming explanatory power, counternarrative is not only possible but necessary. As the Vietnam veteran and author James R. McDonough wrote in his memoir, *Platoon Leader*, "There were no typical experiences. If anything was typical about the Vietnam experience, it was that it was different for everyone."[9]

Oral history reminds us of this truth.

NOTES

INTRODUCTION

1. Hynes, *Soldiers' Tale*, 177–78.
2. Ibid., xiii.
3. Ibid., 177–222.
4. Ibid., 201.
5. Willenson, *Bad War*.
6. Hynes, *Soldiers' Tale*, 221.
7. Ibid., 222.

1. MAKING SOLDIERS: THE BOYS WHO BECAME THE MEN

1. "2,000,000 Will See City's War Parade," *New York Times*, June 12, 1942; "Fifth Ave. Crowd Put at 2,500,000," *New York Times*, June 14, 1942.
2. "Births and Deaths on the Rise This Year," *New York Times*, July 18, 1943.
3. Richard Goldstein, *Helluva Town: The Story of New York City During World War II* (New York: Free Press, 2010), xi.
4. German, *Deep Down in Brooklyn*, 6.
5. Ira Rosenwaike, *Population History of New York City* (Syracuse, N.Y.: Syracuse University Press, 1972), 117.
6. German, *Deep Down in Brooklyn*, 32.
7. Joshua B. Freeman, *Working-Class New York: Life and Labor Since World War II* (New York: New Press, 2000), 29–30.
8. Flanagan, *Born in Brooklyn . . . Raised in the CAV!*, 18.
9. George Q. Flynn, *The Draft, 1940–1973* (Lawrence: University Press of Kansas, 1993), 166–87.

10. Flanagan, *Born in Brooklyn . . . Raised in the CAV!*, 28.
11. George Lankevich, *American Metropolis: A History of New York City* (New York: New York University Press, 1998), 163.
12. Meyer Berger, "Our Changing City," *New York Times*, June 20, 1955.

2. PROFESSIONALISM: RICHARD EGGERS

1. The baseplate holds the mortar in place for firing. The 81-millimeter baseplate weighs approximately twenty-five pounds.

3. FUTILITY: SUE O'NEILL

1. Westheider, *Fighting in Vietnam*, 170.
2. Vuic, *Officer, Nurse, Woman*, 11.
3. Ibid., 45–46.
4. Susan O'Neill, "The Non-matrixed Wife," Peace Corps Writers, accessed July 2, 2012, http://www.peacecorpswriters.org/pages/2005/0501/501pchist.html.
5. O'Neill, *Don't Mean Nothing*, xiii.

4. WAR AND LIES: JOSEPH GIANNINI

1. Blog comment, posted May 18, 2010, at 12:09 a.m., accessed Jan. 20, 2012, http://blog.lemuriabooks.com/2010/04/why-i-write-karl-marlantes/.
2. Raftkeith Eros Baker, private first class, D Company, First Battalion, Third Marines, Third Marine Division, III Marine Amphibious Force, U.S. Marine Corps, Chicago, Illinois, accessed May 1, 2012, www.virtualwall.org/db/BakerRE01a.htm.
3. Pete Bowles, "Man Acquitted of Killing Cop Got Away with Murder; Judge," *Newsday*, April 26, 1990.
4. Trial testimony transcript in possession of the author. Laura Palmer, "Killing Tied to Vet's Flashback," *Houston Chronicle*, July 16, 1990.

5. FOLLOW ME: ANTHONY WALLACE

1. "U.S. War Deaths Highest Since September," *Palm Beach Post*, April 17, 1970.

6. THE BELIEVER: JOAN FUREY

1. A recent dissertation asserts that between seventy-five hundred and eleven thousand military women served in Vietnam. See Jean Dunlavy, "A Band of Sisters: Vietnam Women Veterans' Organization for Rights and Recognition" (PhD diss., Boston University, 2009).
2. Scott, *Vietnam Veterans Since the War: The Politics of PTSD, Agent Orange, and the National Memorial* (Norman: University of Oklahoma Press, 1993), 32.

3. One version of this ad appeared in *The American Journal of Nursing* 68, no. 8 (Aug. 1968): 1778, http://www.jstor.org/stable/3420960.

4. Elizabeth Norman, *Women at War: The Story of Fifty Military Nurses Who Served in Vietnam* (Philadelphia: University of Pennsylvania Press, 1990), 36–37.

5. Approximately 30 percent of the nurses in Vietnam in 1969 were male, like Furey's friend. Vuic, *Officer, Nurse, Woman*, 90.

6. Ralph Blumenthal, "Protesting G.I.'s in Pleiku to Fast on Thanksgiving," *New York Times*, Nov. 24, 1969; Ralph Blumenthal, "100 G.I.'s in Pleiku Fast for Holiday," *New York Times*, Nov. 28, 1969; Vuic, *Officer, Nurse, Woman*, 85.

7. Letter to the editor, *Port Jefferson Record*, Jan. 29, 1970. Grammar and punctuation are presented here as in the original.

8. Norman, *Women at War*, 28.

9. Ibid., 129; Elizabeth M. Norman, "After the Casualties: Vietnam Nurses' Identities and Career Decisions," *Nursing Research* 41, no. 2 (March–April 1992): 110–13.

7. WAR AND LOSS: MIANO, NOWICKI, AND GONZALEZ

1. Stéphane Audoin-Rouzeau and Annette Becker, *14–18: Understanding the Great War* (New York: Hill and Wang, 2000), 203–25.

2. Jim Tutak, Remembrance for Stephen W. Pickett, Vietnam Veterans Memorial Fund, accessed Aug. 12, 2011, http://www.vvmf.org/thewall/anClip=207617.

3. Wisconsin Division of Health, Madison, *Wisconsin Vietnam Veteran Mortality Study* (1986), accessed Aug. 12, 2011, http://dva.state.wi.us/WebForms/Data _Factsheets/VietnamVetMortalityStudy.pdf; Centers for Disease Control, "Current Trends in Postservice Mortality Among Vietnam Veterans," *MMWR Weekly*, Feb. 13, 1987, 61–64, accessed Aug. 12, 2011, http://www.cdc.gov/mmwr/preview /mmwrhtml/00000865.htm; Centers for Disease Control, *Postservice Mortality Among Vietnam Veterans*, accessed Aug. 12, 2011, http://www.cdc.gov/nceh /veterans/default1a.htm.

4. Veterans' Diseases Associated with Agent Orange, accessed July 9, 2012, http://www .publichealth.va.gov/exposures/agentorange/diseases.asp.

5. Larry Mcshane, "Remains of Brooklyn Marine Killed in Action During Vietnam Return Home," New York *Daily News*, March 21, 2009.

8. WELCOME HOME, JIMMY: THE BACOLO TWINS

1. *Data on Vietnam Era Veterans* (Washington, D.C.: Reports & Statistics Service, Office of the Controller, Veterans Administration, 1971), 1.

2. William Barry Furlong, "The Re-entry Problem of the Vietvets," *New York Times*, May 7, 1967.

3. Sandy Goodman, "The Invisible Veterans," *Nation*, June 3, 1968, 723–26.

4. Senate Committee on Veterans Affairs, *A Study of the Problems Facing Vietnam*

Era Veterans on Their Readjustment to Civilian Life, January 31, 1972 (Washington, D.C.: U.S. Government Printing Office, 1972).

5. Robert D. McFadden, "Thousands Here Honor Vietnam Veterans," *New York Times*, April 1, 1973.

6. Charles Wiley, "The Culpability of the Media" (session of the conference Examining the Myths of the Vietnam War), accessed Nov. 12, 2011, http://www.viet-myths.net/Session12T.htm.

9. AGAINST WAR: FRIEDMAN AND LOUIS

1. Nicosia, *Home to War*, 15.

2. Homer Bigart, "War Foes Here Attacked by Construction Workers, City Hall Is Stormed," *New York Times*, May 9, 1970, accessed June 28, 2012.

3. Nicosia, *Home to War*, 227; Hunt, *Turning*, 180–82.

4. Friedman also told the story to the historian Gerald Nicosia. See his account in Nicosia, *Home to War*, 224–26.

5. Statement of Purpose, accessed June 28, 2012, http://www.veteransforpeace.org/who-we-are/our-mission/.

6. "We Always Get a Great Response" (an interview with Fred Louis of the Connecticut chapter of Veterans for Peace at the Veterans Day Parade, Nov. 2006), accessed May 17, 2012, http://www.youtube.com/watch?v=SavMnL1fLb4.

10. BECOMING VETERANS: EDELMAN, GERMAN, AND PAS

1. William E. Farrell, "About New York: Some Who Served and Were Not Treated to Parades," *New York Times*, Jan. 31, 1981.

2. For a longer treatment of this subject, see Scott, *Vietnam Veterans Since the War: The Politics of PTSD, Agent Orange, and the National Memorial*.

3. David W. Dunlap, "Wall to Honor City's Veterans of Vietnam," *New York Times*, May 30, 1984.

4. Minutes, Executive Committee Meetings, series 1, subseries 1, file Oct. 16, 1984, box 1, April 13, 1983–Feb. 7, 1985, New York Vietnam Veterans Memorial Commission Papers, 1983–89, New York City Municipal Archives.

5. Denis Hamill, "Heroic Viet Vets Plan Major March," *New York Daily News*, May 4, 2005.

6. Jane Gross, "New Yorkers Roar Thanks to Veterans," *New York Times*, May 8, 1985.

7. "Vietnam Veterans Give Ex-comrades a Hand Up," *New York Times*, Aug. 11, 1985.

8. Terry Martin, *An American Sunrise: The Vietnam Veterans Leadership Program: A History of ACTION's Three-Year Veteran's Initiative: Technical Report* (Washington, D.C.: ACTION, 1984), 67, 68, 69–72.

9. Hagopian, *Vietnam War in American Memory*, 217–18.

10. Gene Gitelson to Robert M. Sellar (IBM), March 11, 1987, Rockefeller Archive,

Collection DLM a, series 2.2, projects, box 185, folder 1713, Vietnam Veterans Leadership Program, Gene Gitelson, 1986–92; "Vietnam Veterans Give Ex-comrades a Hand Up."

11. "Vietnam Veterans Give Ex-comrades a Hand Up."
12. Gitelson to Sellar, March 11, 1987.
13. Ibid.
14. Hagopian, *Vietnam War in American Memory*, 218.
15. Minutes, Executive Committee Meetings, series 1, subseries 1, box 2, file Oct. 7, 1986, New York Vietnam Veterans Memorial Commission Papers, 1983–89, New York City Municipal Archives.

12. TWONESS: HERBERT SWEAT

1. W.E.B. Du Bois, *The Souls of Black Folk: Essays and Sketches* (Chicago: A. C. McClurg, 1903), p. 4.
2. George N. Katsiaficas, *The Imagination of the New Left: A Global Analysis of 1968* (Boston: South End Press, 1987), 141; "Pentagon to Crack Down on Deserters," *Gettysburg Times*, Sept. 16, 1970.
3. Whitney M. Young Jr., "A Report from Vietnam (Fourth of Four Articles)," *New York Amsterdam News*, Sept. 10, 1966.
4. *Soldiers of Misfortune, Homeless Veterans in New York City* (Research and Liaison Unit, Office of the Comptroller, City of New York, 1982).
5. Bernard Edelman to Ed Koch, Feb. 5, 1988, Mayor's Office of Veterans' Affairs, image 00029, roll 41129, Koch Papers, New York City Municipal Archives.
6. "U.S. Opens a New Center for Homeless Veterans," *New York Times*, May 15, 1988.
7. "Nation's Homeless Veterans Battle a New Foe: Defeatism," *New York Times*, Dec. 30, 1987; Robert Rosenheck and Peggy Gallup, "Vietnam Era and Vietnam Combat Veterans Among the Homeless," *American Journal of Public Health* 81, no. 1 (May 1991): 643–46.
8. "Man Fatally Stabbed in Homeless Shelter," *New York Times*, Aug. 9, 1993.

13. LONG ROAD HOME: NEIL KENNY

1. Leslie Roberts, "Vietnam's Psychological Toll," *Science*, July 8, 1988, 159–61.
2. "Mayor Announces 3 Housing Projects; Gets State Rebuke," *New York Times*, June 14, 1943.
3. "Contracts Signed for City Housing," *New York Times*, March 27, 1945; "Low-Rent Housing Project Planned for Lower East Side," *New York Times*, Feb. 25, 1948.
4. John Prados and Ray W. Stubbe, *Valley of Decision: The Siege of Khe Sanh* (Boston: Houghton Mifflin, 1991), 505–6.
5. Kenny knows that Ratliff's official records indicate that he was killed on July 3, 1968. He is, however, firm in associating the death with the fourth, possibly

because what took place on the third in Vietnam took place on the fourth in the United States.

6. "Headquarters U.S. Military Assistance Command Vietnam—Monthly Summary: December 1968–February 15, 1969," box 02, folder 01, Glenn Helm Collection, Vietnam Center and Archive, Texas Tech University, accessed April 21, 2012, www.vietnam.ttu.edu/virtualarchive/items.php?item=1070201007.

7. "Command Chronology, December 1, 1968," folder 060, U.S. Marine Corps History Division Vietnam War Documents Collection, Vietnam Center and Archive, Texas Tech University, accessed April 21, 2012, www.vietnam.ttu.edu/virtualarchive /items.php?item=1201060223.

8. Staff Study, *New York City's Financial Crisis: An Evaluation of Its Economic Impact and Proposed Policy Solutions,* Joint Economic Committee of the Congress of the United States (Washington, D.C.: Government Printing Office, U.S. 1975, accessed April 21, 2012, http://fraser.stlouisfed.org/docs/historical/jec/1975jec_nyfinanc .pdf.

9. William Clayton Wray, private first class, L Company, Third Battalion, Twenty-Sixth Marines, First Marine Division, III Marine Amphibious Force, U.S. Marine Corps, Plattsburgh, New York, June 2, 1948, to Sept. 23, 1968, accessed May 19, 2012, www.virtualwall.org/dw/WrayWC01a.htm.

10. Workman tells his story in Jeremiah Workman with John R. Bruning, *Shadow of the Sword: A Marine's Journey of War, Heroism, and Redemption* (New York: Ballantine Books, 2009).

14. LEADERSHIP: VINCE McGOWAN

1. Monica Surfaro, "Veterans Caught in City Welfare Battle," *New York Times,* Oct. 13, 1974.

2. Dean, *Shook Over Hell.*

3. U.S. Department of Labor, Bureau of Labor Statistics, Middle Atlantic Regional Office, *New York City in Transition: Population, Jobs, Prices, and Pay in a Decade of Change,* Regional Report 34, July 1973, Robert F. Wagner Documents Collection, box 060278, folder 18, Wagner Archives, accessed Jan. 11, 2011, www.laguardiawagnerarchive.lagcc.cuny.edu/FileBrowser.aspx?LinkToFile =FILES_DOC/WAGNER_FILES/06.021.0058.060278.18.PDF.

16. LIVING MEMORIALS

1. U.S. Department of Interior, *The National Parks Index, 2009–2011,* 8, accessed May 19, 2012, http://www.nps.gov/history/history/online_books/nps/index2009 _11.pdf.

2. David Glassberg, *Sense of History: The Place of the Past in American Life* (Amherst: University of Massachusetts Press, 2001), 29.

A NOTE ON METHOD

1. Jerome Bruner, "Life as Narrative," *Social Research* 71, no. 3 (2004): 691–710.
2. Dan P. McAdams, "The Psychology of Life Stories," *Review of General Psychology* 5, no. 2 (2001): 100–22.
3. The literature about narrative life history research is large and growing. For an overview, see D. Jean Clandinin, *Handbook of Narrative Inquiry: Mapping a Methodology* (Thousand Oaks, Calif.: Sage, 2007).
4. Annette Wieviorka, *The Era of the Witness* (Ithaca, N.Y.: Cornell University Press, 2006), 132.
5. Alessandro Portelli, "What Makes Oral History Different," in *The Death of Luigi Trastulli, and Other Stories*, 51.
6. Maynes, Pierce, and Laslett, *Telling Stories*, 41.
7. See also Nigel C. Hunt, *Memory, War, and Trauma* (Cambridge, U.K.: Cambridge University Press, 2010); and Abrams, *Oral History Theory*.
8. See, for example, Ashok Jansari and Alan J. Parkin, "Things That Go Bump in Your Life: Explaining the Reminiscence Bump in Autobiographical Memory," *Psychology and Aging* 11, no. 1 (March 1996): 85–91; and Alison Holmes and Martin A. Conway, "Generation Identity and the Reminiscence Bump: Memory for Public and Private Events," *Journal of Adult Development* 6, no. 1 (1999): 21–34.
9. James R. McDonough, *Platoon Leader* (Novato, Calif.: Presidio Press, 1985), 1.

RECOMMENDED READING

VIETNAM WAR, GENERAL

Anderson, David L. *The Vietnam War*. New York: Palgrave Macmillan, 2005.

Bradley, Mark Philip. *Vietnam at War*. New York: Oxford University Press, 2009.

Hagopian, Patrick. *The Vietnam War in American Memory: Veterans, Memorials, and the Politics of Healing*. Amherst: University of Massachusetts Press, 2009.

Hess, Gary R. *Vietnam and the United States: Origins and Legacy of War*. Boston: Twayne, 1990.

Hynes, Samuel Lynn. *The Soldiers' Tale: Bearing Witness to Modern War*. New York: Penguin Books, 1998.

Karnow, Stanley. *Vietnam: A History*. New York: Viking, 1983. 2nd ed., New York: Penguin, 1997.

Lawrence, Mark Atwood. *The Vietnam War: A Concise International History*. New York: Oxford University Press, 2008.

Logevall, Fredrik. *The Origins of the Vietnam War*. New York: Longman, 2001.

MacPherson, Myra. *Long Time Passing: Vietnam and the Haunted Generation*. Garden City, N.Y.: Doubleday, 1984.

Prados, John. *Vietnam: The History of an Unwinnable War, 1945–1975*. Lawrence: University Press of Kansas, 2009.

Schulzinger, Robert D. *A Time for War: The United States and Vietnam, 1941–1975*. New York: Oxford University Press, 1997.

Summers, Harry. *On Strategy: The Vietnam War in Context*. Novato, Calif.: Presidio, 1982.

Vuic, Kara Dixon. *Officer, Nurse, Woman: The Army Nurse Corps in the Vietnam War*. Baltimore: Johns Hopkins University Press, 2010.

RECOMMENDED READING

Westheider, James. *Fighting in Vietnam: The Experiences of the U.S. Soldier.* Mechanicsburg, Pa.: Stackpole Books, 2007.

Wiest, Andrew. *The Vietnam War, 1956–1975.* Oxford: Osprey, 2002.

Young, Marilyn B. *The Vietnam Wars, 1945–1990.* New York: HarperCollins, 1991.

VIETNAM VETERANS

Bonior, David E., Steven M. Champlin, and Timothy S. Kolly. *The Vietnam Veteran: A History of Neglect.* New York: Praeger, 1984.

Boulanger, Ghislaine, and Charles Kadushin. *The Vietnam Veteran Redefined: Fact and Fiction.* Hillsdale, N.J.: L. Erlbaum, 1986.

Brende, Joel Osler, and Erwin Randolph Parson. *Vietnam Veterans: The Road to Recovery.* New York: Plenum Press, 1985.

Dean, Eric T. *Shook Over Hell: Post-traumatic Stress, Vietnam, and the Civil War.* Cambridge, Mass.: Harvard University Press, 1997.

Hunt, Andrew E. *The Turning: A History of Vietnam Veterans Against the War.* New York: New York University Press, 1999.

Lifton, Robert Jay. *Home from the War: Vietnam Veterans: Neither Victims nor Executioners.* New York: Simon and Schuster, 1973.

Moser, Richard R. *The New Winter Soldiers: GI and Veteran Dissent During the Vietnam Era.* New Brunswick, N.J.: Rutgers University Press, 1996.

Nelson, Deborah. *The War Behind Me: Vietnam Veterans Confront the Truth About U.S. War Crimes.* New York: Basic Books, 2008.

Nicosia, Gerald. *Home to War: A History of the Vietnam Veterans' Movement.* New York: Crown, 2001.

Palmer, Laura. *Shrapnel in the Heart: Letters and Remembrances from the Vietnam Veterans Memorial.* New York: Random House, 1987.

Polner, Murray. *No Victory Parades: The Return of the Vietnam Veteran.* New York: Holt, Rinehart and Winston, 1971.

Scott, Wilbur J. *Vietnam Veterans Since the War: The Politics of PTSD, Agent Orange, and the National Memorial.* Norman: University of Oklahoma Press, 2004.

Shay, Jonathan. *Achilles in Vietnam: Combat Trauma and the Undoing of Character.* New York: Atheneum, 1994.

Starr, Paul, Ralph Nader, James F. Henry, and Raymond P. Bonner. *The Discarded Army: Veterans After Vietnam: The Nader Report on Vietnam Veterans and the Veterans Administration.* New York: Charterhouse, 1973.

The Vietnam Veteran in Contemporary Society: Collected Materials Pertaining to the Young Veterans. Washington, D.C.: Department of Medicine and Surgery, Veterans Administration, 1972.

RECOMMENDED READING

VIETNAM WAR, ORAL HISTORY

Appy, Christian G. *Patriots: The Vietnam War Remembered from All Sides*. New York: Viking, 2003.

Baker, Mark. *Nam: The Vietnam War in the Words of the Men and Women Who Fought There*. New York: W. Morrow, 1981.

Engelmann, Larry. *Tears Before the Rain: An Oral History of the Fall of South Vietnam*. New York: Oxford University Press, 1990.

Fawcett, Bill. *Hunters and Shooters: An Oral History of the U.S. Navy Seals in Vietnam*. New York: W. Morrow, 1995.

Gioglio, Gerald R. *Days of Decision: An Oral History of Conscientious Objectors in the Military During the Vietnam War*. Trenton, N.J.: Broken Rifle Press, 1989.

Lehrack, Otto J. *No Shining Armor: The Marines at War in Vietnam: An Oral History*. Lawrence: University Press of Kansas, 1992.

Marshall, Kathryn. *In the Combat Zone: An Oral History of American Women in Vietnam, 1966–1975*. Boston: Little, Brown, 1987.

Maurer, Harry. *Strange Ground: Americans in Vietnam, 1945–1975, an Oral History*. New York: H. Holt, 1989.

Santoli, Al. *Everything We Had: An Oral History of the Vietnam War*. New York: Random House, 1981.

———. *Leading the Way: How Vietnam Veterans Rebuilt the U.S. Military: An Oral History*. New York: Ballantine Books, 1993.

Terry, Wallace. *Bloods: An Oral History of the Vietnam War*. New York: Random House, 1984.

Tollefson, James W. *The Strength Not to Fight: An Oral History of Conscientious Objectors of the Vietnam War*. Boston: Little, Brown, 1993.

Willenson, Kim. *The Bad War: An Oral History of the Vietnam War*. New York: New American Library, 1987.

MEMOIRS AND FICTION BY VETERANS INTERVIEWED FOR THIS BOOK

Flanagan, John. *Born in Brooklyn . . . Raised in the CAV!* Bloomington, Ind.: Xlibris, 2001.

German, Ed. *Deep Down in Brooklyn*. Bloomington, Ind.: AuthorHouse, 2011.

O'Neill, Susan. *Don't Mean Nothing: Short Stories of Vietnam*. Amherst: University of Massachusetts Press, 2004.

ORAL HISTORY, THEORY

Abrams, Lynn. *Oral History Theory*. New York: Routledge, 2010.

Frisch, Michael. *A Shared Authority: Essays on the Craft and Meaning of Oral History and Public History*. Albany: State University of New York Press, 1990.

Gluck, Sherna Berger, and Daphne Patai, eds. *Women's Words: The Feminist Practice of Oral History*. New York: Routledge, 1991.

RECOMMENDED READING

Grele, Ronald J., ed. *Envelopes of Sound: The Art of Oral History.* New York: Praeger, 1991.

Maynes, Mary Jo, Jennifer L. Pierce, and Barbara Laslett. *Telling Stories: The Use of Personal Narratives in the Social Sciences and History.* Ithaca, N.Y.: Cornell University Press, 2008.

Perks, Robert, and Alistair Thomson, eds. *The Oral History Reader.* New York: Routledge, 1998.

Portelli, Alessandro. *The Battle of Valle Giulia: Oral History and the Art of Dialogue.* Madison: University of Wisconsin Press, 1997.

———. *The Death of Luigi Trastulli, and Other Stories: Form and Meaning in Oral History.* Albany: State University of New York Press, 1991.

Thomson, Alistair. *Anzac Memories: Living with the Legend.* Oxford: Oxford University Press, 1994.

Tonkin, Elizabeth. *Narrating Our Pasts: The Social Construction of Oral History.* Cambridge, U.K.: Cambridge University Press, 1992.

ACKNOWLEDGMENTS

I would like to thank the following individuals for taking the time to speak with me about this project, whether officially as interviewees or in other capacities. These people generously gave me hours of their time and energy. Many are veterans, some are not. Several have passed away in the years it took to complete this project. Without them this book simply would not exist: Carol S. Aljets, Barbara Allier, Frank Arce, James Bacolo, Mauro Bacolo, Barry Berger, James Best, Jason Bianco, Edward Blanco, Louis H. Blumengarten, Larry Boyken, James Bradley, Thomas Brinson, Thomas Brooks, Henry Burke, Kevin Burns, Don Buzney, Victor Candelaria, John Canney, Frank Careccia, Larry Cary, Joe Casal, Lucylee Chiles, Michael Chirieleison, Arthur Chitty, James Clark, Grant Coates, Anthony Cochran, Stuart Cohen, Lee Covino, Anthony D'Aleo, Ken Dalton, Ed Daniels, Rudolf Dent, Frank DeSantis, Paul DeSaro, Martin V. D'Giff, Thomas Dimitry, John Di Sanza, Carl Dix, Isaac Dweck, Charles Eaddy, Bernard Edelman, Richard Eggers, Emile Ercolino, Francisco Esquilin, Gerald Faulk, Joseph Ferrandino, Paula Fichtner, Barry Fingerhut, Israel Fishman, Sandy Fishman and Elisa Andrews, John Flanagan, Dominick Florio, Tom Fox, Frank Freeman, Danny Friedman, Joan Furey, Jim Gabe, Robert Garguilo, Thomas J. Garvey, Bruce Geiger, Ed German, Joseph Giannini, Karen Gleeson, Tom Glenn, David Glick, Stephen M. Gluck, Mike Gold, Steven Gombas, Jose Gonzalez, Robert Gratz, Richard Green, Robert Greene, William Gribben, Wayne Griffith, Martin Grosso, Pat Gualtieri, Mike Guerin, Hector Guzman, Herman Guzman, Jerome Hall, Robert Hall, John and Denis Hamill, Thomas Harnisher, Richard Harris, William Harris, Alex Heitlinger, Allen Higgins, Samuel Himmelstein, Michael Hipscher, Boyce Holt, Benjamin Homes, Mike Horan, Matthew Iocavelli, Joanne Izzo, William Jacob, Ron Jensen, Peter Katopes, Kenneth Katta, Milton Katz, Joseph Kearney, Ann L. Kelsey, Jack Kenigsberger, Neil Kenny, Bruce Kessler, Michael King, Rita King, Paul Knox, Jerome Krase, Walter Kudlacki, Fred LaVentua, Christopher Leach, Carmine Lengua, Hector

Leon, Gary Levine, Louieco G. Lewis, Philip Lockit, Joseph M. Logan, Fred Louis, Peter Mahoney, Andrew Manicone, Louis Marcello, James J. Markson, Nancy Martin, Peter Martin, Wade Martin, Luigi Masu, Nick L. Mazzella, Sue McAnanama, William A. McCloud, Vince McGowan, Jim McKee, James McMillan, Brian J. McPadden, Peter Meloro, Ray Mesk, Denney Meyer, Victoria Miano, Joy Molfetto, Edward Molineaux, Patrick Mooney, Joel Murov, Kathy Mussen, Manny Napolitano, Stephen Neftleberg, Tin Nguyen, Joseph Nigro, Yuri Niyazov, Lana Noone, Bridget Nowicki, Denis O'Keefe, Robert Oliva, Laurence Olivo, Paul O'Neill, Susan O'Neill, Pippin Parker, Alexander Pas, David Pereplyotchik, Glenn Petersen, Joseph Piazza, Andrew Pietri, Anthony Pinkard, John Platania, Ronald Powers, Robert Ptachik, Angel Ramirez, Juan Ramos, Dorothy Ratigan, Daniel Rice, Ernesto C. Rigby, John Rinaldi, Ray Robertson, Joseph M. Rup Jr., Andy Salimury, Joe Sanchez Picon, Robert Santos, John Sartorius, John Scarimbolo, Auggie Scarinio, William Schank, Barry Schechter, Susan Schnall, James Schrang, Leonard Sciascia, Paul Sheridan, Richard Sheridan, Barbara M. Simmons, Gerald Singer, Albert Singerman, Philip Skolnick, John Slater, Ron Sleeis, Jay Small, Carrie Spearman, Jack Squeo, Mary Beth Stack, William D. Stack Jr., Amadeo Stephanelli, Christopher Strunk, Herbert Sweat, Ralph Testa, Rudy Thompson, Pastor Toro, Kristin Tsafos, Kristina Vaskys, Lucian Vecchio, Anthony Velez, Carlos Velez, Anthony Wallace, Allen E. Walters, Ed White, Arnold Willence, Van Wilson, David Woodrow, and Michael Yates.

The following individuals, who were at one time students of mine, collected interviews and transcribed and offered assistance, for which I am grateful: Christine Sciascia, Eric Smith, Suella Vainstein, Matthew Gherman, Ruben Valencia, Claire Heitlinger, Nicole Lebenson, Rebecca McIvor, David Imparato, Yakov Herman, Linda Schwartz, Brant Levin, Kemile Jackson, Ancil Richardson, and Nathan Wilson.

I would like to thank the following colleagues for their constant encouragement and help: Alan Brinkley, Mike Foley, Robert David Johnson, Andy Meyer, Steven Remy, and David Troyansky.

Julie McGarvey and Jennifer Farbar provided invaluable editorial and intellectual support.

Then there are those whose contributions can't be categorized: Adriana and Gabriella Napoli, Dorothy Napoli, Michael and Judy Schwartz, Joan and Larry Adelman, Stephanie Sargent and Ralph Bernstein, Philip Shaw, Peter Schilling, James Rich, Alice Kenny, and Nikki Giannini.

Gay Culverhouse was instrumental in making this book possible.

The acknowledgments for this work would be incomplete without the name of the late professor James Shenton of Columbia University. Jim, a World War II combat medic, was my teacher and mentor. "War never leaves you," he once said to me. "It lives in your bones."

Printed in the USA
CPSIA information can be obtained
at www.ICGtesting.com
LVHW091139150724
785511LV00005B/431

9 780809 031535